Interregional Migration, National Policy, and Social Justice

Interregional Migration, National Policy, and Social Justice

Gordon L. Clark

ROWMAN & ALLANHELD
Totowa, New Jersey

ROWMAN & ALLANHELD

Published in the United States of America in 1983
by Rowman & Allanheld, Publishers
(A division of Littlefield, Adams & Company)
81 Adams Drive, Totowa, New Jersey 07512

Library of Congress Cataloging in Publication Data

Clark, Gordon L.
  Interregional migration, national policy, and social justice.

  Bibliography: p.
  Includes index.
  1. Migration, Internal—United States. 2. Labor
mobility—United States. 3. Urban policy—United States. 4. Social justice. 5. United
States. Dept. of Housing and Urban Development. The President's national urban
policy report. 6. United States. Panel on Policies and Prospects for Metropolitan and
Nonmetropolitan America. Urban America in the eighties. I. Title.
HB1965.C53 1983   304.8′0973   83-3170
ISBN 0-86598-124-8

83 84 85/ 10 9 8 7 6 5 4 3 2 1

Printed in the United States of America

For John Lynch

Contents

Tables

Preface

I began this study with modest intentions. My goal was to evaluate the report presented by President Carter's Panel on Policies and Prospects for Metropolitan and Nonmetropolitan America (part of President Carter's Commission for a National Agenda for the Eighties) in the last days of the Carter administration, *Urban America in the Eighties.* I believe, and I argue in this book, that its recommendations regarding national urban policy and interregional migration to be simplistic ideology and to be fundamentally flawed in terms of its assumptions, evidence, and logic. As ideology, the report attempts to legitimate a narrow role for national policy, more appropriate for an earlier era of laissez-faire capitalism than the complex and interdependent spatial economy of today. The report is essentially a neo-conservative manifesto: against government intervention in the spatial structure of the American economy, and for the supposed virtues of the free market. As such, the panel explicitly supports "winning" regions and argues for market solutions to the problems of regional and industrial decline in the Northeast and Midwest. According to the panel, the free market, as embodied in the system of interregional migration, works better than governments in allocating labor and welfare across the spatial economy. Their evidence on the patterns and impacts of interregional labor migration is at best weak, at worst nonexistent. The panel blithely assumed that spatial labor markets are efficient, in terms of the spatial-temporal allocation of labor, and equitable, in terms of the "fair" spatial distribution of income where the evidence does not in fact support either assumption.

At the time I was preparing my critique of *Urban America in the*

Eighties (UA in the 80s), the Reagan administration was grappling with the design and the implementation of a national urban policy. Their attempts at formulating an urban policy that is plausible set within the conservative agenda of President Reagan have been somewhat problematic. The 1982 *President's National Urban Policy Report (President's NUPR),* prepared by the U.S. Department of Housing and Urban Development, was soundly criticized by city mayors, and it has not been able to garner broad bipartisan support in Congress. Rhetoric of a "New Federalism," coupled with the Reagan Administration's observed reluctance to become involved in significant policy initiatives regarding areas such as the South Bronx, might lead one to dismiss the Republican urban "policy" as a mere charade. To do so, however, would be a mistake. The President's urban policy report promotes an urban America in very similar terms to the *Urban America in the Eighties* report. And it does so in terms that are more explicit, especially with regard to the primacy of national economic growth, and more detailed, especially with regard to the proper roles of federal, state, and local governments. It proposes market solutions only hinted at by the *Urban America in the Eighties* panel, and assumes an extraordinary faith in the "justness" of private behavior in the aggregate.

In just a few years, the conservative urban agenda has been given both official and unofficial blessing. When linked to the resurgence in political conservatism, as illustrated in George Gilder's recent book *Wealth and Poverty,* the doctrines of market solutions and of a circumscribed role for government intervention have claimed a central place in the national debate over the "proper" urban policy. There have been few attempts to assess the veracity of the conservative agenda as yet, and no effective critique has been mounted against its assumptions and values.

In part, the goal of this book is to reconsider the conservative agenda, especially with regard to issues of interregional migration and national policy focusing in particular upon the panel report, *Urban America in the Eighties* and the more recent (1982) *President's National Urban Policy Report.* Mounting an effective critique requires an analysis of assumptions, evidence, and logic. My initial approach was to use original research results of previous and ongoing studies of the dynamics of interstate labor migration in order to demonstrate the inadequacy of the conservative agenda. In this context, there should be no doubt as to my conclusions; conservatives' assumptions of efficiency and equity in the spatial labor market cannot be empirically sustained. Consequently, the potential role of government policy in fostering the economic welfare of urban America is necessarily more complex and more important than is assumed by the Reagan administration.

As I developed my critique of the conservative urban agenda it became obvious that current modes of policy analysis, especially with regard to questions of national economic efficiency and regional welfare, are generally quite inadequate. Part of the explanation of this inadequacy stems from an uncritical acceptance of national efficiency as the key national policy goal. Conservatives relegate regional welfare to secondary importance. Its place on the policy agenda is saved only by some analysts who envisage the possibility of "trading-off" between national economic efficiency and regional equity. As I suggest in later chapters of this book, the trade-off notion is fundamentally flawed, presuming as it does an unreasonable conception of social justice as being divisible, incremental, and separable from other substantive social goals. Further, the very idea of national efficiency as a policy objective confuses means with ends; only those with a vested interest in securing the hegemonic power of the nation state would support national efficiency as the primary end in and of itself. National economic efficiency should be thought of as a means to securing other goals. In these terms, it is then extremely odd to think of "trading-off" a means with an end.

To sustain these arguments, the study expanded into an analysis of the ends of national policy, especially with regard to its significance vis-à-vis regional welfare. Inevitably, this meant an evaluation of the proper role of national public policy, and the most appropriate definition of social justice as it relates to interregional migration: hence, the second part to the title of this study. In seeking a rethinking of the notion of regional welfare, I have reviewed recent debates in political philosophy and applied their findings and methods of analysis to the problems at hand. I cannot claim to have developed a wholly original or definitive model of regional welfare, but I hope that the questions raised, and the framework presented, will provide the basis for further inquiry into the role of national urban policy in structuring the distribution of people and jobs. In these terms, my evaluation of the recently articulated conservative urban agenda offers not only a critique, but also a way beyond the confused and reactionary neo-conservative notion of free market "(in)justice."

A project of this sort depends on the assistance and often high level of involvement of many others. In particular I would like to acknowledge Dr. Kenneth Ballard of Pacific, Gas, and Electric (and previously the Bureau of Economic Analysis of the U.S. Department of Commerce) who was co-author with me on three studies that contributed to much of Chapter 3. These papers were published in *Environment and Planning A* (1980), *Economic Geography* (1981), and *Regional Studies* (1981). Meric Gertler of the University of Toronto was co-author of an article that contributed to Chapter 4, which was published in the *Annals, Association of American Geographers* (1983). John Whiteman of Harvard University co-authored an article which forms the basis of Chapter 5, and was published in *Environment and Planning A* (1983). Thanks very much to Ken, Meric, and John for their substantial and generous contributions to this work. Dr. Royce Hanson of the National Academy of Sciences, Professor Brian Berry of Carnegie–Mellon University and John Whiteman provided indepth comments on a previous draft of this book. Professors William Alonso and Victor Solo, both of Harvard University, commented on sections of Chapters 4 and 5. Thanks as well, but not least, to Professor David Kennedy of the Harvard Law School for entreé to some of the less accessible fine points of legal philosophy and institutional analysis.

Finally, I owe an intellectual debt to Ronald Dworkin and a debt of friendship to John Lynch, to whom this book is dedicated.

The Ph.D Program in Urban Planning at Harvard University's Graduate School of Design provided funds for a research assistant, Takatoshi Tabuchi, and computer analysis during 1981/82. This book was written while the author was a National Research Council Fellow (funded by the Andrew Mellon Foundation) at the National Academy of Sciences, Washington, D.C., during the academic year 1981/82, while on leave from the John F. Kennedy School of Government, Harvard University. Background research was conducted during 1979/81 through the support provided by the National Science Foundation for a study of U.S. population redistribution and regional growth (Grant SES 7909370). The views and opinions expressed in this study are, of course, solely the author's.

ONE

Interregional Migration and Policy Analysis

It is a commonplace observation that America is a country of migrants. America was created by migrants of virtually all nationalities, and it continues to attract migrants from many countries. By virtue of two hundred years of immigration, the economic and social histories of so many villages and towns of other countries are intertwined with the growth and development of the American urban system.[1] Frontiers and settlements were systematically expanded and built in America by successive generations of adventurous migrants. And even today, the experiences of southern Italian villagers during the early decades of this century (for example) have their images reflected in Central American immigration to the United States. Immigration is a common fact close to the experience of many Americans and their families. It is perhaps this fact that helps us understand the significance attached by American society to concepts such as "the natural right of free mobility."[2]

As America is a country of immigrants, it is also a country that has placed a high premium on the freedom of internal mobility. When linked to notions of individualism, freedom, and the promise of progress (Pole 1980), internal mobility can be interpreted both as one element necessary for the sustenance of individual freedom and as a component of national growth. Geographical mobility ensures that individuals need not be ensnared by a repressive or paternalistic local government.[3] It facilitates individual choice and, for Nozick

(1974) among many others, it is the means of sustaining American decentralized democracy. From this conception of individual liberty (or the "freedom of locomotion" as it was termed by Blackstone in his *Commentaries on the Laws of England* and noted in the Fourteenth Amendment of the U.S. Constitution; *see* Berger 1977), it has been a short step to generalizing individual mobility as a necessary condition of national progress.[4] The earliest debates over the form and character of America promoted this notion against other more conservative and traditional forms of community life (Rossiter 1982). And today, this notion is expressed as an article of faith, an ideological tenet of American life, whether in academic writings (Nozick 1974) or in more pragmatic social policy. It is no surprise that these images dominate both the *Urban America in the Eighties* Panel report and the 1982 *President's National Urban Policy Report.*

Even so, in terms of explicit public policy, an internal interregional-assisted migration program remains to be implemented; this is despite the fact that for many years the federal government has promoted spatial market integration and economic interdependence. Through active government involvement, implemented by institutions such as the Supreme Court and Interstate Commerce Commission (Clark 1981a), and as a pervasive ideological assumption of the necessary "goodness" of individual liberty, the goal of free mobility has become an accepted fact of American society. The history of Supreme Court adjudication provides some evidence for this judgment. In a review devoted to the issue, Rosenheim (1969) suggested that much of the litigation in the United States concerning mobility could be traced to an early denial of English Poor Laws that has had a continued residual influence on questions such as the distribution of the welfare burden and migration. This influence has been evidenced by a constitutional interest in sustaining mobility rights per se which, according to Houseman (1979), implies the existence of a fundamental right of mobility. The Poor Laws provided that localities were responsible for their poor, migration of the destitute was prohibited, and a residence test was to be used to designate those eligible for alms. To a limited degree, the United States still has vestiges of this system despite the fact that the Poor Laws were repealed in England in 1834 (the Poor Law Amendment Act). For example, unemployment insurance policies in many states still require a proxy residence requirement in that eligibility is tied to previous periods of employment in the particular state. Also, residence tests for local welfare relief were often used prior to 1935 in the United States as a means of restricting the local welfare burden.

The Social Security Act of 1935 reduced minimum residence requirements, homogenized intrastate variations in work relief benefits and conditions, and encouraged states to respond to the plight of the large number of unemployed workers moving throughout the states looking for work.[5] Even so, institutional barriers still exist to a degree and reflect a *conditional* mobility policy; conditional on the expected burden that out-of-state unemployed workers and welfare recipients could place on state welfare agencies. As well, there are marked differences between states in their commitment to funding and providing welfare for their citizens. Hamermesh (1977), in a study of interstate unemployment insurance differences, concluded that the extent of these variations makes it "impossible to . . . comprehend the nuances of all state programs." (p.2) The leading case of *Shapiro v. Thompson,* 394 US 618 (1969), has been used by some researchers to press the argument for a completely free mobility system. The majority opinion of the Supreme Court in that case was premised on notions of the right to travel, and on the Equal Protection Clause. Welfare recipients in particular were the people most affected by this decision, especially those who depend on federal matching grants. Otherwise, there has been remarkably little litigation over institutional barriers to mobility, perhaps because a high level of economic growth since 1945 has made the financing issue of only secondary importance. It is only recently that these issues have been revived and have been applied to unemployed auto workers.[6]

Americans migrate each year in numbers and rates that go far beyond those in most advanced western countries.[7] Frontiers remain to be conquered, and the spatial reach of economic growth to be expanded. Historically, there has been an intimate association between the volume and structure of migration, the spatial development of the economy, and the overall economic growth of the nation. Williamson and Lindert (1980) made the point with respect to U.S. spatial economic growth in the nineteenth century, as did Greenwood (1981) with respect to recent economic trends. The promise of America for individual advancement has, in part, been the option to migrate, to improve one's own chances of economic success by changing location. At the same time individual mobility and freedom of choice have been seen as synonymous with the economic development of the whole nation. To the extent that individuals seek to improve their own economic welfare through relocation, it has been assumed that the whole nation benefits. Aggregate explanations of national welfare then assume as a basic tenet the fundamental importance of mobility. This theme dominates interpretations of the economic history of the United States, and it remains a central public policy issue today. For example, in the report of the President's Commission for a National Agenda for the Eighties, *Urban America in the Eighties,* the panel made a strong argument to the effect that, as national vitality must take precedence over the interests of localities, rapid and unfettered interregional migration is a basic means for attaining high levels of national growth.[8]

Yet not all people migrate, nor do they necessarily want to migrate despite appearances and rhetoric to the contrary. Place and community remain, for many people, important social values that presume the necessity for a specific context in which personal interactions should take place. Even though immediate urban neighborhoods have lost much of their earlier nineteenth century meaning as the primary locus of interaction, larger community-wide associations remain important for most peoples' social networks (Clark 1982a). In contrast, rapid and continuous migration implies a hyper-individualism or utilitarianism at odds with more traditional (and valued) conceptions of a "good" society. Communitarian ideals are of course the "flip side" of individualism. Mobility is a threat to the possibility of a viable social and political community. In addition, continual mobility implies personal alienation from the immediate community.

Interregional migration also implies a specific geography of costs and benefits, affecting the economic fabric of all localities. For destinations, migrants represent added fiscal burdens for local governments and financial districts that provide local public goods and services. Of course, such migrants also represent an expanding market for local merchants and a work force for local producers. Consequently, public costs of rapid in-migration are often not absorbed in the private market. For the localities left behind (and for their residents), out-migration represents a loss of income, employment, and the more highly educated population (Parr 1966). The welfare and income distribution of communities are positively and negatively affected by migration. It is difficult to show that *on net,* the social benefits of interregional migration outweigh the costs to those communities affected, whatever the benefits to those individuals directly involved. With the collapse of the traditionally important secondary industries of the Midwest, such as steel and automobiles, and the massive growth of the Southwest, these questions of local versus individual welfare have gained increasing importance.[9] Poverty stalks the industrial Midwest threatening those who will not migrate, those who cannot migrate, and reinforcing the decline of the regional economy.

To some extent, the federal government has recognized the importance of these issues by intervening to protect the economic well-being of existing communities. Through direct job creation, capital subsidies to private employers, public job training, and infrastructure investment, the federal government has in the past attempted to bring jobs to people. In doing so, the federal government has promoted a specific spatial and economic pattern of development premised upon a policy goal of maintaining populations in place. To the extent these policies have been successful, the federal government may well have compromised broader national goals of economic growth and spatial economic interdependence. This policy predicament isn't simply a confusion of policy design, nor is it evidence that, for whatever reasons, simultaneous attempts at maximizing national economic growth and improving the welfare of individuals where they live is impossible. Rather, it is primarily the product of competing values, of ideological differences concerning the rights of people to employment where they live.

Philosophically, the notion of a right to employment is a contentious topic, although in past years the public record has shown clear support for such an idea, both in abstract terms and, more concretely, in actual federal legislation. For example, the Employment Act of 1946 (15 USC 1021–1025) set a national goal of achieving employment opportunities for all able and willing persons seeking work. In 1978, the Full Employment and Balanced Growth Act (the Humphrey-Hawkins Bill) stated the case more forcefully by not only enunciating specific employment goals, but actually enacting programs designed to accomplish full employment. Debate rages, however, over what seems on the surface to be a simple legislative commitment. One of the central unresolved issues is inherently spatial in nature, and it concerns whether or not individuals have a right to employment where they currently reside. The question for public policy is whether or not an individual's current place of residence (defined technically to include the spatial extent of the local labor market) ought to be the locus of federal job creation programs.

While some in Congress promote a communitarian view, others contend that an individual's current place of residence should simply be viewed as a residual: as a spatial outcome of market forces (assuming mobile capital and labor) from past phases of growth whose "optimal" locational solution under previous conditions of production and exchange may no longer be relevant in the current period. This latter conceptualization tends to diminish the importance of place of residence in the short run and especially in the long run, and promotes individual mobility as the solution to national growth problems. Interestingly enough, this latter view has received support from both ends of the political spectrum. (*See,* for example, Bluestone and Harrison 1982 for the radical, albeit pessimistic view, and McKenzie 1981 for the conservative view.) While radicals and conservatives alike agree on the imperatives of market capitalism, there is widespread debate over the proper role of public policy. In reaction, radicals have prescribed "runaway plant" legislation and similar constraints on the mobility of capital, while conservatives have tended to prescribe programs which encourage the mobility of labor and minimize the job search time for the unemployed; the goal being to somehow rationalize the spatial distribution of production and thus to maximize national productive efficiency regardless of its spatial dimension.

This debate over place versus people prosperity is well recognized in the academic literature. Theorists, from a number of disciplines, have in recent years, become skeptical of claims of the uniqueness of spatial location in determining the proper allocation of economic resources. Space may be as much an intervening and manipulable variable in conflicts between capital and labor.[10] These issues have also arisen in the political arena through recognition of the on-going process of economic growth and massive re-arrangement of the geography of prosperity in the United States. In this context, the

Urban America in the Eighties panel report and the 1982 *President's National Urban Policy Report* have added significantly to a critical evaluation of the people and places debate already occuring in the academic literature.

Public policy, not surprisingly, reflects these debates. On one hand, the time-lags inherent in labor adjustment to the map of new economic opportunities have encouraged cushioning policies; on the other hand, it has been argued that these types of policies are neither efficient nor in the national interest. In response, a variety of different policy tools have been developed. For example, the Economic Development Administration focused upon place prosperity, targeting the needy according to locational aggregates; the Comprehensive Employment and Training Act programs were targeted on people prosperity, but used place-related aggregates to disburse funds; and, the Job Search Relocation Assistance Project was targeted almost entirely upon individuals without regard to the location implications of assisted migration vis-à-vis the prosperity of origins and destinations.

These cross-currents in policies and values dominate contemporary debate over the appropriate design of national urban and regional policy. Advocates of maximum national growth and of a market-oriented people-to-jobs policy have become very powerful in a political milieu that can only be described as conservative. Yet, there remain powerful objections to these notions. Policies that promote individual mobility may fail to help those most in need, and it is entirely possible that by promoting migration, the problems of the older industrial Midwest will be exacerbated. Furthermore, the communitarian vision has made strong claims for the maintenance of communities suffering severe economic dislocation. Not only is there a clash of policy, but there is also an implied clash of values.

This study is concerned with re-evaluating the evidence, processes, and policies of interregional migration in the United States. Given the contending value positions, and their policy tools of taking people to jobs and jobs to people, I want to re-examine what we know about geographical mobility and to establish what should be the corresponding mix of public policies. So much of research and policy are implicitly prefaced on a belief in one or the other value position. Thus, it must be acknowledged that the methodological tools of economists and geographers are dominated by individually oriented utility maximization models. In academic analysis, we so often begin with the individual decision and end with individual and aggregate outcomes. Rarely do we integrate the local context into our analytical models of migration. For example, we have little understanding of how local conditions affect and condition migration decisions, how migration itself is initiated, and how public policy might affect the context and the geographical patterns of labor.

There is an implied trap in orthodox models of migration; the conception that individual decisions take precedence over social values. By concentrating so much on the migration decision, there has been a tendency to believe the rhetoric of those who assert the equivalence between individual mobility and national economic prosperity. A conscious analysis of public policy must take seriously alternative value positions. Thus, our methodology must be designed to allow for contending normative goals.

EVALUATING PUBLIC POLICY

In the previous section, I briefly reviewed the apparently unresolved debate between those who advocate maximum national economic growth strategies of labor mobility ("people-to-jobs") and those who advocate assisted local economic development ("jobs-to-people"). Before evaluating the case made by the protagonists in the debate and especially the *UA in the 80s* report and the 1982 *President's NUPR,* I shall outline the methodology I will be using in this evaluation. Conventionally, public policy analysis supposes that these types of debates can be resolved through the judicious use of social science, theory and methods. By scientifically evaluating contending hypotheses or propositions regarding the policy problem at hand, it is supposed that the optimal policy will be determined (Stokey and Zeckhauser 1978). The basis of this methodology is typically empirical, wherein facts are collected, sifted, and applied to distinguishing the veracity of each claim. Even after evaluation, if a less than optimal policy is chosen to be implemented by the political process, the policy scientist's role is as an accountant; determining the costs and benefits of such a choice, both in terms of the opportunities foregone and of the distribution of the burden of such policy choices.

Although there are many views of the definitive model of policy science, the orthodox view can be summarized in the following caricature: public policy decisions are often irrational and consequently wrong. Those making policy decisions are overly influenced by political considerations and are often unaware of the implications or unintended consequences of their decisions (Vernon 1979). Accordingly, social scientists are essential to the policy making process for the following reasons. First, social scientists provide independent and objective information on the nature of the policy problem and on the implications of following alternative policy options; social science methodology is logical and rational, and thus superior to untrained intuitive decision making. Second, social science enables rational choices as to the best policies or solutions to the identified problems (Stokey and Zeckhauser 1978). Implied here, of course, is the division of academics from direct involvement in the political process and their importance in the substantive issues of evaluation and problem solving. Academics, according to the rational model, accept the status quo as their research context, and define the most efficient resolution to the identified problem.

In practice, there are a variety of ways in which social science is perceived to bring about rational policy making. Once a significant policy problem is identified (presumably politically), existing social research and results are applied to its solution. Social science knowledge is used as either a means of informing decision makers as to the appropriateness of alternative policies and/or as an ex post check of the desirability of proposed policy solutions. Thus social science information is assumed to be more objective, rigorous, and complete than the information possessed by the typical policy maker. Emphasis is on the quantified and objectively stated goals and objectives. Alternatives are also quantitatively evaluated and the results "feedback" into policy definition and analysis.[11] Notice, however, that in practice, the policy analyst may also become involved in problem definition and political response as legitimacy for making correct policy decisions shifts from the policy maker to the advisor. The constraint on this process is that available scholarly research may not be readily identifiable or even applicable to the problem at hand.

Consequently, a second mode of involvement by social science in policy making may be direct, action-oriented research where the policy scientist is hired to analyze the problem and to recommend action (Goldberg 1977). Here, previously developed and refined social science techniques are applied to real world problems (as defined politically by sponsoring institutions) on the understanding that the social scientist is to remain independent and objective. In both instances, social science performs a number of functions; it provides the missing information without which "good" decisions cannot be made or contemplated; it identifies the appropriate means for achieving the desired goals; and it provides the correct information on the best approach to solving the problem (Weiss 1978). Rational problem solving is thought to be the application of the best of social science theory and practice to significant problems of the day.

This brief sketch of the policy analysis model is obviously incomplete, and it stylizes the actual practical problems of policy analysis such as inadequate information and poorly articulated goals and objectives. Nevertheless, this so-called rational policy framework depends very much on using "the facts" to distinguish between good and bad policy. For those seeking an ultimate truth, this framework appears as the most objective means of making policy choices, unencumbered by supposedly distorting and subjective value positions.

It is common in the policy analysis literature to see reference to a dichotomy of facts and values, as if a distinction can be made between what is true or a fact (as in reality), and what is mere opinion. For example, in a recent survey of research in quantitative geography, Wrigley and Bennett (1981) argued that researchers must be careful to distinguish between policy preferences (normative ideals) and the facts. Their concern was that the facts can be, in some manner, massaged to fit preferences. Related to this view is the argument that facts can be objectively determined, even if researchers disagree on values. The approach taken in this study, departs significantly from this conventional dichotomous treatment of facts and values, insisting that they cannot so easily be separated, that there can be no neutral facts.[12]

To understand what I mean by policy analysis and evaluation, a brief review is needed of the underlying logic of my argument concerning the fact-value connection. In the first place, I would argue that facts presuppose values: either the facts we collect are so determined by the problem at hand, or the standards by which we judge whether or not a fact is a fact are themselves determined by exogenous values of what makes a fact. Few would disagree that the problem at hand often supposes, by its very nature, the facts necessary to adjudicate competing hypotheses. But at the same time, such an argument presupposes an agreed-upon definition of the policy problem. This is, of course, precisely the issue for many of the protagonists in the people-to-jobs and jobs-to-people debate. On the former side, the problem is thought to be sustaining long-run national economic growth so that employment and income are maximized (but, obviously, without regard to the resulting map of economic opportunities). On the latter, the problem is thought to be in sustaining local employment opportunities, wherein the location of employment is the crucial distinguishing feature. It is difficult to envision the "facts" that would resolve such a debate because there is no obvious commonality between the two positions capable of sustaining empirical research.

At this point, one might counter by arguing that there is a role for evaluating the comparative costs and benefits of these two options. To do so would require a common metric for evaluation, and a common ordering of the significance of the derived "facts." Both requirements are fatal to the logic of the rational public policy analysis model. A common metric presupposes criteria set outside, and agreed to by proponents of both sides to the debate. If this metric is essentially a higher order objective, then there must be a value system that determines such an hierarchy. For example, if the jobs-to-people versus people-to-jobs debate is to be evaluated according to their respective contributions to maximizing total income and employment, this ordering, where maximum income and employment are ranked first and local prosperity and national growth are ranked second, must be justified. In this instance, the primacy of one goal over another must be ultimately derived from a normative value position. There can be no neutral, third-party evaluative criteria, as there can be no neutral but shared facts, that would distinguish between competing values.

Also problematic is the question of judging the significance of facts derived from a common, yet third-party metric. A set of standards are required to make sense of what a collection of facts would mean in a specific instance. Before going further into the question of standards, we must also recognize that facts are wholly contextual. The Kantian notion is that facts arise out of experience and social interaction. We cannot know the truth about the world because what we know is actually socially designed or constructed. Social intercourse defines in a hierarchical fashion what is significant and what is merely mundane; by extension, social intercourse simultaneously defines a system of values that orders reality in a descriptive fashion. Facts are actually structured according to the logic of society.

To the extent that society is non-homogeneous, wrought by social conflict and inequality, then the system of values itself will be a point of social antagonism and may not be capable of integration. Appeal to third-party, higher-order consensual values presupposes a particular political view of society that may not be realistic (however much it may be desired). A related issue, one recognized by Wittgenstein, is that the very language that we use to describe the world, our "facts," is intimately bound within the social context. Competing values have competing languages of description; inevitably there cannot be a one-to-one correspondence of terms, as there cannot be a one-to-one correspondence in interpretation.

Facts cannot, then, stand on their own. Their significance and applicability come out of a specific social setting, plagued by the schisms existing in society itself. If these arguments have not convinced the reader of the relative nature of facts, perhaps the problems of interpreting supposedly common facts will. Take, for example, an instance of labor migration, and assume for the moment that we can observe that person A migrated from place i to place j during a given year. How might this "fact" be interpreted? Those schooled in human capital theory would immediately suggest that the person moved because the discounted utility of migration (accounting for costs over a specific time horizon) was greater than remaining at place j. Implied is an assumption that the move was voluntary, and necessarily of benefit (however measured) to the individual involved. Yet, it is entirely plausible that person A was forced to migrate. The corporation employing him threatened dismissal if he did not move to j and begin work at a company plant with no increase in wage or salary. This type of explanation is associated with those (*see* McKay and Whitelaw 1977) who have emphasized the importance of corporate human resource policies in allocating labor in time and space rather than conventional notions of individual free choice or utility maximization.

That person A moved from i to j is the fact, but its meaning is subject to interpretation. Bluntly, in the first interpretation, migration was voluntary, and in the second instance it was coerced. The language describing migration is different as are the implied values. It might be protested at this point that my example is limited because more information is available in the second instance to describe the "fact."

However, recognition of the importance of this new information is based upon the logic of the theory of migration that researchers utilize. Because of the structural quality of human capital theory it does not recognize as important, corporate labor policy. It is a theory based upon assumptions of individual utility maximization that assumes non-coercive labor markets. "Facts" and the descriptions of facts is inherently an interpretive process, set within a specific and an a priori defined logic. It is often argued that new facts are basic to the evolution of science; by comparing facts with expectations, new advances are made. This logic assumes again that facts are neutral. Instead of assuming that facts sustain theory, it is better to assume that facts are created by theory and are interpreted with respect to specific value positions (Brest 1982; cf. Fiss 1982).

If facts are relative and interpretations based upon values, how then should the existence of contending theories of migration and the appropriate roles for public policy be understood, let alone evaluated? At the most general level, it is clear that interpretations must have specific social settings. Accordingly, interpretations must be thought of as structured and designed, rather than arbitrarily or idiosyncratically assembled. Furthermore, interpretations inevitably have a purpose: most ideally as explanation, more realistically as the legitimization and reinforcement of a specific point of view. Because of the social context of interpretation, how specific modes of interpretation are designed must reflect the positions, values, and goals of those who are involved in the process of interpretation. And, since values themselves are highly specific to social position, there exist (however loosely organized) discrete "interpretive communities" (a term coined by Fish 1980). This is not to suggest that all interpretation is explicitly, ideological and self-serving. Rather, all interpretive acts are inherently socially defined and support of a particular interpretation is itself a political act. There can be no neutrality in this social process: naiveté is not an adequate defense.

Evaluation of contending public policy options must then recognize the determining role of values and social context. That is, any policy evaluation must recognize the origins and agendas of particular proposals in the social system itself. This goal is a matter of bringing out into the open the underlying premises and assumptions of particular options, indicating where possible the substantive differences and irreconcilabilities of different options. As we shall see in discussing alternative interregional migration policy options, not all policy goals and their instruments conflict with one another despite their surface antagonisms. Furthermore, indicating the underlying normative positions of public policy enables evaluation with respect to other, perhaps more important, policy goals. Our ability to recognize commonalities, irreconcilabilities, and associations with other normative goals is an important evaluative tool, without which the political system may be unable to distinguish between crucial and incidental policy decisions. Of course, it should be immediately apparent that some public policy conflicts cannot be rationalized or reconciled, rather recognition of the underlying value positions will specify the crucial issues.

Not only will I attempt to shed light on the underlying value positions of the conservative urban policy agenda, as it concerns interregional migration, I will also evaluate their assumptions in the light of evidence and theory. To do so, fairly at least, will require an explicit recognition of how the "facts" of interregional migration should be interpreted, and the types of standards I shall use to judge the veracity of their assumptions.[13] In the first instance, this will require a discussion of the principal methodological assumptions of conventional migration theory, and of the use of facts derived according to their own terms. I cannot hope to provide interpretations consistent with the spirit of neoclassical economic theory; after all, I am employing a critique. Nonetheless, given my acceptance of their definition of "the problem" of interregional migration (spatial-temporal allocative efficiency), I hope to provide an *internal* critique of the assumptions of the conservative agenda. Second, the standards I will use to evaluate the evidence on migration will be largely derived from conventional policy analysis. In particular, four standards will guide my analysis—coherence (or logic), simplicity, comprehensiveness, and instrumental effectiveness.[14] Conventionally, the last standard, often termed predictability, is thought to be superior to the others.

Coherence refers to the systematic manner in which an argument or hypothesis is developed. Implied in such a notion is consistency in assumptions, logic, and interpretation. Without coherence of assumptions between different instances of application, no theory could hope to be an adequate explanation of diverse but related phenomena. Similarly, the logic of argument must be consistent from specific suppositions to hypotheses and then to empirical analysis. Finally, interpretations of facts derived from initial assumptions of significance and so on must relate to underlying value premises. Otherwise, interpretations will not only be inconsistent with respect to the "facts," but also with respect to the underlying logic of basic principles. Simplicity is analogous to parsimony. In statistics (*see* Box and Jenkins 1976), this property refers to description of the underlying process using the minimum of parameters. By analogy, simplicity is adequate description through the minimal use of propositions and/ or hypotheses. Generality of argument is one strategy wherein each case or event can be described by higher order principles. Comprehensiveness is a constraint on simplicity. For example, in statistics parsimony is constrained by measures of closeness of description. For instance, in time-series analysis the objective is to describe a series through the smallest number of parameters while simultaneously minimizing the errors of under- or overestimation.

In this study, comprehensiveness will have a more particular meaning than simply generality or completeness of description. In conjunction with instrumental efficacy, it shall refer to the extent that an argument or hypothesis is able to *effectively* deal with the most difficult cases. I shall use as the most important standard of explanation the extent to which a given argument is able to deal with the most difficult issues. For example, the fact that most people move, especially when they are young and in the early phases of their working lives, may not help explain why a small group does not move despite living in the worst of conditions. Another example might be the causal links between migration and capital growth: although we observe that migration and economic growth are inter-related, this does not help in the extreme (or hard) cases where the direction of causality is the crucial (but unknown) policy variable. Does out-migration lead economic decline, or does in-migration lead capital growth? Both examples are the subject of subsequent empirical and theoretical analysis in this study.

Dworkin (1978) referred to these difficult cases as "hard" cases. His argument, which I follow here, was twofold. First, whatever the generality of a model or theory, its ultimate usefulness is determined by how well it can deal with exceptions. This view is obviously at odds with those who suppose that generality is the crucial criterion. For example, to be crude about it, a statistical model of out-migration from a specific region may predict 95% of all variation (a coefficient of determination, $r^2 = 0.95$), but it may be unable to explain the other 5%, perhaps the most crucial elements of the whole domain. In later chapters, I will argue that whatever the generality of si-multaneous equation models of labor migration and economic growth (*see,* for example, Greenwood 1981), they fail conspicuously to predict what *causes* regional economic growth in the most volatile instances. Second, Dworkin (1978) also suggested that the hard cases are the most interesting cases because they reflect back upon the whole theory; its coherence, comprehensiveness, and simplicity. A similar point has been made by McKay (1980) concerning Arrow's Theorem—paradoxes are the bases of theoretical development, because of their very ambiguity and incoherence.[15]

Thus, in my evaluation of the conservative agenda vis-à-vis in-terregional migration, I shall confront the hard cases and use them to reflect upon the adequacy of the whole. Where possible, this will be in the terms, the language, and the "facts" of conventional neoclassical migration theory. Wherever possible, I want to be fair to the fact-value nexus that forms its basis. My choice of these standards for internal evaluation are obviously not neutral for, following my earlier argument, there can be no neutral standards of objectivity. Wherever appropriate, I have included standards shared by protagonists on both sides of the policy debate. In this respect, coherence, simplicity, and comprehensiveness might be thought as consensual. The final criterion, however, the most important one in my analysis, predictability vis-à-vis the most difficult cases, departs from traditional methodology. Arguments in defense of my choice have been suggested above and reflect a more general methodological argument that goes beyond this particular policy debate. Concern for the underlying fact-value nexus has also suggested an evaluative methodology that seeks to make clear the commonalities and irreconcilabilities between contending value positions. No ultimate consensual or integrative logic will be suggested for determining good and bad value positions.

I wish to clearly distinguish my position from a churlish nihilism by this extended discussion of the bases of evaluation. Some writers have suggested that if all values are relative, then there are no objective standards of good and bad, everything is permitted, and consequently nothing is worth doing (Rosen 1969). In this sense, nihilism in policy evaluation might come about simply because of the incapacity of researchers and policy analysts to decide upon specific value positions. This isn't what I intend; my critique is designed as an internal analysis (accepting a specific fact-value nexus) using standards of evaluation derived from shared and specific values, and as an external analysis which seeks to devine the political nature of different value positions. In this manner, I seek to avoid the easy nihilism of relativism.

OVERVIEW

My argument proceeds in the following manner. In Chapter 2, I review the underlying philosophical and conceptual bases of American public policy as it pertains to interregional migration and economic growth. Much of the chapter focuses upon the report of the *UA in the 80s* Panel report and on the 1982 *President's NUPR*. I note that these reports have been proposed as an agenda for immediate public policy in the form of claims made by President Reagan regarding "New Federalism." A critical argument is mounted against the basic assumptions of these two reports. First, I argue that the notion of minimal government intervention in the spatial economy is at once naive and nihilistic. It is naive because the government cannot be neutral; just by enforcing the rules of exchange it creates a distinct geography of public policy impacts. It is nihilistic because both reports mistake poor public policy with governmental incapacity. Serious welfare and efficiency problems remain to be addressed, and they will not be solved by the rhetoric of government restraint, however fashionable it may be.

Second, I also argue that both reports are seriously amiss in terms of their assumptions regarding the meaning of notions such as maximum national efficiency. This notion can only be understood with reference to some underlying normative goal. For example, national efficiency might be interpreted to mean "a bigger pie," or as an instrument for attaining other goals such as "freedom of choice." The assertion of the inherent "good" of national efficiency cannot be sustained in the terms of the conservative agenda, and consequently the reports reviewed here loose their self-proclaimed images of neutrality and consensual legitimacy. Finally, the reports are also criticized for their ignorance of the facts of interregional migration. This chapter is essentially an analysis of the coherence of the conservative agenda in terms of their assumptions and interpretation.

In Chapter 3 I review and report on original research results concerning the patterns and consequences of interregional migration, focusing throughout upon the "hard cases." The market efficiency of labor migration is the focus of this chapter, especially with regard to the sensitivity of migration to economic determinants. It is shown that the volume of out-migration from depressed areas is quite adaptive to fluctuations in local prosperity relative to national indicators. It is also shown that the volume of in-migration to rapidly growing areas is also very adaptive to local economic conditions. At first sight at least, labor migration is shown to be an efficient response to the appropriate determining variables. It is also shown that the spatial allocation and efficient distribution of labor through migration is much more problematic. Out-migrants from depressed areas do not necessarily go to rapidly growing areas, and in-migrants to growing areas often come from other growth regions of the United States. The spatial allocation of labor is poorly coordinated and synchronized. More disturbing is the further finding that labor migration has variable impacts on local (and, in the aggregate, national) prosperity. At times, in-migration causes relative decreases in local wages (and, hence, convergence in interregional welfare), and in other instances in-migration causes relative increases in local wages (divergence) in regional welfare. Similarly, out-migration causes lower and, in other instances, higher relative wages. It is just as plausible that interregional migration might lower, as well as increase, total income in the entire spatial system. Thus, we must be wary of ascribing to a market phenomenon, such as migration, powers of efficiency and welfare that are assumed to create a beneficial map of greater income and more job opportunities. The suppositions of the *UA in the 80s* Panel report and the 1982 *President's NUPR* concerning the efficiency of market solutions are open to severe question, specifically in terms of their own logic and predictions.

This analysis leads on to Chapter 4 in which I consider, in more technical detail, the relationships between migration and regional economic growth. The central question in this chapter is the extent of causality between gross migration and capital growth. I show that in the "hard cases," local growth and decline, it is capital growth or decline that determines labor migration. For these very hard cases, where spatio-economic processes are highly unstable and subject to massive shifts in population and resources, it is local investment that determines the map of economic prosperity. For localities characterized by average economic growth, migration and capital growth operate simultaneously.

The implications of these results are twofold. First, we should be wary of ascribing "freedom of choice" to migrants when in fact they have to follow the spatial and temporal paths of capital growth. That is, much of the migration of people to the Southwest has been in response to the creation/destruction of jobs in the Southwest/Midwest. Limited choice in job opportunities and their location may imply that labor is *forced* to migrate, rather than choosing to migrate (the latter being the crucial assumption of the conservative agenda). Second, to the extent that the location of capital can be controlled or channeled to particular areas, then migration itself will similarly be affected. Of course, this does not mean that there need be a closely synchronized relationship between origins and destinations (see Chapter 3); rather, the opportunity exists for national public policy to play a more conscious determining role in the fortunes of specific areas of the spatial economy.

Recognition of the importance of capital mobility in determining the pattern and structure of labor migration is followed in Chapter 5 by a theoretical analysis of the rigidities of labor migration. I argue that poor people do not move for quite rational and economic reasons. The costs of searching, information, and mobility are shown to disadvantage poor people. Similarly, the available jobs also are shown to have a determining role in the mobility option. At origins, the types of occupations determine work histories, income, and available contacts while destination job opportunities determine the potential of outside workers finding appropriate employment. The consequences of this type of analysis are threefold. First, there are impediments to individual mobility that are beyond individual control. People are often caught in a *context*—a locality—that forces them to follow certain paths and not follow others. It is the *force* of circumstance, not physical coercion that is at issue here. Second, as a consequence there is a two-tiered system of migration: a choice-oriented stream that, because of employer demand and recruiting practices, is able to more easily adapt to the changing map of economic opportunities; and a context-oriented stream that is caught by circumstances. Third, the design and implementation of public policy has to be adept at isolating the character of clients from the specific circumstance that the client reflects. Of course, even here public policy has to decide on a role vis-à-vis the desirability of government intervention, that goes beyond a simple rhetorical statement regarding "small government."

These arguments concerning the internal coherence, the comprehensiveness, and the predictive powers of conventional theories of interregional migration set the stage of Chapter 6 in which I deal in depth with public policy options. Two contending policy options are presented: that of sustaining community integrity (facilitating local economic growth and thereby personal welfare); and, that of maximizing individual mobility (encouraging people-to-jobs adaption). The context for this analysis is the Michigan city of Flint; a city that can be best described as undergoing a depression and whose future (and that of its residents) looks very bleak. I argue that if American society values "free choice" above all else, then government policy must be more responsive to the choice of individuals not to move as to the choice of moving. Since capital growth can contribute to the growth of the locality (in terms of migration and population growth), then there are options for greater involvement of the federal government in *creating* better local environments. It should also be noted that individuals may choose to relocate, but because of the force of circumstances be prevented from following their choice. Here government policy could also play an active role.

By way of illustration, I examine Canadian policies that facilitate interregional migration for their usefulness in the American context. The Job Search Relocation Assistance Project, of the U.S. Department of Labor is also noted. My conclusion is that the extent of government intervention depends very much upon normative assumptions regarding the "good" society. In so doing, I also argue the case for a interventionist strategy focused upon community integrity and individual choice. This analysis is then *external,* concerned with different fact-value combinations, and different normative ideals of government policy.

In Chapter 7, the conclusion, I propose a framework for analyzing questions of welfare and equality, and the role of public policy. It is based on two propositions. First, I argue that the trade-off notion, wherein consensual agreement is reached amongst competing policy goals through compromise on the full meaning of specific goals, is basically inadequate. Trade-offs assume incrementality of values and choices between competing substantive values. Without resorting to a simpleminded characterization, I presume trade-offs to signify 40% equality and 60% efficiency. Values are rarely so divisible; more often they are absolute categories so that we either have justice (or some other goal) or we don't: there may be no possible in-between positions. Second, I also argue that there are sets of policy goals that are more congruent than others. Instead of proposing arbitrary mixes of policies, governments propose recipes, specific combinations of goals and values. The use of the word *recipe* is quite deliberate as it indicates that there are "best combinations" (in a normative sense) of public policies. Thus, there are no trade-offs, rather political choices between recipes of substantive policy goals. Finally, I also argue that in combination, particular policy tools can have distinctive outcomes depending on the recipe or specific mix of values.

These propositions are then developed in accordance with the policy options considered in Chapter 6. Community integrity and maximum mobility options are evaluated with respect to a normative model of equality and justice. This model is premised on individual welfare as the primary, but not the sole, datum point for evaluating "good" and "bad" outcomes. Social standards of resource equality are the devices for measuring equality. As such, the proposed model is a non-utilitarian model that is social or contextual, not individualistic and universal. Given equality of resources, the analysis then reintroduces questions of mobility, locational preference and choice. By using an envy test (wherein equality of resources is maintained over the experiential time of individuals to the point where they are indifferent between alternative distributions), it is shown that some people may well prefer to live in places like Flint despite their reduced economic options. Only by maintaining the choice option (mobility in response to relative deprivation) can community integrity be morally justified. Thus, it is shown that regional welfare need not be thought of as a constraint on an otherwise "bigger pie," rather it can be thought of as one ingredient in a recipe for overall social justice.

My goal in this monograph is to elaborate upon the assumptions and philosophical bases of current public policy options. To do so requires some detective work, especially with regard to isolating the philosophical meanings of policy options such as embodies in the *UA in the 80s* Panel report. Thus, there may be some disagreement over my characterizations. If so, this can only benefit the debate over policy, for too much academic research has naively taken quite sterile definitions of "good" policy as given. This detective work also requires a framework, a mode for organizing research. There may be debate over the usefulness of this framework. Well and good! More empirical and less philosophical are the research results presented in this monograph. Even here, however, there is bound to be debate, especially since the methods and data used are quite different from conventional modes of analysis.

NOTES

1. See, for example, the recent paper by Ostergren (1981) on the links between Swedish towns and villages and their counterparts in Minnesota. Piore (1979b) discussed more generally the nature of U.S. immigration from Italian regions.

2. Houseman (1979) has provided an in-depth account of this doctrine and its basis in the U.S. Constitution.

3. Pole (1980, p. 6) noted that de Tocqueville was quite conscious of the liberating potential of migration from the possible arbitrary control of government. Voluntary residence in a particular jurisdiction is then taken to indicate consent to the laws, even norms of legitimate behavior. From this position, notions of exit, voice, and loyalty have been inflated to represent a theory of local government legitimacy (Clark and Dear 1984).

4. Blackstone contended that there is a trinity of absolute rights. The first concerned personal security, the second personal property, and most significantly for our purposes, personal liberty "the power of locomotion, of changing situations or moving one's person to whatsoever place one's own inclination may direct" (quoted in Berger 1977, p. 21).

5. H.R. report No. 369 77th Congress 1st Session (1941) *Report of the Select Committee of the House of Representatives Investigation of the Interstate Migration of Destitute Citizens,* Washington, D.C.

6. See *Fisher v. Reiser* 610 F.2d 629 (9th Cir. 1979) on a case related to the relevance of place of residence as a condition for receiving workers' compensation.

7. Details on different propensities to migrate by country are shown in Rogers (1979).

8. *Urban America in the Eighties* (1980, p. 5).

9. See Poole (1981) on the importance of people moving to jobs from the conservative perspective of the Washington, D.C. based Heritage Foundation. For a more general and balanced review of the issue see the recent report by the National Research Council's Committee on National Urban Policy (1982).

10. See for example Clark (1980a) and Soja (1980) on the spatial dialectics of power and inequality. Their argument was that regional inequality need not be a *necessary* condition for the reproduction of capitalism. Rather, that location is an active variable in the relations between labor and capital that may at time result in greater or lesser spatial inequality.

11. For example, Tribe (1973) listed the evaluation procedure used by the National Academy of Engineering for technology planning: (1) identify and refine the subject to be assessed; (2) delineate the scope of the assessment and develop a data base; (3) identify alternative strategies to solve the selected problems. . .; (4) identify parties affected . . .; (5) identify the impacts on the affected parties; (6) evaluate or measure the impacts; (7) compare the pros and cons of alternative strategies. These steps are both focused and systematic, relying upon the nature of the problem at hand as well as the nature and scope of relevant social science methodology. Legitimate policy analysis is presumed to operate *within* the structure of the political processes; serving essentially the institution through which policy outcomes are generated (Tribe 1972). Numerous governmental agencies in the United States have adopted the rational model as the basis for their own planning and policy evaluation, including for example, in the Housing and Urban Development's (HUD) Office of Policy Research and Development.

12. Putnam (1981, ch. 6) argued at length that, philosophically, the supposed fact-value dichotomy is indefensible. He suggested that it has no rational basis, and exists primarily as a cultural institution. He has also conceded however that "even if some better philosopher than I could show by an absolutely conclusive argument (that the dichotomy is indefensible) . . . still the next time you went out into the street, or to a cocktail party . . . you would find someone saying to you 'Is that supposed to be a statement of fact or a value judgement?'"

13. Emphasis upon standards in this context, rather than rules, is quite deliberate. Rules can be either formal (as in law) or informal (as in "accepted behavior") and legitimate specific types of human actions. They seek to be systematic and inclusive regulations that set out the proper extent of behavior (Kennedy 1976). Rules are designed to cover a multiplicity of situations and in doing so are formulated to remove individual discression in response. For example, in situation X, behavior Y is the rule. Standards on the other hand are ethical or normative judgments made about the "value" of certain kinds of behavior or objectives. For example, in situation X, honest behavior is expected. Obviously judgments about the correctness of standards and whether or not prescribed standards are observed, involves moral values. Unlike rules, there is no expectation that there can be simple binary (0 - 1, right - wrong) tests of appropriate behavior.

14. Habermas (1982) makes a distinction between knowledge as in understanding, and knowledge that allows for instrumental action. The former is concerned with the structuration of social thought, the latter with action within a priori defined social networks. Here, I obviously refer to the latter.

15. Arrow's Impossibility Theorem, demonstrates that, given initial and plausible assumptions, there is no ideal rational aggregation device of inidividuals' preferences.

TWO

Community, Efficiency, and Public Policy

Much of this chapter is an evaluation and critique of the underlying assumptions and propositions of the conservative urban policy agenda. As noted earlier, I take this agenda to be represented by the panel report *Urban America in the Eighties,* and the 1982 *President's National Urban Policy Report.* These reports are evaluated on their own terms, and the analysis here is concerned with the internal coherence of the conservative agenda. In beginning with an internal evaluation, recognition is given to conservative claims of the legitimacy and seriousness of their proposals. This presumption of credibility should not, however, be taken as implying my agreement with the underlying assumptions and objectives of the conservative agenda. I do not believe that their case can be sustained, especially on grounds that they claim to best represent their position. I will demonstrate this first by an analysis of the coherence of the conservative agenda, then by an empirical evaluation of their predictive qualities, and finally by an external evaluation vis-à-vis the credibility of their normative vision of reality.

My goal in this chapter isn't exactly the destruction of the con- servative urban agenda. No concealed, hidden, or external truths will be introduced to demonstrate that the conservatives have got it wrong.[1] According to the logic of the previous chapter, this strategy is at once implausible and indeterminant. It is implausible, because destruction appeals to an external and validated truth, an empirical reference point that exists separate from the arguments that *structure* the facts. Such a critique would only perpetuate the myth of "objective" social inquiry, ignoring the fact-value nexus central to all interpretation. Ultimately, this strategy is also indeterminant because it cannot help us in understanding the *mode(s)* of interpretive action; of giving meaning to facts, structure to observation. The escape clause for those wishing to avoid destruction is to simply claim that the critic has misinterpreted either the facts or the underlying arguments. That is, for whatever reasons, the critic has mistaken the truth. And, since there may be no common standards of adjudication, destructive criticism often ends at an impasse with neither side willing or able to give up their particular vision of the "truth," and with no way of going forward in the critical evaluation of alternative interpretations (Leitch 1983).

In an internal evaluation of the conservative argument, I am essentially deconstructing the logical structure of the conservative position.[2] I am concerned with how the conservative argument is made, what facts they choose to employ, and what they have to assume in order to structure their own interpretation of reality. In this way the conservative agenda will be evaluated according to what it proclaims to be true with respect to urban processes, and the method by which the conservative position is presented. Some literary critics have referred to this internal analysis as a *double-reading* of the text (*see* especially Norris 1982). Rather than assuming the authority of the author to be the primary mode of interpretation, the reader evaluates the manner in which interpretation is structured, looking for false moves, assumptions and internal inconsistencies. The existence of *internal* contradictions, of irreconcilabilities and inconsistencies is, according to this logic, damning evidence that may lead the reader to conclude that the underlying argument is fatuous. I will be helped in this task, figuratively speaking, by Ronald Dworkin's (1980b) critique of the notion of efficiency.

URBAN POLICY AND THE ROLE OF GOVERNMENT

The Carter administation was in many ways the final expression of some ten years of debate over the proper role and design of national urban policy in America. Even though it was criticized by some academics as being only a smorgasbord of unrelated activities, and that it was limited by a modest level of funding, the Carter administration's urban policy sought to reverse "the deterioration of urban life in the United States."[3] To that end, the Executive Branch took an active role in formulating and defending urban policy; so much so that the Department of Housing and Urban Development (HUD) had an unprecedented Cabinet and bureaucratic role in structuring domestic policy itself. Rather than simply administering entitlement programs, such as housing subsidies, and presiding over a small but active bureaucracy, assistant secretaries were encouraged to think of their roles in a larger context. The Carter administration focused upon four general areas: employment and economic development; fiscal assistance; housing and community development; and, most important, coordination of federal program activities.[4] This last aspect was often emphasized by the President, who in doing so defined the role of government to be a crucial lever in encouraging public response.

One consequence of this essentially activist role was the formation of the Urban Impact Assessment Policy (Circular A–116), wherein other departments such as Defense (not traditionally interested in the plight of cities) were required to submit urban impact assessments of new and existing programs. In short order, the profile of HUD was raised to heights of power and influence unknown in previous administrations (Hanson 1982). National and urban policy was to be coordinated and to be made consistent, and the larger conflicts between various departments' agendas were to be considered in terms of their spatial outcomes.[5] In this way, national and urban policy making was to be formally integrated (Clark 1980b). For example, the urban implications of defense procurement policies became not only a matter for those localities directly affected, the underlying spatial pattern also became a matter of public policy. Less contentious, but as important, were the evaluations of the urban impacts of tax policies and anti-recessionary programs (Glickman 1979).

Underlying this ideal-type policy (for that is what it was, given that it remained largely experimental and did not survive the Reagan transition), was a proposed redefinition of the role of government vis-à-vis urban problems. Previous administrations had been quite concerned with urban policy but in a largely ad hoc manner. Although many policies had been designed and implemented (such as the Model Cities Program of Nixon; *see* Hanson 1982), HUD remained very much an institution of response to previously identified problems, even those of other agencies. In this respect, its agenda was similar to the Department of Health, Education and Welfare (HEW) because by responding to urban problems it was fulfilling a welfare function.

Programmatically, and in terms of expenditure powers, HUD did not of course grow to rival departments such as HEW (primarily because of its smaller entitlement programs). The Carter administration evolved a strategy of intervention that was both more general *and* activist. By virtue of the Urban Impact Assessment program it recognized that government actions could have a pervasive and a large impact on not only the economy's performance but also its very geographical and structural (sectoral) character.[6] Thus, to the extent that the federal government's various actions could be coordinated and focused on the economic landscape, the very fabric of urban America could be permanently changed for the better of all citizens, and especially the disadvantaged in the inner cities. President Carter proclaimed that the federal government had a "clear duty" to lead urban revitalization, in part by making existing programs more sensitive to local needs, as well as by providing for the needs of particularly distressed communities.

This positive and active leverage role, promoted by and for the federal government, had its antecedents in the Democratic Party and the Great Society programs of the Johnson administration. Reflected in the "positive force" notion is a (liberal) conception of the state as a means of transforming society for the benefit of those most disadvantaged. To understand what is implied in this conception of the state, we should recognize that there are three principal ways of defining the role of the state in society. One is essentially functionalist; the state is defined according to what the state does. In these terms, the state is simply an ensemble of administrative, bureaucratic, and legislative agencies. It is composed of the Department of the Treasury, the Justice Department, and the Congress that legislates on matters concerning individual rights and duties. These examples can be extended to many areas of social welfare, defense, economic planning, and of course urban welfare. The point is that the state is more than government; it is an institution that functions in the realm of collective social activity, and it may have no direct links to the democratic process.

A second approach is essentially realist, wherein the state is described in terms of how it acts. For example, it provides defense, police, justice, education, and so forth. Taken more broadly, however, the realist position also describes the motivations of state actions. For example, both conservatives and radicals often argue that the state acts on behalf of the ruling elite or special interest groups (*see* Huntington 1981 and Ely 1980). The realist position is different from the functionalist position in that the state's actions are given an intent or purpose whereas the functionalist position is that the state is what the state does.

The third approach is basically normative and describes what the state should do. For example, liberal political theory argues that the state should represent the interests of all citizens, or, as a subset, that the state should preserve the freedom of all citizens (Tribe 1980). The realist approach could also be described as idealist in that the state's role is defined with respect to utopian visions of society. According to the liberal agenda, the state is thought to be an agent or positive force, a means of sustaining certain values and achieving particular social goals. Conservatives, such as Berger (1977), have supposed, on the other hand, that the positive force analogy is a threat to the established order, and that the proper role of the state is to minimize its intervention in the private lives of citizens.

All three definitions make the point that the state is an institution autonomous, to a greater or lesser extent, from the structure of society. For Choper (1980), a constitutional conservative, the intervention of the judiciary in legislative matters is a normative question, but for Wilson (1980), who could be thought of as a realist, it is a fact of life that must be retained as a central element of any empirical investigation. It is also useful to note that the basic difference between the first two definitions and the third is their very different analytical perspectives. The former considers the state as the primary object of enquiry; the latter views the state from the perspective of society. Nordlinger (1981) has termed these analytical perspectives as, respectively, *state-centered* and *society-centered* models of the state.[7]

To understand the liberal notion of the state as a positive force in initiating social change requires a brief appreciation of the differences between state-centered and society-centered theories of the state. The latter theory would suppose that the source of change in state policy is derived out of society, that the state cannot change society in ways counter to existing social values. Society-centered theories see the state as very much a product of society. Theorists of democratic participation, such as represented by Verba and Nie (1972), argue that the state *responds* to social goals, and even if it attempts to radically alter society, the democratic structure would force the state back to the status quo. More philosophically, society-centered democratic theories would deny that a state capable of altering society in this way would be in fact democratic; more likely, it would be totalitarian. State-centered theorists emphasize the power of the state as an institution. For example, Wilson (1980) has suggested that through the leverage this power gives the state over society, society itself can be modified. Liberal policy of the 1960s and 1970s conceived the state in very similar terms. Without control of the state, social change might not be possible. It was this notion that was a cornerstone of the Johnson administration.

Despite President Carter's claim to conservatism and for the necessity of a smaller role for government, the underlying principles that guided the formation of urban policy in the last half of his administration were traditionally liberal. To be sure, deregulation and cutbacks in government expenditures and programs were major objectives behind Carter's administration, yet even within that agenda government actions were seen for their potential—their enabling power in altering society. It is then ironic that the President's Commission for a National Agenda for the Eighties, and, in particular, the report *Urban America in the Eighties: Perspectives and Prospects* should have appeared in the last phases of the Carter administration because, unlike the Urban Impact Assessment Program and the underlying philosophy of the domestic policy staff, this report was strongly critical of government intervention. It was the antithesis of the activist philosophy embodied in programs such as Urban Impact Assessment.

To be more specific, the report *UA in the 80s* is much more consistent with traditional conservative doctrine and in particular President Reagan's philosophy that governments should not initiate change in the underlying structure of society or in the economy. Stressed throughout the report is an assertion that the government is relatively powerless to alter the underlying patterns of economic transformation. The report deliberately attempts to counter the notion that the government can use its size and position in the economy to alter local (geographical) outcomes. According to this logic, governments can and should only facilitate change. More than anything else, the report is a restatement of conservative political beliefs, so popular in American history (*see* L. Hartz 1955), that governments should maintain a low profile consistent with society-centered theories of the state. Moreover, with respect to that tradition, the report reasserts the overall preeminence of the national interest over diverse, competing, and essentially anarchical local interests. Not that local interests are denied: quite the contrary, they are recognized as unique and ultimately as the cornerstone of American decentralized democracy. The central point of the report is its claim that the nation is best served by maximum national growth: urban policy, like welfare policy, is seen in this light as an unnecessary encumbrance. At the level of political philosophy, it is no wonder that liberal and democratic party groups summarily rejected the *Urban America in the Eighties* report and saw it quite plainly as an embarassment to the outgoing President.

Yet, it is quite obvious that the report came at an auspicious time. It could hardly be more in tune with the Reagan agenda: a minimal role for government, local responsibility for local problems, restructuring of the American economy, and the destruction of national social programs. Implied in the recommendations of the panel is a clear conception of the proper relationship between national and urban policy put summarily as: "Ultimately, the federal government's concern for national economic vitality should take precedence over the competition for advantage among communities and localities" (p. 5). As such it is a manifesto for reordering national urban policy and a blueprint for a much reduced role for federal intervention in urban problems. For these reasons, and the policy prescriptions that were recommended by the panel members, I wish to detail the basic argument of the report as a prelude for analytical enquiry into the possible relationships between local and national welfare, and ultimately the supposed role of the federal government vis-à-vis interregional migration.

The *UA in the 80s* report argued for a much reduced role for federal intervention in urban areas in three steps. First, it was observed that non-metropolitan and sunbelt economic growth has occurred despite the federal government's attempts to bolster the economies of older northern and central cities. According to the panel, a structural and geographical transformation of the economy has occurred quite independently of the federal government. The flow of population out of urban developed areas is argued to be a *consequence* of the shift toward a post-industrial economy that is characterized by extremely efficient information processing and transfer technologies which obviate the need for traditional spatial forms such as urban agglomeration. The characteristics of this transformation are thought to be many and varied. For example, the shift to a service economy, according to the report, means that the advantages of urban areas for heavy durables manufacturing firms (market, low transportation costs, skilled labor, linkages with other input firms, etc.) are no longer as critical in determining the location of those firms concerned with manufacturing (this point has been made in detail by Stanback and Noyelle 1982). Obviously cities are a barometer of these changes, but only that. The economy is changing its spatial form or glove; what is left is an outmoded form of spatial economic organization that will *naturally* adapt—if given a chance by less government intervention (or so the argument goes)!

Second, it was also observed that the fiscal and economic distress of the cities is in large part a function of the poor performance of the national economy (*see* Vernez et al. 1977 for more detail and evidence). Low, even negative productivity, a flood of cheaper imports, the volatility in the U.S. dollar on foreign exchanges and the poor performance of basic industries were all noted to have had quite severe and differentiated spatial impacts. The report then asserted that it is inevitable that winners and losers are created in such an environment, both sectorally and spatially. Finally, in line with this logic, the panel noted that policies which seek to maximize economic performance also create differential local impacts and distress.[8]

These propositions depend on one basic assumption: in the aggregate the economy *creates* the conditions under which the urban system operates or functions. In the jargon of regional econometric modeling, the report assumes a top-down economic-spatial system.[9] Rather than the aggregate economy being composed (summed-up) by its constituent elements (the urban system), it apparently has an independent existence. In reading this section and argument of the *Urban America in the Eighties* report it is apparent that the panel was unaware of the well-known description of the national economy being a system of cities, composed and created out of the separate and interdependent functions of each economic and geographical unit (*see* Berry 1964).

It is of course true that the top-down conceptualization of the spatial economy has some utility in describing impacts and modeling the behavior of urban areas separately and in relation to national economic performance. This approach enables comparisons between areas in their patterns of economic behavior relative to a "norm." But as a conceptual device for describing the spatial economy in general it has a basic flaw: it inevitably introduces the prospect for a conflict between the interests of a region and the interests of the nation. This was in fact the third stage to their argument. The *UA in the 80s* report suggested that policies which seek to restore the economic vitality of older industrial urban areas undermine maximum national economic growth. In essence, policies of urban reindustrialization [to invert Bluestone and Harrison's (1982) terms] subtract from the potential level of national economic growth. No empirical evidence was introduced to support the claim and despite its apparent rhetorical appeal, this assertion was based on a fallacy that the whole (the performance of the national economy) is more than the sum total of its parts (urban economic growth). This assertion may or may not be true, by redistributing wealth to poor areas, overall economic performance may suffer. In the end, the veracity of the argument depends on many factors not introduced—like real evidence.

Having made this argument, the panel asked whether or not a reconciliation can be made between the imperatives of maximum national economic growth and urban "health". In brief, the answer had two parts. No, if it means bolstering older (worthless) areas and their economies. Yes, if it means finding new roles for all urban areas. Redistribution of people, jobs, and economic activity is necessary, according to the report, for national prosperity. Transformation of all areas will help the nation reach its potential. From this conclusion it is a short step to policy, and the policy responses were entirely predictable. The government should facilitate spatial and sectoral economic transformation and not attempt to reverse these trends. Appropriate policies would encourage labor mobility, capital restructuring, and access of the unemployed and disadvantaged to the areas of new growth. The panel argued that the *natural* path of spatial redistribution must be accommodated by policies which are based on a *people-to-jobs* conception, not a *jobs-to-people* one. It is not too strong to suggest that the report assumed the economy to have a *will* or *design* that is natural or immutable, in their terms a process that should not be interfered with. This places the "laws of economics" in the metaphysical realm, close to divine natural order.[10]

Throughout, the report emphasized that the underlying trends should not be tampered with, that relocation must be facilitated and that any actions hindering this process will place the whole national economy in jeopardy. Thus, policies of local economic development were seen to be counterproductive and ultimately doomed to failure. Accordingly, such policies apparently ignore the larger context—the fundamental importance of national growth and the irreversibility of economic trends. More specifically, the panel also argued that aggregate policies are unable to account for or deal with the uniqueness of local conditions. No one federal policy would be adept in anticipating or responding to the diversity of local conditions. If this is to be the federal role, the report argued, then even states and local communities must also be encouraged to facilitate these trends, not to attempt to counter them (*see* Carleson 1981; cf. Nathan 1981). In the extreme, the report calls for the dismantling of urban policy: urban impact assessment is claimed to have been counterproductive; national urban programs encourage conflict between areas over grants and public facilities; grants to places reduce migration potentials;

and, without exhausting the list, national urban policies set the government in an adversarial relationship with business, and do not encourage the public-private partnerships so necessary for national economic growth.[11]

So, what should the federal government do in terms of urban areas? What is the minimal role prescribed by the report? There are two dimensions noted by the panel. First, the federal government must facilitate the structural and geographical transformation of the economy by ensuring the efficiency of migration (adaptability to changing local conditions; directionality vis-à-vis the expanding demand for labor; and speed in response to new economic opportunities, etc.). To the extent that spatial impediments to the efficient functioning of the national economy exist, then the federal government must intervene to provide the conditions for maximum economic growth. Those familiar with the history of government intervention in the spatial economic development of the U.S. economy will immediately recognize this option as the conservative policy agenda (*see* Clark 1981a). Second, the report also emphasized the need for the government to help and compensate those most affected by these changing economic times. For example the report suggested that "where disadvantage and inequality are selective and cumulative, federal efforts should be expended to ameliorate these consequences in ways that *are consistent with developmental trends within the society and economy as a whole*" (p. 101, emphasis added).

There are many similarities between the 1982 *President's NUPR* and the *UA in the 80s* report, specifically in terms of their assumptions, arguments, and philosophy. Secretary of HUD Samuel Pierce, in his letter of transmittal of the 1982 *President's NUPR* to President Reagan, noted the priorities of the administration's urban policy to be (a) greater emphasis on economic growth; (b) a proper balance of responsibilities between different tiers of government; (c) encouragement of private sector initiatives; (d) encouragement of local leadership; and (e) experimental enterprise zones.[12] Whatever the importance of each priority, it was immediately apparent from the report that maximum national economic growth was to be the principal objective. This ordering of priorities was expressed in a number of ways. In the overview to the report it was stated that "if cities are to prosper, our economy must be healthy and vital" (p. 3). Accordingly, a strong national economy was argued to be a *precondition* for an adequate and productive urban policy (a "top-down" conception).

A more oblique reference to the same issue was made in Chapter 1 of the report where it was noted that the administration's Economic Recovery Program would prompt a turnaround in the country's economic competitiveness. To the extent that the program works, said the report, then economic growth "will directly strengthen the economy of cities and thereby cure many related problems" (p. 1-10). To bolster their argument, the *Urban Policy Report* also quoted the

Joint Economic Committee of Congress to the same effect.[13] Without going into the detail of the Economic Recovery Act, the major elements to this program were the stabilization of the money supply, income and corporate tax cuts, incentives for greater private saving and investment, and the reduction of federal regulations and spending.[14] While the tax cut was implemented during 1982, the prospects for reductions in federal government spending were bleak, since the federal deficit assumed record proportions and unemployment reached over 10% and much higher in specific states.[15] Throughout the urban policy report, the primacy of national economic growth was stressed and re-stressed, and previous urban policies (often unnamed) of other administrations (also often unnamed, but presumably Republican and Democrat) were blamed for having seriously compromised this goal. For example, in the early sections of Chapter 1, it was noted that, compared to other countries, the U.S. has had a very poor record on productivity growth. And earlier in the report it was asserted that interventionist urban policy may have forestalled economic growth. Only by reading through to Chapter 2 did it become clear that a prime example was the Economic Development Administration's aid to the steel industry during the Carter Administration.

Through a discussion of the evolution of the urban economic system it also became apparent that the 1982 *Urban Policy Report* agreed in almost every respect with the *UA in the 80s* report. The Reagan administration's argument also proceeded in three stages. First, it was argued that the urban agglomeration of the late nineteenth and early twentieth centuries was a function of industrial and transportation technology. Localization of production was due to the type of activity, especially in the heavy secondary industries sectors, and the tremendous costs of transporting raw materials. By focusing upon the steel industry, the report made an argument that could be characterized as Weberian: the pull of resources mediated by the costs of transportation and the need to locate close to markets. By then invoking agglomeration and external economies, the report argued that the resulting urban system was both efficient and inherently maximized national economic growth.

The second stage to the administration's argument was a discussion of the transformation of the economy away from a heavy secondary industry concentration to a high-technology and service-oriented economy. In large part, the means of this transformation was thought by the report to be significant changes in transportation technology and increasing real income. Both trends, according to the report, fostered spatial deconcentration and decentralization. Thus, as transportation became cheaper, the national economy became more integrated and interdependent, goods could be shipped further and production could be dispersed from close proximity to markets. Likewise, households could relocate from the center cities, thereby improving their material standards of living. In all this description, the report emphasized that not only did the market enable strong economic growth, it was also able to transform itself (spatially and sectorally) so that real standards of living increased.

The third stage of the argument had essentially a dual message: intervention by the federal government to offset or divert this market process has both failed and reduced the effectiveness of the market. Like the *UA in the 80s* report, the Reagan administration believed (and probably still believes) that the federal government is not strong enough to control the market. In particular, "[t]he effectiveness of these (interventionist and ameliorative) policies was somewhat limited, however, because the economic forces propelling jobs and populations dispersal have been so strong" (p. 1–7). From that point, the report emphasized that intervention only slows the market, causes unnecessary disruptions and, in the long run, creates greater hardship. Again, the *natural* market is thought to be more virtuous, and certainly more efficient than the federal government. For example, in Chapter 2 the report stated, without qualification or evidence, "the private market is more efficient than Federal program administrators in allocating dollars among alternative uses" (p. 2–16). Thus, again like the *UA in the 80s* report, the market is given an *intent* and *design* of almost a metaphysical character.

So as to demonstrate the strengths of the market, and the apparent inability of the federal government to sustain local economic growth, the report noted the turnaround of the New England economy over the past decade. Quite rightly, the report pointed out that even as late as 1975/76, few analysts had confidence in the New England economy. Despite attempts at job creation and EDA-type subsidies, traditional sectors continued to decline. In contrast, without apparent public assistance, the high-technology sector began its meteoric growth. What this phenomenon has proved is more debatable than the Reagan administration cares to allow. Suggestions that this example is the model for growth in other areas of the country have not been closely examined. Already in some quarters, alarm has been expressed about the possibility of a mercantilist type of competition between other areas of the United States for high-technology firms. In fact, the evidence of one sector's growth in an era of economic stagnation may simply serve to focus the economic development agencies of many states on the type of competition justly criticized by the federal government. In any event, one example is hardly the evidence necessary to convince many politicians and citizens of the Midwest that their economy is likely to turn around in the next decade, let alone over the balance of this century.[16]

Policies promoted by the report included Urban Enterprise Zones[17] and Urban Development Action Grants (the latter already an active and successful program administered by the Department of Housing and Urban Development). Despite the familiarity of Urban Development Action Grants to many local economic planners, as leverage devices for encouraging private investment in targeted areas, the rationale for their importance offered by the report has a particular market-oriented basis. In Chapter 1, the authors of the report argued that there are indeed good opportunities for development in many depressed centers. The problem, according to the report, has been that individual firms have been unwilling to take the first risk. Thus the government has to start the process and, according to this logic, "demonstrate the viability of investments in certain depressed urban areas." Yet again the market is to be the vehicle for urban economic development conditional upon the need to make urban policies compatible with the overall priority of maximum national economic growth.

This was exactly the same logic employed by the panel in the *UA in the 80s* report: policies must be designed to assist economic adjustment, not hinder the naturally efficient allocative mechanisms of the market. The role of state and local governments in this new era of laissez faire was argued by the President's report to be (a) greater concentration on making their areas attractive to investors by reducing unnecessary regulation, taxes, and an antagonistic attitude to business, while (b) facilitating and encouraging economic transformation as it occurs at the regional, national, and international levels (*see* Ch. 4 of the panel report). In these terms, it is apparent that the agenda for state and local governments was the same as for the national government—the promotion of maximum national economic growth.

The *UA in the 80s* is an extraordinary document, both for its conservative tenor (especially given the fact that President Carter initiated the study), and for its conception of the role of urban policy in the national arena. And, like the 1982 President's Urban Report, the *UA in the 80s* was incredibly nihilistic in that it argues that national policy cannot change the underlying economic trends of the economy (although the reason is at best unclear) and that interventionist policies inevitably fail because they cannot be adequately targeted to local experience. One is left wondering if this meant that the New Deal must have failed and economic catastrophes such as the Depression of the 1930s, of the Appalachians during the 1950s, and of the Midwest today, must necessarily be endured. Both reports are also incredibly simplistic in their naturalistic notions of immutable economic laws. The metaphysics of conservative doctrine has come to replace logical argument. And last but not least, both argued for the primacy of maximum national economic welfare against local interests, assuming an implausible conception of the spatial economic system: top-down as opposed to the more logical notion of bottom-up.

At the same time, Carter's panel and the Reagan administration presumed much about the patterns of interregional migration and economic growth without actually providing empirical evidence for their conclusions. For example, the trends in migration between the Northeast and Southwest are thought to be so stable and fixed that intervention to change these patterns would inevitably fail. But there is virtually no evidence introduced in either report to prove this assertion. If it could be shown that labor force migration is extremely volatile in both its volume over time and its geographical patterns, then surely both reports would be compromised on their own fact-value terms (coherence). Similarly, it is also assumed that labor migration inevitably benefits places that attract large numbers of migrants; that, in fact, the overall spatial economic system benefits (on net) in the long run by an efficient market allocation of labor. Yet, again there is virtually no real evidence to back up these assertions, and if interregional migration does not bestow benefits on destination areas then both reports, even the whole conservative agenda, would be compromised. The point is that these reports, which recommend such drastic policy conclusions, *must* be consistent and sure of their facts. Instead, we are forced to accept their "facts" on face value—no evidence is actually presented!

In subsequent chapters, the "facts" of interregional migration and regional growth are explored in more detail. Chapter 3 reviews the evidence on the impacts of migration on wages and income for both prosperous and declining areas. Then, in Chapter 4, the relationships between migration and capital investment are considered in depth. In both chapters, the evidence, based upon the conceptual frameworks implicit in the conservative agenda, is contrary to the assumptions of both reports. Not only do the reports assert recommendations without substantive evidence to back their assumptions, their evidence, consistent with their fact-value nexus, directly challenges the validity of their assertions.

NATIONAL WEALTH AND JUSTICE

Time and again throughout both reports the reader's attention is drawn to the supposed fundamental importance of ensuring maximum national economic growth. The reader is often warned that urban policy compromises this goal; that the basic objective of the government must be to stand above the local (parochial) concerns, by ensuring the development of the national economy. Through maximizing economic growth, it is often contended that national income and wealth will expand to the limits imposed by technology and resources.[18] Although maximum economic growth and wealth are never really defined in both reports, given their specific value positions, these two related goals might be best interpreted in terms of Posner's (1981, p. 61) terms, who noted that "the wealth of society is the aggregate satisfaction of those preferences (the only ones that have ethical weight in a system of wealth maximization) that are backed up by money, that is, that are registered in a market." In the *UA in the 80s* report, maximum national wealth is conceived as a goal in its own right that can be measured either directly, as in output, productivity, and income, or indirectly, as in a proper accounting of the opportunity costs of alternative policies.

Despite their assumptions, not everything can be traded or given a price. Posner (1981) has suggested that many attributes of wealth can be analyzed using a hypothetical or shadow market so that prices can be imputed, if not directly measured. Underlying this notion, however, is a further technical device used by economists to ensure maximum economic growth and welfare: efficiency itself. By the efficient functioning of the spatial economy, national economic growth is achieved. According to Just et al. (1982, p. 11), economic efficiency has to do with ensuring the maximum production of desired goods given a set of resources, technology, and income distribution.[19] They explicitly distinguish between equity and efficiency, and they argue that efficiency is simply the best use of resources for a given end.

Efficiency is then a means to an end and, in simple terms, an efficient solution is one in which a given product is produced at minimum cost (assuming that prices reflect the true value of inputs and their relative scarcity). Musgrave and Musgrave (1978, p. 63) noted three particular rules of efficiency: (a) given an amount of input X, Y should be produced in the largest amounts possible; (b) the rate at which two customers (A and B) are willing to trade the last unit of X for additional units of Y should be the same; and (c) the marginal rate of substitution of X for Y in consumption should be the same as the marginal rates of transformation in production. For example, to the extent that the demand and supply of labor are allocated in the most efficient manner vis-à-vis the spatial configuration of production and demand, then national wealth will be maximized.

Because it is the sum of all individual actions and outcomes that determines the national level of welfare, an efficient solution must take into account the *relative* place of individuals vis-à-vis their productive capacities. An efficient arrangement in these terms is one in which there can be no rearrangement that will leave someone better off without worsening the position of others. Conventionally, this definition is the Pareto efficiency notion. Put another way, one allocation of resources is Pareto superior to another if at least one person is made better off and no other person is made worse off (Posner 1981, p. 88). Whatever the merits of this conception of efficiency, and there is some debate over this issue because of its denial of the underlying pattern of income and wealth as well as the concept of needs, it does provide a datum point for evaluating alternative strategies of production and allocation.[20] The Pareto superior standard in particular allows for a ranking of policy options, indicating whether or not each option is an improvement over the other in terms of total utility. Thus some standard or calculation is required to make a judgment, and in terms of utilitarian theory this also means that individual utilities must be comparable and additive (Coleman 1980).

There is of course wide debate over the possibility of individually based, summed social welfare functions (Arrow 1951). It would be misleading, however, to suggest that both reports necessarily meant to invoke this strict definition of welfare. Rather, emphasis in both was placed on the macroeconomic characteristics of the aggregate spatial system; maximum national welfare is measurable as market prices, output, income, and labor productivity. Furthermore, the extent to which an urban policy inhibits labor and capital mobility and creates less than optimal national economic growth, then in these terms the cost of such policies could presumably be measured in terms of the potential economic growth foregone and in the real cost of implementing such a policy. Thus, a calculation is made between the most efficient solution and other options, the difference between the strict welfare definition and the conservative agenda is that rather than dealing with individual utilities, the metric of policy analysis is explicitly numeraire and based on aggregate indicators.[21] From this perspective, an internal one concerning their logic, it could be concluded that both reports are a poor imitation of *good* neoclassical economic analysis. Such a characterization would be unfair because other writers, such as Posner (1981), have also attempted to generalize the notion of wealth maximization to cover public policy issues while at the same time returning to the notions of efficiency and Pareto superiority.

In reality of course, few situations are readily adaptable to the Pareto-superior criterion. Most issues of policy require some decision over who will benefit and who will lose. The conception of a zero-sum game, so popular these days as a characterization of society (Thurow, 1980), does pose a real dilemma for policy analysis. In this context, it is conventionally thought that the goal must be to minimize losses or at least compensate those who lose while broader national goals are being pursued. And, this conception of compensation is a central facet of both the *UA in the 80s* report and the President's Urban Report. But this notion involves more than simply accommodating losers. Emphasis upon efficiency and the rule of Pareto superiority also implies that compensation itself must be consistent with the goals of maximum wealth. For example, where the *UA in the 80s* report mentioned compensation (as on p. 101), it also noted that such compensation must be "consistent with developmental trends within the society and economy as a whole." This is also an argument made continually by the Reagan administration![22] The result of such a conditional compensation provision is that targeted and limited policies of help may be more preferable than general, nationwide categorical programs of entitlement. To put the matter bluntly, trade adjustment subsidies in specific areas may be preferable to CETA public service employment in all areas.

The type of compensation principle implied by the *UA in the 80s,* and perhaps by the President's report, is clearly the Kaldor-Hicks principle. This requires that if some are made worse off by a reallocation of resources, or by a new policy of efficiency, the resulting increase in aggregate wealth must be such that the losers can be fully compensated. Some writers, such as Posner (1981, p. 91) have referred to this notion as *Potential Pareto Superiority,* in that if compensation actually does take place and the resulting increase in aggregate wealth more than matches the losses incurred by some citizens, then the overall distribution may be *Pareto superior.* Notice that the issue here, as for the report, is not increased welfare in the sense of redistribution or individual well-being: it is strictly one of wealth maximization. That is the fundamental goal of policy makers. To the extent that efficiency may require greater (ex ante) inequality in order to maximize national wealth, the economic and spatial system may be polarized so that there are many more losers than gainers. Compensation, along the lines of the Kaldor-Hicks principle, is an ex-post policy. After having achieved the policy goal, governments may intervene (as long as efficiency is not compromised) to help those most affected.

There are, of course, many difficulties with the Kaldor-Hicks principle. For instance, it refers only to potential compensation; in reality, full compensation may not be implemented, even though "efficiency" may lead to greater overall wealth. The Kaldor-Hicks principle may simply legitimate a policy of spatial inequality without providing the means to evaluate its consequences. As well, more technically, it is quite conceivable that a situation will arise in which two or more distributions are Kaldor-Hicks efficient, but there is no way of making a definitive judgment. The Scitovsky (1941) paradox is in fact a demonstration of this possibility. Total output (in terms of dollars expended) may be exactly the same in two cases, but the underlying composition of the output (its allocation amongst different bundles of goods) may be different. More problematic would be the generation of the same output through markedly different income distributions. For example, it is plausible that complete spatial-economic concentration would produce the same amount of total wealth as complete spatial-economic deconcentration. In reality, there may be no uniquely efficient solutions, whatever the initial presumption in favor of Kaldor-Hicks compensation. To break such an impasse another rule would have to be invoked, presumably one that was based on distributional or justice-related issues, anathema to efficiency-oriented welfare economists and apparently to the conservative urban agenda.

Further, there is a problem of measurement. How do we know how much to compensate loser locations, and what level of sacrifice is needed to ensure maximum national wealth? For theorists who are solely market-oriented, the level of compensation is presumably easy to decide upon—local income loss, employment potential, and future advancement all could have dollar assignments. It remains difficult to show how one Kaldor-Hicks solution is different from another unless there is some further investigation of what wealth itself means, how important are (in terms of substantive justice) questions of redistribution, and what are the actual impacts of alternative wealth maximizing policies.

From this perspective, it is apparent that maximum national economic growth must have a stronger meaning. Thus, what is implied in the conservative agenda by these terms? The simplest answer, and one bolstered by the work of Posner (1981) on market efficiency and outcomes, is quite plainly the highest per dollar volume of output, production, productivity, etc. Putting it crudely, maximum wealth is in fact the maximization of national income, given exogenous constraints imposed by limited natural resources. Of course, this implies that wealth can be measured, quantified, and given a true measure. Despite the obvious problems of measurement (what do prices really mean?) maximum wealth is given a contemporary meaning. For all the clarity of this answer, however, another more problematic question immediately comes to mind: Why is this goal so important? Why should it be the central goal of the federal government before which urban policy (among so many other social and welfare policies) is to be sacrificed? What is implied by the goal of maximum wealth? And, to what extent can an investigation of its meaning discover consensual foundations that will attract the support of all society as implied in the report? For the panel members and the writers of the President's report, the answers are apparently self-evident; for readers of both reports, however, the answers (propositions) are at best confused and at worst unknown.

The difficulty we have in answering these questions is that these reports never *directly* address the issue. So, we are left to derive and to interpret a set of different possible answers. Here I shall concentrate on a set of summary propositions, derived from Dworkin (1980a), that I hope best reflects the intent of the conservative agenda.[23] Notice that all propositions may be implied in the reports, it is a question of emphasis.

Proposition I—*maximum social wealth is a desired goal in and of itself.*[24] This could be interpreted as meaning that, like individuals, a society that has more wealth is obviously better off. The panel who wrote the *UA in the 80s* report often personified American society in these terms. For example, on page 4 it stated that "[the panel] believes that this nation should reconcile *itself* to these redistribution patterns" (emphasis added). By treating the nation as an individual it is, of course, possible to argue that more income is better, but such personification is incredibly naive. Surely the nation is at the very minimum the sum of its citizens: they are the ones that benefit or lose from alternative policies; and, they are the ones who materially create wealth. Once again the strategy of top-down analysis, in this case society to the individual, creates a philosophical impasse. One can hardly take it seriously unless what is really implied is that the federal government is made stronger, wealthier, and more powerful because of national growth (see Clark 1981a on this issue).

Here what may be implied is a state-centered, perhaps realist, model of the state (albeit designed to achieve conservative goals). To hypothesize for the moment, social wealth is generated by the state so as to further its own goals and agendas. In this type of model, state agencies are goal-oriented organizations that collectively seek to maximize their power and minimize their dependence upon other organizations. Wilson (1980) argued of course that state agencies often deal in a hostile environment with competition from other agencies, such as interference from political managers and demanding client groups. In order to maintain control and autonomy, state agencies seek to rationalize and differentiate their tasks in relation to threats from outside (the agency or state structure in general). Internal or bureaucratic power can be achieved by concentrating the power of task definition and diffusing responsibility. On the other hand, external power can be achieved by gaining control over financial and personnel resources—the goal in general being to sustain autonomy. For a panel and President committed to minimizing the influence of government, this characterization questions exactly what kind of intervention is held to be inappropriate. Perhaps the reality is, as a number of Reagan critics have suggested, that a strong national government is a prerequisite for conservatives to alter society according to their own agendas.

Proposition II—*maximum wealth is a worthy goal because it makes everyone better off.* Despite assertions to the contrary in the President's report, the truth of this proposition is *not* self-evident. Clearly spatial and individual inequality are considered to be inevitable and necessary, by the panel and in the President's urban report, to maximize national wealth. To the extent that the Kaldor-Hicks criterion is actually used to design policy, and full compensation is proportionally allocated to those affected, then it is possible that this proposition could be valid. In whatever way, these are quite restrictive assumptions that may or may not (and most likely not) be met in reality. This proposition is also premised on an assumption that economic growth creates benefits for all individuals. It is just as plausible that economic growth bolsters the wealth of elites and impoverishes the masses. There are no automatic or natural tendencies in the economy of income equalization or redistribution. Sharing wealth depends on public policy and intervention—compensation is one avenue, progressive taxation another. It is plain that compensation is a specific policy prescription of both reports; conditional, of course, upon the achievement of maximum national growth. Nonetheless, it is not obvious that by maximizing wealth the inequality deemed necessary for its generation will be fully or even partially compensated. This remains very much a political issue, perhaps more so than a strictly economic argument.

An argument that is often made along these same lines suggests that even if current generations of workers are not fully compensated for their sacrifices, in the long run future generations will benefit. By maximizing wealth now, in the future there will be more to be redistributed; thus, it is an intergenerational act of altruism and a transfer of wealth (or so the argument goes). The central question here, like the above, is the actual distribution of wealth in the future. If no redistribution takes place and if inequality (absolute and relative) remains the same, then the sacrifice would not have been worthwhile. To some extent, the *UA in the 80s* Panel believed this proposition to be of some merit. The report discussed the long-run benefits to the nation (presumably its citizens, not the nation personified) of a structural transformation in the 1980s (*see* Chapter 5, p. 53). Assuming that they do not commit a fallacy of national personification (I will be generous here), the panel obviously believed that in the long run all citizens will be better off. Notice that in attempting to understand the implications of this proposition, it is necessary to consider wealth maximization in terms of distribution—a conception of justice is required but never acknowledged.

More generally, this last observation is consistent with an argument by Calabresi (1980, p. 536) to the effect that "it is hard to see how an increase in wealth constitutes an improvement in society unless it furthers some other goal like utility or equality." In our context, this means that the claim that wealth maximization as a goal in and of itself is basically flawed. To understand what wealth maximization means we have to invoke some other unstated goal such as redistribution. And yet, the only obvious claim for redistribution made by both reports is for ex post compensation. At this level we can hardly be blamed for imagining that the underlying rationale for wealth maximization might be the benefit of the elites of society or of the state located in rapidly growing regions of the country. Some critics of the reports have in fact suggested that this is simply a conservative agenda for redistribution—away from the disadvantaged to the rich. Thus there may be *no* underlying conception of justice to legitimate the necessary sacrifices, and the dismantling of jobs-to-people–based urban policy. Without an explicit agenda for redistribution and justice, it is hard to escape this type of conclusion unless we suggest that the Reagan administration is naive or mistaken.

Proposition III—*maximum wealth is a worthy goal because it enables the achievement of other substantive goals.*[25] Here wealth maximization is assumed to be an instrument (just as efficiency is an instrument of wealth maximization), a means of attaining other social goals. This makes explicit what was noted to be implicit in Proposition II. What kinds of goals would be best served by maximizing wealth? The Reagan administration and Carter's panel were again less than direct in defining the likely results of wealth maximization. At times they noted that by improving access to the economic system, and by improving the overall vitality of the national economy, the fortunes of the numerous poor, disadvantaged, and unskilled would be substantially improved. Further, by removing barriers to mobility, all those seeking jobs would, according to the conservative position, substantially benefit, as would the nation. It is not clear, however, that all these goals would be best served by a national policy of wealth maximization. For example, public service employment targeted to areas in distress often improves the fortunes of the unemployed, and certainly their income. It is readily apparent that wealth maximization as an instrument for other goals may not be very effective or even appropriate in specific instances.

More general goals that may be instrumentally achieved through wealth maximization might include security, liberty, opportunity, and autonomy. It may be that wealth maximization provides the conditions for individual freedom in pursuing their other essentially *contingent* goals. For example, by maximizing wealth individuals may be able to explore every opportunity for advancement and creative development. Also, if the immediate imperatives of finding employment were removed or made less problematic, then individuals may have more freedom in attaining their desires for self-fulfillment. Posner (1981) argued more to the point that wealth maximization is coincident with, and enables, individual consensual behavior, distinct from the inherently coercive requirements of having to take certain jobs to survive. These dimensions are central to American ideals, and one might ask whether or not these are the goals (albeit implicit) in the conservative position. The evidence is vague. For the most part, the *UA in the 80s* panel, for example, was content to assert the importance of opportunity and freedom. These notions rarely entered into the underlying argument of either report.

Proposition IV—*maximum wealth is a surrogate for other worthy goals.* Again the evidence is weak with respect to conservative interest or even acknowledgment of this issue. Two issues do, however, bear scrutiny. First, a strong argument is made by both reports against interjurisdictional conflicts over resources, jobs, and prosperity. By focusing on the national agenda of wealth maximization, it was argued that localities will be dissuaded from pursuing their own costly wars of relative prosperity. In this context, wealth maximization may be a surrogate for other policies that remove institutional, racial, and economic barriers to upward and geographical mobility. By forcing groups and governments to justify their policies in terms of efficiency, other more pernicious practices of exclusion may be forced out. Consequently, wealth maximization in this context would be a false target (Dworkin 1980a).

Of these four propositions, the last two are clearly more sophisticated and would be less obvious in the *UA in the 80s* report and the President's urban report by their very nature. (Proposition IV looks very much like David Stockman's Trojan Horse analogy.) With the best of intentions, I would like to think that the writers of both reports based their recommendations on these last two criteria; however, the evidence is very weak for such a supposition. For the most part, in both reports, national wealth maximization is conceived of in terms of its absolute meaning. Its instrumentality is rarely acknowledged. More often simplistic assertions claim that the nation (sometimes itself personified, at other times all *its* people) would be better off with more wealth. The necessity for an explicit justice conception underlying wealth maximization is not ever recognized even though Propositions I through IV are unintelligible without such a "value." Although compensation is the key element in terms of redistribution, even this notion is flawed because it cannot be shown that compensation will be Kaldor-Hicks efficient. In terms of the internal coherence and logic of the conservative urban policy agenda, it is fundamentally compromised on three counts:

1. The goal of maximum national wealth (that is, economic growth) is not legitimated on any substantive grounds. No justice or equity goals will be clearly served by its advancement.

2. The meaning attached to wealth maximization (that is, maximum national economic growth) is at best simplistic, and at worst a cynical means of legitimating further inequality in the interests of state or social elites.

3. Both reports fail to substantiate an empirical case that an activist ("liberal") urban policy of the jobs-to-people type is necessarily counter to national economic policy objectives, despite their claims that there is an inevitable trade-off between local equity and national efficiency.

EQUITY AND EFFICIENCY

Failure of the conservative urban agenda to produce consistent and substantive meanings for the legitimacy of goals such as national maximum wealth opens up for debate the meaning of equity and efficiency in the urban policy context. For the sake of clarity and consistency in argument, I want to review briefly how these terms have been utilized in public policy and what general propositions can be made concerning the design of urban and national policy. Inconsistency and lack of coherence of the conservative agenda also reopens for debate the issue of the proper role of government in the urban economic system and with respect to questions of individual welfare. Here I want to suggest a set of guidelines for analysis that will form an extended agenda of research and theoretical inquiry in the future. It is not intended at this point to propose specific policy options for the federal government vis-à-vis urban and national problems. This will be left for another occasion. A more meaningful theoretical context is required if we are to understand in subsequent chapters how interregional migration may be associated with regional equity and national efficiency. To that end, we first need to consider the relationship between equity and efficiency in very general and conceptual terms.

It is often said in the academic and policy-related literature that a trade-off exists between regional equity and national efficiency. For example, Alonso (1971) argued that regional welfare might require less national efficiency: that for whatever reasons, to attain maximum national growth may require economic activity to be concentrated in specific regions of the economy. At the most simplistic and naive level, national economic growth is simply measured by output, and Alonso (1971) indicated that by shifting investment capital away from production to consumption, so as to raise the welfare of a given set of regions, potential national output would probably decline. Efficiency in these terms is like Posner's (1981) description of a means to an end. The trade-off between efficiency and equity according to Alonso is then actually a trade-off between two goals—national growth versus regional welfare. Now my argument in the previous section suggested that maximum national growth has very little substantive meaning in and of itself (especially if notions of justice are introduced). It is either an instrument or a surrogate for other substantive values. Thus, the discussion by Alonso and the empirical analyses of Williamson (1965) among many others of national efficiency must be seen as being either extremely vague about the substantive values underlying their analysis or as largely irrelevant if no substantive values were involved. But what of the notion of trade-off itself? Does this have any real meaning?

It is quite odd to think of a trade-off between justice and efficiency at the national or, as we shall see, at any other level. Why would a person be interested in efficiency unless that person subscribed to the view that wealth maximization was the central goal of society? Only in this instance could one conceive of a trade-off because efficiency would be designed to maximize overall wealth. But, as we have seen, the goal of maximum national wealth cannot be substantially sustained unless it is taken to mean something else. Thus the idea of a trade-off is the more general problem of arranging/ordering the priorities of a nation. Similarly, it would only make sense for a society to compromise on one priority vis-à-vis another if both were components of society's underlying normative values. It is difficult to imagine compromising an underlying value by a goal that was unimportant or peripheral to its basic ideals. Thus the concept of a trade-off between what Alonso and others have termed efficiency and equity makes no real sense except at the most superficial and naive level. It is superficial because it hides an underlying and more difficult problem of ordering goals. It is naive because it presumes efficiency to have a substantive meaning in terms of a quantitative measure of output, and not justice.

It is of course possible that to the extent substantive values or goals are divisible (we prefer more freedom not less, as opposed to absolute freedom versus no freedom), then public policy may order and segment conflicting goals. It should, however, also be recognized that if the substantive values are absolutes (like equality before the law) then no ordering may be possible; all contending values and their representative policies would have to be accepted. In this context, the values that give purpose to notions such as efficiency and wealth maximization may be in conflict with one another.

Extending this logic further, it is entirely plausible that different groups may have both different interpretations of existing conceptions of justice and emphasize different principles. Thus the conception of a general consensual principle, such as wealth maximization, being able to mobilize and garner the support of all groups in society is again suspect. The conservative attempt to define such an objective fails precisely because it does not recognize underlying social dis-agreements over the interpretation of what constitutes preferred spatial or welfare outcomes. The danger is that this principle will be used by conservatives such as Reagan to coerce dissident local groups, against their own interests, into accepting greater inequality. Consensual definitions of the ultimate "good" of a society are inherently political and should be recognized as such before proposing public policies that change the underlying patterns of wealth and equity.

At this point it is well worth recognizing an implied argument in much of the above. That is, conflicts over justice are basically conflicts over substantive outcomes and efficiency rules are, axiomatically, tools for achieving a priori stated ends. Without belaboring the point, it is obvious that I consider efficiency to be simply a means to an end. I emphasize this point because it is ultimately quite contentious. Tullock (1980), for example, would argue that efficiency is a neutral principle (as opposed to an ethical claim) on which social institutions should be based. The associated argument is that as long as the procedures that enable action are efficient and just, then outcomes should not matter. For example, imagine that a policy was designed such that the coordination between labor demand and labor supply was more efficient. That is, knowledge of job opportunities in other areas was readily available, as was assistance (in the form of repayable loans) for migration. Efficiency would presumably be judged by the speed of response by a worker who was searching for a job to the notice of alternative opportunities and his subsequent move. Whether or not all labor migrates, or even whether or not any labor migrates, would be unimportant. As long as the procedures were efficient, so the argument goes, outcomes will be socially *optimal*. Unlike the wealth maximization argument no final outcome is given as the objective of public policy, rather that is left to individuals.

This is an attractive notion because it circumvents the problems of defining the social "good." Moreover, it implicitly makes the argument that people should be left to make their own decisions: the role of government is to facilitate action, not to intervene to create a certain distribution. In consequence, debates over substantive moral issues are left to the political process, and the role of the government is closely circumscribed. In terms of urban policy and interregional migration, we could imagine a set of policies that would, at first sight at least, be consistent with such a policy. Above, I noted the possible policy option of facilitating the speed of response of those that wish to migrate through tools such as information banking, mobility grants, and the like. Whether or not this would lead to the decline of older urban areas and the rapid growth of the sunbelt would be unimportant, according to this logic. Another option might be to make unemployment insurance transferable between states so that those that wish to search for another job in another state may do so without losing their entitlements. Again, this policy has the virtue of appearing neutral with respect to outcomes, and efficient with respect to the procedures whereby individual choices are made. Without exaggeration, this is the basis of the conservative urban policy agenda outlined above.

There are two fundamental flaws in this logic. First, rules or procedures of efficiency (or anything else, including law—*see* Tribe 1980) are never neutral with respect to outcomes. By speeding up the responses of migrants to economic opportunities elsewhere, this inevitably creates impacts at origins and destinations. Now a pro-cedural- or process-based efficiency expert might claim these impacts to be unimportant. Alternatively, such an expert may place respon-sibility for dealing with these outcomes in the political arena. After all, it is in the political arena that competing substantive values are given order and priority. If so, then the procedural claim would dissolve into other issues, notably the question of compensation. Given an efficiency rule, should not those most adversely affected be compensated, perhaps according to the Kaldor-Hicks criterion? Immediately, it is obvious that we have returned to the initial fallacy: wealth maximization, or efficiency, conceived as a unique solution, separable from questions of composition and distribution. The prob-lems of that particular conception of the ultimate "good" of society immediately come into play. For example, what does procedural efficiency mean? What does it represent in terms of substantive values, and so on?

Second, and related, is the problem that procedural efficiency must inevitably be premised on substantive values. For example, imagine our procedural policy of efficient migration applied only to the unemployed. What would justify such a policy? One answer might be that because the unemployed are more in need, they require more help. Surely a substantive value position! Alternatively, imagine that assisted migration was available to all regardless of status. Would not that solve the substantive issue? Clearly not, for by treating all people equally is in itself a *substantive* goal. Values are inherent in any procedural policy if these policies are to have any meaning. Consequently, for a policy to be at all effective substantive choices must be made before implementation. It is only with reference outcomes that procedures can be given a distinct character (Tribe 1980). If there was no intent or at least no perceived goal, then the policy itself would be ineffective and a shambles. Procedural efficiency is not a means of circumventing questions of substantive justice. Like questions of wealth maximization, we need another justice-oriented theory to give it a specific meaning and ultimately to give specific procedural policies their very shape.

A "GOOD" URBAN POLICY

If the reader has taken my argument at all seriously, the title to this section will immediately appear incongruous. After all, in the previous sections I have argued against the hollow conceptions of national wealth maximization and economic efficiency that so dominate current conservative opinion on urban and national policy. A "good" policy has to be ultimately based on substantive values arrived at in the political arena. The principal problem of the conservative agenda, in terms of its internal coherence, is precisely the lack of recognition of the substantive meanings attached to concepts such as efficiency. If, on the other hand, specific meanings were to be attached, there would be immediate implications for distributive equity. The conservative appeal to supposedly neutral, consensual values of efficiency cannot work.

The lessons to be drawn from this discussion are in two areas. First, and most obviously, we should not despair of designing a better urban policy even though the substantive questions of concern are ultimately politically derived. By considering the conservative agenda in its own terms, I sought to evaluate it within a particular fact-value (if you like, substantive) nexus. Assuming for the moment that the conservative position has some political legitimacy (as it obviously has in the Reagan administration), then the logic of a given position must be coherent and consistent. That the conservative agenda is not, at least in terms of deriving substantive interpretations of key organizing concepts, demonstrates the utility of a more general evaluative framework for judging the adequacy of specific public policy agendas. Of course, this does not mean that there are "truths" to be discovered that would invalidate one position and crown another. The evaluative framework itself has particular substantive assumptions that may or may not be debatable. But of course that is the point. We should not be seduced by an easy nihilism that suggests because everything is relative, nothing can be decided.

From our evaluation of the conservative agenda it has become apparent that a good policy, whether radical or conservative, should be able to sustain its own internal logic. In particular, three basic propositions summarize internal coherence with respect to public policy design.

1. *Goals must be articulated first in terms of substantive outcomes, only then in terms of means.* That is, there must be a clear specification of what is to be achieved by a specific policy, and how such an outcome will further a given goal. Too often the conservative agenda confused means with ends, so much so that in some interpretations the conservative argument proposes a trade-off between a means (like national efficiency) and an end (like urban welfare). This distinction between ends and means also implies a distinction between outcomes and procedures. That is, a procedure cannot be an end in itself: to understand its desirability, we must evaluate what it attempts to achieve. In these terms, for example, maximizing the speed of adjustment of labor to the changing geography of demand is only desirable if by doing so the welfare of those involved or affected is improved. The ultimate fallacy of the conservative agenda is to suppose that the market is desirable for itself, and not for what it can or cannot achieve. Their argument for market capitalism often supposes that the market is the best form of spatial organization without directly evaluating the desirability of its outcomes. It may well be that the market is quite poor at spatially allocating labor, and thus reduces individual and regional welfare. If welfare is after all the desired goal, then the market may not be the best *means* of achieving the desired outcome.

2. *Goals must be articulated in terms of their distributive consequences.* By implication of the above proposition, the desirability of alternative goals can only be adjudicated with respect to their distributive consequences. To assume that there are unique, best solutions is to ignore the issue of composition and the fact that even *Pareto superiority* is premised upon the *given* distribution. Both facets are important because, in the first instance, welfare does not have a single specific meaning. It is composed of many material dimensions such as income, employment, and environmental amenity, as well as non-material aspects such as safety, social identity, and social association. The 1982 *President's National Urban Policy Report* did recognize some subtleties of what urban welfare can mean emphasizing issues such as crime. And yet, this report so poorly articulates its own interpretation of wealth and national prosperity that the links between what goals and distributive consequences are virtually non-existent. More problematic is the fact that different distributions imply different efficiency procedures and different, but Pareto superior, outcomes. To deny otherwise is to attempt to legitimate specific distributions that may reflect more underlying political agendas than simple-minded analysis (Bebchuk 1980).

3. *Goals must be hierarchically arranged so as to enable adjudication in instances of conflict and non-commensurability.* This issue was implicitly recognized in the President's urban policy report—the primacy of national economic growth was its fundamental goal. Of course, the fact that such a goal is unintelligible makes its primacy of dubious virtue. The more general point is that priority setting allows for the separation of competing values, and it is a more realistic device for making policy choices than supposing trade-offs will solve the policy dilemma. This similarly recognizes that values and goals may not be divisible, that they may be absolute rather than incremental.

So far the requirements for a "good" policy have been articulated in terms that relate to the internal coherence and logic of given, or alternative, value positions. These criteria are also inherently value positions, and are based upon the initial discussion in Chapter 1, concerning the standards of policy adjudication. In large part, these standards are reflective of more general epistemological propositions central to the structure of the social sciences. For example, few academics would argue with the necessity for making ends-means distinctions, but we can take this apparent idea of consensus too far. For instance, my emphasis upon the intimate connection between procedures and substantive outcomes is a debatable point, currently at the center of controversy in constitutional adjudication (Ely 1980; cf. Fiss 1982). Furthermore, the notion that it is the distributive consequences of policies that determine their ultimate meaning is a crucial, but debatable, point in welfare economics (*see* for example Mishan 1982 on this debate, and his recantation of the proposition that cost-benefit analysis is neutral between substantive outcomes).

The final issue that requires emphasis is my argument that there are particular fact-value nexes that are inherently distinctive and non-commensurable. Debates over policies and their appropriateness may ultimately revolve around fundamentally opposed conceptions of the desired goal. There may be no neutral or common metric that will allow comparison. Therefore, how one chooses to interpret, for example, maximum national welfare will ultimately determine the "facts" necessary to support such an argument. In this respect, many choices over "best" policy will be political choices. Otherwise, if goals are commensurable, then much of the debate will revolve around "means" or "procedures."

The second major lesson to be learnt from our internal evaluation of the conservative urban agenda is that policy implies, even depends, on empirical propositions concerning reality. The "fact-value" nexus is a continual interaction between assertion, evidence, and interpretation. As I noted in Chapter 1, this occurs even though many facts are evidently well-known and shared by opposing value positions. For example, the problem with the assertion (made in the *President's*

NUPR) that the market works if given a chance, and that the "turn around" of the New England economy is a case in point, in that its meaning derives from a priori assumptions. It could as easily be argued that the New England phenomenon is the exception that proves the rule—namely that in general, the market does not work. And, once we begin specifying alternative explanations it becomes impossible to disentangle "fact" from "value." By its very nature the "fact" when interpreted sustains like "facts."

This issue leads then to a fourth and fifth proposition regarding the design of "good" urban policy. Both relate to empirical issues, although being based upon my own a priori arguments, and the conceptualization introduced in Chapter 1.

4. *Internal coherence of a given fact-value position presupposes consistency in terms of the "facts" of the argument.* Otherwise, the actual coherence of the argument must be suspect. Implied then is an assumption that incommensurable facts threaten the veracity of the argument, not in the traditional sense of proof and disproof, but rather in the sense of the logic of the argument.

5. *External validity* (that is, in relation to other competing theories) *depends upon accommodating peripheral paradoxes—the exceptions.* Thus, like critical theorists, I suggest that interpretation can only be judged as successful and unsuccessful, not correct and incorrect.

For public policy questions, then, empirical analysis allows us to demonstrate the inadequacies and failures of policy, not the ultimate determination of good and bad policy. Given our early propositions that policies are chosen in specific political contexts, especially with regard to questions of distribution, these propositions are entirely consistent. Note, however, that within specific fact-value nexes, empirical analysis can be used to discriminate between good and bad policy instruments. In this context, good and bad refer to predictability and instrumental effectiveness. Thus, the extent to which maximum national economic growth can be achieved either through spatial agglomeration or decentralization should be empirically determined. Which tool is chosen, however, will of course again depend upon distributional issues.

NOTES

1. This argument should not be taken to suggest that destructive criticism is totally useless or of no consequence. In point of fact, destructive criticism is an invaluable tool for sorting one's own values and preconceptions, and establishing one's own *relative* position vis-à-vis contending interpretations. Leitch (1983, p. 67) noted Heidegger's belief that "the strategy of destruction is two-faced. In one aspect tradition conceals truth by preserving only deadened truths (which appear insidiously as self-evident to us) [and] destruction renews tradition by conserving selected materials of value."

2. The notion of deconstruction has become very popular in recent years among

academic literary critics (*see,* for example, Fish 1980), and those concerned with building a structuralist interpretation of capitalist language and ideology (*see,* for example, Ryan 1982). I prefer to use the term in the sense that any argument is relative; it is built upon assumption and interpretation which are inextricably set *within* the social context of experience (Hookway 1978). Deconstruction is then a critical social act that aims to establish the internal arrangement of an argument.

3. Kain (1978) argued that the Carter program lacked coherence and failed conspicuously in diagnosing the causes of urban distress. Moreover, Kain argued that the Carter administration "mistakenly identified central city population and employment declines as the principal causes of urban distress" (p. 3). The spirited debate over the causes of decline that accompanied the Carter initiatives (*see* Downs 1979 and Wolman and Merget 1980 for examples), tended to overshadow the fact that under Carter funding for HUD activities remained modest and hardly rose in real terms. For the fiscal year of 1979, the administration planned to increase funding of the urban package by only some $742 million (Congressional Quarterly 1978, p. 117), hardly a massive commitment when compared to the Reagan administration's proposals of a $44 billion increase in defense appropriations and a $13.3 billion decrease in education, employment, and social services appropriations for the fiscal year 1983 (Congressional Budget Office 1982, p. 158; Office of Management and Budget 1981, p. 108). Yet, in these terms, and in hindsight, the Carter administration begins to look like the "golden era" of federal commitment to urban problems.

4. Through the Urban Development Action Grants (UDAG), begun in 1978, and the Community Development Block Grants (CBDG), consolidated in 1974, HUD aimed to influence the life of low and moderate income people in severely distressed areas. These programs were designed to be adaptive to local conditions and priorities, although in aggregate their funding levels were again quite modest. The conservative National Tax Limitation Committee (1981) sought to portray UDAG and CBDG programs as "pork-barrel politics," more related to city-machine politics than the plight of inner-city residents. Even in the Reagan administration, these programs have survived, if not prospered, because of their decentralized design and implementation capacity.

5. A new agency called the Inter-Agency Coordinating Council (IACC) was established under Carter to coordinate departmental responsibilities as they affected urban areas. Through direct White House involvement the IACC was successful in "breaking through bureaucratic logjams" (Executive Summary, 1980 *President's National Urban Policy Report,* p. 5). It was, of course, dismantled early in the Reagan administration.

6. During the Carter administration there was a great deal of debate over the spatial impacts of federal spending. Some commentators contended that the Southwest was growing largely because it was receiving a greater share than its due of federal outlays (especially on defense). Others contended that the Northeast received more than its share of welfare expenditures leading to rigidities in labor adjustment to economic opportunities (*see* Bartlett 1982). This debate surfaced in the *National Journal* (Pierce 1976), and was joined by Senator Daniel Patrick Moynihan (1977) amongst others (including Vehorn 1977, and the Congressional Budget Office 1977). Whatever the merits of each side, the debate served to focus attention on the *impacts* of government and the potential role for directed spatial appropriations and transfers in rearranging the geography of growth and decline in a systematic manner.

7. State-centered analysis implies a theory of the state as an institution. With the exception of neoclassical economic models of individual rationality within organizations, most theories of the state are based upon notions of power and control. For example, Wilson (1980) applied essentially Weberian concepts of authority and rationalization to describe how state bureaucracies are controlled by rules and procedures, and by a hierarchical separation of responsibility and implementation.

8. Donald Hicks (1982), the principal staff officer (and researcher) of the *Urban America in the Eighties* panel, has recently argued that these impacts are inevitable

and should be appreciated for what they will bring, long-run sustained economic growth, rather than for their immediate effects, such as urban decay and poverty. His argument is vintage Reagan in its intent and assumptions—short-run denial of the obvious problems of urban America (tremendous unemployment in the inner cities), and naive optimism in the long-run inevitability of growth. He goes so far to suggest that policies of urban renewal will only imperil the larger economy.

9. See Ballard et al. (1980) and Miernyk (1982) on the different approaches to interregional model-building, and in particular the contrasts between top-down (which dominates regional science) and bottom-up techniques.

10. Piore (1981) has been particularly critical of economists who fail to recognize that markets are institutional devices for facilitating exchange. A market is no more natural than a price.

11. It should be acknowledged that the Carter administration did in fact promote the concept of private-public partnerships, both as a conceptual device for encouraging private investment in urban areas as well as a policy which brought together national business and government leaders to work-out possible partnerships that would facilitate government plans (*see*, 1978 *President's National Urban Policy Report*, p. 91 and the final report of the *Urban and Regional Policy Group*, 1978, p. II–8).

12. July 8th, 1982, Secretary of Housing and Urban Development, Washington, D.C. (p. 1).

13. U.S. Congress (1980), Joint Economic Committee, *State and Local Finance: Adjustment in a Changing Economy* (Washington, D.C.), p. 15.

14. According to President Reagan the program for economic recovery was "based on sound expenditure, tax, regulatory, and monetary policies. It (sought) properly functioning markets, free play of wages and prices, reduced government spending and borrowing, a stable and reliable monetary framework, and reduced government barriers to risk-taking and enterprise" (p. 1). The optimism and naiveté of the President's claims are, in hindsight, incredible, especially given the drastic increases in unemployment through 1982. For example, Reagan claimed that "the U.S. economy faces no insurmountable barriers to sustained growth. It confronts no permanently disabling tradeoffs between inflation and unemployment, between high interest rates and high taxes, or between recession and hyperinflation" (*America's New Beginning: A Program for Economic Recovery*, 1981, p. 1). Even then, many labor representatives, including Lane Kirkland of the AFL-CIO, claimed that the Republican vision was new only in terms of rhetoric, and that higher unemployment was inevitable as restrictive monetary policy sought to lower inflation.

15. By October 1982, national unemployment rate was 10.1% while in the midwest unemployment reached closer to 16%. For example, Michigan had a measured unemployment rate of 15.9%, Ohio, 12.7% and Illinois 12.5% (*Boston Globe,* October 9th, 1982, pp. 1–6).

16. Kuhn's (1982) study of the New England computer industry provides a stark contrast to the enthusiasm of the Reagan urban policy report. Not only does it appear that the computer industry is highly location specific—in terms of resource requirements and entrepreneurial capital—its effects on the local labor has been of mixed blessings. Affirmative action is negligible: skills are either of tremendous importance (especially in research and development), or of little consequence (as in assembling). Bimodal stratification of the labor market is hardly a benefit if those caught at the lower end of the scale are those already unemployed and those that enter at higher levels are already very well educated and highly trained. Dispersal of the computer industry is likely to spin off the lower-tier functions; the benefits to host communities may be illusory.

17. It should be emphasized that the Reagan administration considered the enterprise zone concept to be an experiment, not a fully fledged program applicable to the most distressed pockets of urban areas (GAO 1982). Over three years, the administration proposes to establish up to 75 such zones (Joint Committee on Taxation 1982). And, although the intent was to encourage the formation of new businesses in

these zones, there has been no comprehensive policy proposed that would enable discrimination between new and relocated businesses—one of the issues that has been of concern to British planners (Barnes 1982).

18. See Musgrave and Musgrave (1978) for a restatement of this basic argument of neoclassical economics and its relationship to scarcity.

19. Just et al. (1982, p. 11) also argued that there are many different economically efficient outcomes corresponding to different income distributions. They also argued that there are no objective standards for choosing the appropriate income distribution. They write that the choice of income distribution "is a political matter that can be solved only by value judgments through the political process."

20. Bebchuk (1980), for example, argued that notions of datum points, base lines, and the like are essentially devices that ensure the legitimacy of the status quo.

21. Prices as indicators have at least two fundamental drawbacks. For one thing, prices do not reflect *value* except in quite restricted instances, most typically in neoclassical equilibrium. In the second instance, prices imply that the only goods/ products of worth are those that are exchanged in the market, or for which a price can be imputed. Coleman (1980) among many others has suggested in this context that prices are only a narrow version of wealth.

22. For example, on pp. 1–12 the 1982 *President's National Urban Policy Report* argued that policies such as UDAG and enterprise zones are "designed to help communities that are losing jobs to assume new economic functions compatible with the changes occurring in the larger economic order of which the community is part. [Such policies] speed rather than slow social and economic adjustment in a manner consistent with the interests of the community and [n]ation as a whole."

23. Dworkin's (1980a) argument was made in response to Posner (1980) who argued that the maximum national wealth is indeed valuable in its own right. In this section, I follow Dworkin's (1980a) logic very closely and apply it to understanding the assumptions of the conservative urban agenda.

24. Dworkin (1980a, p. 195) noted that there are two versions of this claim. The first (termed *immodest* by Dworkin) is the idea that social wealth is the only component of social value; the second, is that social wealth is just one aspect of social value.

25. See Dworkin (1980a, p. 195) for a fuller treatment of this argument, especially as regards its instrumental quality.

THREE

Consequences of Interregional Migration

INTRODUCTION

The conservative national urban policy agenda, outlined in detail in the previous chapter, assumed many facts and made many undocumented assertions about the functioning of the spatial economic system. These assumptions were of course consistent with the arguments made in the *UA in the 80s* panel report and in the 1982 *President's NUPR*. Briefly, their arguments depended upon three assumptions concerning how the economic system behaves. First, it was contended that if the market is unfettered, if it is allowed to operate "naturally," then it will work to efficiently allocate resources over space and time. Second, it was argued in both reports that the trends in spatial-economic development are so pervasive that little can be done to alter them, and indeed if attempts are made to change the path of trends then the whole economy will suffer even more in the long run (Muller 1981b). Third, as a consequence of these assertions, it was then argued that by allowing the market to work, national economic growth would be maximized, and by implication (assuming Pareto optimality coupled with some kind of Kaldor-Hicks compensation device), so would be individual welfare. The question before us is to what extent these assumed "facts" are actually plausible. In this chapter, I shall internally evaluate the coherence and consistency of the conservative urban policy agenda, assuming for the moment (in fairness to their argument) that the underlying logic is sound; is the same true of their facts?

While much recent debate in the public policy arena has been framed with regard to the causes and consequences of interregional migration, this perspective is in direct contrast with the debates of the late 1960s and early 1970s that were more concerned with the significance of amenities (climate, the quality-of-life, etc.) in determining the volume of migration and the set of destinations. During that era, migration for employment was accepted as a basic determinant of migration but migration in terms of destinations was at the same time very much ignored. The crucial question was, given employment, how did tastes for leisure and climate (amenities in Mueller's 1981 terms), for example, condition the choice of destination. The freedom of choice between equally growing areas of different opportunities of employment is not as central to policy discussions today. The luxury of being able to accommodate idiosyncracies of life-style by migrating to unique ensembles of culture and social attributes has disappeared (if it ever existed!). In an era of national economic stagnation and higher unemployment, migration for economic rewards has assumed a much greater importance, both for the individuals and households involved, and for the allocative efficiency of the spatial economic system in general.

In this chapter, I deal specifically with two issues that were raised previously regarding the aggregate consequences of interregional labor migration. If we take seriously for the moment the notion that efficiency in the form of wealth maximization is a legitimate goal in its own right, then a legitimate question is whether or not interregional migration is in fact efficient. That is, does migration contribute to wage equalization between regions? Do migrants go to the "correct" destinations (high wage areas) from the "correct" origins (low wage areas)? Does migration increase or decrease employment and unemployment? And, does migration cause increases or decreases in aggregate income? All these questions deal with the impacts of migration. Just as relevant are questions that deal with the determinants of migration. Do migrants in the aggregate respond, as predicted by neoclassical theory, to high wages and job opportunities? In this context, the relevant question becomes: does the migration process appear to be the same for growing and declining areas? Obviously, all of these questions are interrelated. They are separate dimensions of what is conventionally termed spatial-economic allocative market efficiency. At the same time, we need a more general understanding of the spatial and temporal patterns of labor migration, both in terms of trends and in terms of market outcomes.

The framework implied by questions of efficiency and the spatial allocation of labor requires an analysis that takes the basic terms and concepts of the conservative urban agenda to be given and then addresses the veracity of their assumptions. Again it is important to stress that by internally evaluating the conservative argument, it is not implied that I necessarily agree with either the theoretical or empirical propositions that go with the conservative agenda. The object of this chapter remains as the *critical* evaluation of the internal consistency of the conservative urban agenda.

IMPACT OF MIGRATION ON WAGES

First, I shall consider the question of interregional wage equalization and market equilibrium.[1] Models of interstate wage disparities are typically framed in terms of the long run. Wage levels are linked to the process of regional economic growth and decline. State income and wages are derivative of the structure of economic growth models that are based upon notions such as resource endowment, the availability of capital, and the relative productivity of labor. Two competing theories are used to explain interregional growth and welfare disparities: the neoclassical model, which predicts wage convergence and factor equilibrium (described here as the competitive market model after Borts and Stein 1964), and the cumulative disequilibrium model (associated principally with Myrdal 1957; and Kaldor 1970), which predicts inequality and divergence of interregional wage differentials.

Borts and Stein's (1964) explanation of differential interregional economic growth was based upon four assumptions: pure competition exists in each region; each region produces the same output using the same production function; labor tends to flow from low wage to high wage regions; and, the growth of capital is a function of the marginal product of capital (MPC) in each region. Assuming pure competition, there is thought to be a negative relationship between the real wage (the marginal product of labor) and the MPC. Based upon these assumptions, two implications were suggested: first, low wage regions will experience relatively rapid economic growth as capital flows in and labor flows out; and, second, low wage regions will also experience relatively rapid growth in wages because of the growth in the marginal product of labor and in the capital-labor ratio.

Whether or not these implications are borne out in reality depends upon the supply characteristics of labor in the low wage and high wage regions. For example, if labor is not responsive to interregional wage differentials, then economic growth could still occur in low wage regions without inducing spatial factor price equilibrium. Labor would have to be both responsive to interregional wage differentials and actually move to the correct destinations (high wage regions) for the expectations of the model to be achieved. Of course, individuals may improve their wages by migrating without necessarily moving to high wage regions (DaVanzo and Hosek 1981).

While the neoclassical model predicts long-run equilibrium, Kaldor's (1970) model predicts that initial regional economic disparities are generally reinforced and that regional economic divergence rather than convergence is the rule. Kaldor's argument was extended by Dixon and Thirlwall (1976) and depends upon what has been termed the "Verdoorn effect." Briefly, the Verdoorn effect is interpreted in terms of cumulative causation wherein regions maintain their position through increasing returns to scale. As a result, wage increases will then be offset through increased labor productivity (a product of increasing capital intensity). The model is also export- and demand-oriented, implying that leading regions come to dominate other low wage regions by virtue of their product cycles and return on capital invested (Rees 1979). There is a very important role for labor in this process. For regional growth to be maintained, prices must be competitive within an integrated interregional market system. The price, availability, and productivity of labor are important components of export commodity pricing. Like the neoclassical model, the demand and supply of labor are important elements of the Kaldorian model. Given increasing returns to scale in the high wage regions, however, migration of labor from low to high wage regions in the Kaldorian model would simply reinforce the dominance of the spatio-economic core.

Evidence on the roles and relative significance of different labor market variables (employment, unemployment, and migration) on interstate wage relativities are difficult to find despite all the theoretical literature and policy studies, such as the *UA in the 80s* panel report, that assume efficient neoclassical regional adjustment scenarios. In Clark and Ballard (1981), relative interstate average wages were explored in a short-term time series model that incorporated both labor demand and supply characteristics. Given the discussion above concerning alternative wage and regional growth theories and the role of labor, the empirical relationship analyzed was specified as:

$$(W_r/W_n)_t = f[(E_r/E_n),(U_r/U_n),(M_r/L_r)]_t \qquad (3.1)$$

Equation 3.1 linked state wages (W_r) relative to the nation (W_n) at a particular point in time (t) to the levels of relative employment (E_r/E_n), unemployment (U_r/U_n), and migration relative to the local labor force (M_r/L_r), also at time (t). The dependent variable (W_r/W_n) was a relative measure for two reasons. First, to enable cross-state comparisons, which is made possible because state average wages are normalized according to the national average; and, second, to enable analysis of state average wage adjustment vis-à-vis the national average and thus implicitly the degree of regional wage convergence or divergence. Essentially, the time series model enabled empirical analysis of the role of different labor variables in determining changes in the ratio of state to national average wages.[2] Average state wages (W_r) were defined as the level of total employee compensation divided by the total number of employees for each state and year.

The sources of data were the Bureau of Economic Analysis and the Bureau of Labor Statistics.

For a firm, there are two sources of labor supply in the short run: those already unemployed and looking for work, and in-migrants from outside the region. The relationship between unemployment and money wages has often been noted (summarized in Phillips 1958) and applied to regional economic models (*see* Clark 1981b). In recent years, however, this empirical relationship has been subject to severe criticisms. Many commentators at the national level have noted the phenomena of "sticky" wages, inflationary expectations and stagflation. Moreover, public policy has been shown to be severely compromised if based upon this supposedly stable trade-off (Blanchard 1980). In the regional context, Kraft et al. (1971) demonstrated that there is apparently little relationship between the level of wages and the level of unemployment for different regions of the United States. It is just as questionable at the regional level as it is at the national level, whether or not the labor market can be usefully characterized in simple price-quantity relationships (Clark 1983).

Migration may have a variety of effects on local average wages. For example, in-migration (as new hires to local firms) could increase wages if the level of local labor demand was already very high. Wages may be increased so as to hire and attract new workers from outside the labor market. Such increases could have further spill over effects as local revenue is increased (through consumption spending) and as firms attempt to hire even more employees. On the other hand, in-migration, if not directly linked to the level of demand, could induce a decline in average local wages as labor supply is increased relative to demand. Out-migration could also have a variety of effects, such as reducing labor supply and thus increasing wages, or decreasing average wages as high wage earners leave and are not immediately replaced. The latter case may occur if more senior workers quit their jobs for opportunities elsewhere and are replaced by younger or less skilled workers who do not command the same average hourly wage rate. Out-migration could also be viewed as potential quits to the firm and local labor market. If the volume of out-migration is large enough, wages in the local area may have to rise so as to hold on to the labor force (especially if labor demand is already high).

Gross migration sources are much harder to find than the more traditional employment measures. In fact, to adequately test for the impact of migration in this context, migration needs to be disaggregated by employment status, age, gross flow (in- and out-migration), and year. The Continuous Work History Sample (CWHS) of the Social Security Administration (SSA) and the Bureau of Economic Analysis (BEA) is perhaps the best, and only, temporal source for such types of data.[3]

The results of analysis established the following conclusions. First, employment growth was an important factor in promoting local wage rate increases for both the neoclassical market equilibrium and Kaldorian cumulative inequality models. In all states for which analysis was conducted, except Michigan, Oregon, and Colorado, either the short-run current (differenced one period) or long-run dynamic (Koyck distributed-lag) employment variable was *the* major factor in determining the ratio of state to national average wages. In seven states, in fact, the employment parameter was the only significant determinant of relative wages. The actual impacts of regional employment growth on wage relativities were, however, mixed. Sometimes the effects were negative, implying that as employment increased in state (r) relative to the nation, average wages tended to fall relative to the nation; and sometimes the effects were positive, implying that relative employment growth caused relative wage increases. The implication of this finding was that short-run employment growth or decline more often has negative rather than positive effects, something not predicted by neoclassical theory. It was also observed, however, that states with significant long-run dynamic employment variables (Koyck distributed-lag structures) typically had positive signs.

Results concerning the significance and signs of the unemployment variable had fewer surprises, and they were somewhat consistent with expectations. A little over half the states were significantly affected by the rate of unemployment, the implication being that as unemployment in state (r) rises relative to national unemployment, average wages tend to fall. This result was expected. The actual values were quite small, indicating that, relative to other variables such as employment or even labor migration, local unemployment was not as important in determining relative wages as perhaps one might assume. In three states (Michigan, Oregon, and Colorado), unemployment and a migration variable were the sole determinants of wages. It is also apparent, however, that, in just less than twenty states, unemployment was not significant at all. All areas of the country were represented in this group, as were fast growing states (Florida, for example) and slower growing or declining states (such as Minnesota).

The migration variables, crucial for the conservative policy agenda, also had variable effects on relative wages. In some states in- and out-migration caused increases in relative wages. In other states, migration caused declines in relative wages. Typically, the impact of the migration variables was larger than unemployment and thus ranked second in terms of actual importance in determining relative state wages. Overall, these results did not completely reject or force the acceptance of either the competitive market or cumulative causation models of regional growth and wage determination. In some states, employment growth may increase average relative wages while in others average relative wages may decline. Further, in-migration may not decrease average relative wages as out-migration may not lead to an increase in average relative wages. In fact, in-migration may increase relative wages as out-migration may decrease average wages. It is apparent that the aggregate effects of labor market determinants on interstate wage relativities may be quite variable. And, it is also clear from these results of this study that the negative and positive effects of migration are not consistent with regard to regional economic growth. That is, in-migration to a growing area could, apparently, cause increases or decreases in wage disparities. Consequently, any policy that presumes that economic growth will automatically bring about increases in average relative wages and wage equalization would be seriously misplaced. Further, any policy that ignored the substantial short-run impact of migration on relative wages would also be seriously compromised.

The conservative urban agenda and many researchers, including the recent study of interregional economic growth prospects by the Joint Center of Urban Studies at Harvard University (Jackson et al. 1981), believe, almost without question, that labor migration leads to interregional wage equalization. Moreover, there is an automatic assumption that labor migration efficiently adjusts to changing economic circumstances. The results obtained by Clark and Ballard (1981) seriously questioned these assumptions on two grounds. First, this study was quite original in that the role of migration in labor market adjustment was directly considered rather than inferred through cross-sectional analysis. Although many would suggest that declines in the rate of wage increases are the product of migration (*see* Borts and Stein 1964), no one could actually demonstrate this until Clark and Ballard's analysis. But in directly testing the real impacts of migration, the methods of inference used by most researchers were shown to be very unreliable. Second, the theoretical expectations of conventional market-oriented researchers, the source of their inferences, were hardly ever met in Clark and Ballard's analysis, in part because the highly restrictive assumptions of the neoclassical model of interregional migration and wages can never be approximated. Yet the policies recommended by the *UA in the 80s* panel report and the 1982 *President's NUPR* presume that in reality the market is an otherwise efficient and optimizing economic system, that in the absence of government intervention it would inevitably lead to optimal results.

MIGRATION AND DEPRESSED AREAS

Most studies of the determinants of interregional migration have used aggregate (county or state) census migration data.[4] Like those models noted above, models of the determinants of migration are typically specified according to assumptions of market competition and factor mobility. Based on the early work of Hicks (1932) on wages and labor allocation, the classical model assumes that labor moves in response to interregional real wage differentials. In the long run, it is argued that labor migration optimally allocates the spatial demand and supply of labor and thus equalizes wage rates across regional labor markets. In the short run, interregional real wage differentials are argued to reflect the relative economic tightness or slackness of local labor markets. Advocates of the competitive model have suggested that there is a certain spatial pattern or directionality to migration—from low-wage areas to high-wage areas. As a result of individual migration decisions, Borts and Stein (1964) asserted that these adjustment processes tend, in the long run, to equalize regional prosperity.

The assumptions of the competitive model are typical of most neoclassical theory. Workers are assumed to maximize their utility; their knowledge of employment and wage opportunities is assumed to be perfect; labor is assumed to be plentiful and homogeneous; regions are equally attractive except for real wage differences; and, it is assumed that there are no significant social or economic costs to the labor adjustment or mobility process. Lowry's (1966) model was, in part, such a model. Origin and destination wage and unemployment characteristics were hypothesized to be the determinants of migration. The Lowry model, incorporating earlier work of Blanco (1963), can be specified in the familiar form as

$$M_{ij} = k[(U_i/U_j)(W_j/W_i)(L_iL_j/D_{ij})] \qquad (3.2)$$

Equation 3.2 links the number of migrants from origin i to destination j (M_{ij}) to their respective unemployment rates (U_i, U_j) and hourly manufacturing money wage rates (W_i, W_j). Also included are the population components of the gravity model (L_i, L_j), the distance component of the gravity model (D_{ij}), and a constant (k).

The results of testing the type of model specified in Equation 3.2 have provided only limited support for the notion that relative wage differences are crucial determinants of migration. Typically, origin parameters have not been statistically significant, especially the unemployment variables, in most empirical tests. Thus it has been argued that the competitive market model is unable to explain much of the economic decision to out-migrate. Although these models have been successful in prediction exercises (possibly because of the inclusion of the gravity terms), it has been argued that they are inadequate as explanations of the out-migration labor-adjustment process (Greenwood 1981).

Empirically, the best predictor of out-migration has been shown to be in-migration, which at first glance seems to be paradoxical since many researchers have argued that migration flows are unidirectional with one flow (in or out) dominating the reverse flow.

Fields (1978) and Renshaw (1978) have claimed that the empirical and estimation problems may be largely questions of specification that are related to the actual testing of empirical relationships rather than being theoretical inadequacies. Field's (1978) solution was to enter the origin and destination variables separately and circumvent the direct link between where migrants come from and where they go to. Many researchers have also argued that perfect information, labor homogeneity, and costless adjustment conflict directly with the reality of the individual decision making process (MacKinnon and Rogerson 1980).

In this context, I want to briefly review the results of one particular study as a way of reflecting back on the adequacy of theory in general. The approach of Clark and Ballard (1980) had two interrelated but separate stages. The first stage was the development of a model that determined the volume of out-migration from a depressed region. The second stage was the utilization of a model that determined the destination of out-migrants. The conceptual approach emphasized "disenchantment" with the originating region rather than the pull of economic opportunities at the destination. Gustavus and Brown (1977) have also developed a model of migration that has two stages: first, a concern for place utility or local attributes (in their case public services and facilities); and second, a model of the choice of destination. They emphasized the twin problems of lack of knowledge and incorrect knowledge of opportunities and concluded that simultaneous origin-destination models may be inappropriate given an individual decision process that considers locations as endogenous opportunity sets.

Related to this logic, the out-migration model developed by Clark and Ballard (1980) was controlled by employment status and age, and was disaggregated by six industry sectors.[5] Consistent with previous analysis, the out-migration model was dynamic and time dependent, and it emphasized the significance of time and uncertainty in making the decision to migrate. The destination model, however, was not disaggregated by industry owing to sampling problems. Attraction variables were defined in a similar manner to the Lowry model, although the estimation procedure combined a Koyck distributed-lag function in a cross-sectional regression model.[6]

The model of out-migration used by Clark and Ballard (1980) in that paper can be defined as:

$$M_t^{i,r} = b_1 + b_2 \sum_{j=0}^{p} w_j \Delta E_{t-j}^{i,r} + b_3 \sum_{j=0}^{k} w_j (U_{t-j}^r / U_{t-j}^N)$$
$$+ b_4 \sum_{j=0}^{m} w_j (W_{t-j}^{i,r} / W_{t-j}^{i,N}) + u_t \qquad (3.3)$$

where p, k, and m are the number of lags in the Koyck distributed-lag and the variables are the number of migrants from industry i and the Appalachian region ($M^{i,r}$); the negative change in the number of employees in industry i in region r ($\Delta E^{i,r}$); the unemployment rates in region r (U^r) and the United States (U^n); the wage rate for industry i in region r ($W^{i,r}$), and the wage rate for industry i in the United States ($W^{i,n}$). Other parameters included the Koyck distributed-lag term (w_j), the stochastic error term of the estimation (u_t), estimated coefficients ($b_1 - b_4$) and t represented the time period.

So as to illustrate the relative importance of different determining variables with respect to out-migration from depressed areas, the case of Appalachia was chosen to provide a base line of analysis and interpretation. Notice, moreover, that the local determinants were considered in relation to the aggregate context; in particular the national economic system. Thus out-migration from the region was analyzed in relation to the total system—a bottom-up approach.

From the results obtained of this analysis, employment opportunities appeared to be the most consistent and effective determinants of out-migration. In five of the six major industry groups, the employment variable was a significant determinant. Relative wage rates were also important, although not in the wholesale/retail trade sector. The unemployment variable, on the other hand, was generally insignificant and a relatively poor determinant of out-migration. For one of the two industry groups for which the variable was significant, other services, a negative parameter sign was found. This result implied that as local and national unemployment rates converge, out-migration increases! One explanation may be that as short-run aggregate economic conditions improve, relative unemployment disparities may also decrease. This could lead to increased labor-force participation and to increased mobility of the discouraged and chronically unemployed workers.

Given step one, determination of the magnitude of out-migration from the Central Appalachian region, the next step was to analyze the pattern of destinations. The destination model used is summarized below.

$$M^{rs} = b_1 + b_2 G^{rs} + b_3 Q^s + b_4 A^s + u, \tag{3.4}$$

$$\text{where } G^{rs} = P^s / (D^{rs})^a, \tag{3.5}$$

$$Q^s = \Sigma w_j \left\{ \Delta E^s - [\Delta E^N (E^s / E^N)] \right\}_{t-j} \tag{3.6}$$

The terms of these equations were defined as: $M^{r,s}$ equals the number of migrants from the Appalachian region r to destination state s; P^s was the population in state s; ($D^{r,s}$) was the distance from the population centroid of region r to that of state s, where a is the exponent fitted independently in each equation; E^s, the level of employment in state s, and E^N the level of employment in the United States; ΔE^s was the annual change in employment in state s, and ΔE^N the annual change in employment for the United States. A gravity index was also included ($G^{r,s}$) between region r and state s, while A^s was the climate parameter (average temperature). Other variables and parameters were: Q^s the employment opportunity index for state s; a stochastic error term (u), Koyck distribution-lag coefficient (w^j); and estimated coefficients (b_1–b_4). The time period was represented by t.

Equation 3.4 was estimated in a cross-sectional regression model for each year over the period 1958–1975. Emphasis was on the characteristics of the remaining 47 destination states. Because of the small sample size, destinations were not disaggregated by industry type. The form of cross-sectional equation was held constant over the 18 years to enable comparison of the derived parameters.

Not surprisingly, the gravity model component of the determinants of destination were the most important variables for each year. All gravity and employment parameters were significant and had the expected sign—positive. The effect of distance, measured by the parameter a, showed signs of decreasing over the years 1958–1975. There was a strong and steady decline in its value from 2.3 in 1958 to 1.0 in 1975. This implied that the destinations of out-migrants tended to be further away from the Appalachian region than in the past. Evidence for such a trend has not been well documented in the literature. Tarver and McLeod (1976) noted that the average distance of all interstate migrants has increased between the census intervals 1935–1940 and 1965–1970. They concluded, however, that the trend was likely to stabilize in the 1970s. Evidence, based on Clark and Ballard (1980), suggests in fact that the decline in the significance of distance is likely to continue.

The employment variable parameter also showed a distinct pattern. Its value increased until approximately 1963, then it fell, and then it increased to 1969—and it has fallen for each year since 1971. An obvious explanation could be found in the pattern of economic fluctuations and the degree of convergence or divergence between interstate employment growth opportunities. It is entirely plausible that as the national economy booms, relative disparities in interstate employment growth decline, thus reducing the significance of this variable in allocating out-migrants from Appalachia.

The results reported here are important for two reasons. First, it can be shown that out-migration from depressed regions is obviously related to economic opportunities. Hence, one cannot conclude that either people are irrational or migrate without respect to their economic opportunities. This is apparent for both questions of what determines out-migration and where do they go in the economic system. Second, it is also clear that one cannot assume an inevitability to the process of out-migration. If economic opportunities are good in an area relative to the nation, then the volume of out-migration will be less than if local economic conditions were poor relative to the nation. Moreover, because the temporal framework of this analysis was yearly it could also be concluded that out-migration is very adaptive to changes in *relative* economic prosperity. Thus, even for a depressed area the structure and determinants of migration are quite sensitive to spatial patterns and processes. This also implies a great deal more discretion for local economic development planners—the trends in migration have in fact a great potential for volatility!

These results are also important for the light that they shed on conventional understanding of the out-migration process. The Select Committee on Population (1978) concluded that the migratory response to unemployment is weak and uneven. This may be true, but is not the complete picture by any means; other variables such as employment growth are highly significant and consistent in effect. The "pull" and "push" effects of opportunities can be disaggregated (against expectations to the contrary) and the responsiveness of migration to short-run shifts in economic activity implies a great potential for an *active* migration and regional growth policy.

MIGRATION AND GROWING AREAS

Brechling (1973) argued that interregional labor force migration has a major role to play in stabilizing the aggregate economy. He suggested that areas experiencing high economic growth tend to be very tight local labor markets and have relatively high rates of wage increases. These regions may be the wage leaders for the rest of the economy although, in the aggregate, the economy may be experiencing high levels of unemployment. If the unemployed were to be spatially coordinated through interregional migration such that surplus labor was transferred to high-wage–inflation areas, the overall economic system might then approach equilibrium. In this context, migration could be thought as an equilibrating force. The time frame in which this adjustment is to occur is much shorter than the long-run equilibrium conception of Williamson (1965). Migration would have to be sensitive to short-run variations in the interregional distribution of the demand and supply of labor. The relative efficiency of migration in terms of short- versus long-run interregional labor force adjustment is, however, only poorly understood. Few researchers have been able to evaluate the temporal pattern of migration adjustment since short-run adjustment time-series data have not been generally available.

Two hypotheses that bear upon the assumptions made by the conservative agenda can be suggested concerning the role of in-migration and labor force adjustment. First, in-migration to rapidly growing areas is, in fact, responsive to economic opportunities at the destination. Second, in-migrants to high labor demand areas may not come from the correct (labor surplus) regions and, third, interregional labor force migration is not an efficient short-run macrospatial allocation mechanism for labor. The link between migration and labor adjustment to economic conditions over various time frames can be separated into two analytically distinct stages. In the first instance, it is clear that rapid economic growth attracts in-migrants. That is, the volume of in-migrants should be a function of attraction variables such as employment opportunities and turnover characteristics of the local labor market. This does not necessarily imply that in-migrants need come from specific types of origins. The possibility of migration equilibrating a given set of labor markets may still be indeterminant. After determining the volume of in-migrants, the second stage of analysis is a more direct test of the aggregate spatial coordination hypothesis through an analysis of the origins of in-migrants. This two-stage procedure is the same as used in Clark and Ballard (1980), who sought to explain out-migration from a depressed region by first determining the volume of out-migrants and, second, by allocating the out-migrants to specific destinations.

The first step of analysis, in Ballard and Clark's (1981) study, was to determine the short-run responsiveness of in-migration for the following fast-growing states: Arizona, Colorado, Florida, and Texas. The model specified below linked the volume of out-migration to a series of stock and flow of labor market characteristics that were defined relative to national economic performance for the period 1958–1975. General specification of the in-migration adjustment model used is shown below in Equation 3.7:

$$M_t^r = a + b_1 E_t^{r,n} + b_2 L_t^r + b_3 MN_t^r + b_4 D_t + \varepsilon_t, \tag{3.7}$$

where M^r was the volume of in-migration to region r; $E^{r,n}$ the employment growth in region r relative to the nation; L^r a labor turnover proxy for region r; MN^r the population-proportioned regional share of national migration, and D a national "discomfort" index. The stochastic error term was defined as (ε_t); $a, b_1–b_5$ were estimated coefficients; and, t the time period. Explanatory variables included both economic and quality of life factors. Like most migration models, employment opportunity variables were included in the estimation procedure as principal determinants of the level of in-migration, although the employment effect was disaggregated into two components: new employment opportunities,[7] usually created by expanded or relocated industry; and labor turnover, the process of changing jobs and workers.

The turnover variable was used and interpreted as a proxy for the number of workers who voluntarily leave their place of employment. It was assumed that local labor turnover is a positive index of economic opportunity. A variation on local unemployment was chosen because of the lack of comprehensive turnover data for regions of the United States. The key feature of the variable's construction is the word "voluntary." The total number of unemployed for a given region is defined as UN^r. Since workers can only draw unemployment insurance if laid off, UI^r defines the total number of unemployed in that region whose employment termination was involuntary. Thus the difference between UN^r and UI^r was assumed to be those who are voluntarily unemployed—workers who quit to look for a better job.[8]

The third explanatory variable was the population-proportioned regional share of national migration (MN^r). This variable was computed as being the total number of U.S. internal migrants (M^n) multiplied by the share of population in the region (P^r) relative to the nation (P^n). In using this variable, an attempt was made to estimate what might be considered "random" worker migration: that which would occur if the sole determinant of the decision of where to migrate was population. In a multiregional model, this variable might be expected to account for the observed large number of in-migrants to what are considered depressed areas, while in a statistical framework this variable replaced a possible lagged dependent variable on the right-hand side of the equation. The changing level of national migration would, of course, be based on both economic and environmental or social considerations. Finally, the fourth variable attempted to capture the impact of the national unemployment rate and the national inflation rate. This was described as the national "discomfort index."

As should be expected, the Koyck-lagged employment opportunity parameter was most important for all equations and states. The sign of this parameter was typically positive and significant, indicating the strong "pull" of employment growth in determining the level of in-migration to these four states. The labor turnover index had also a positive sign on the parameter although being significant in only two of the four states. The significance of the turnover parameter for Arizona and Florida was also encouraging, since labor opportunities measured by the flexibility of local labor markets have been virtually ignored in much of the empirical literature. The lack of significance of this variable in the two other states was due either to measurement problems (i.e., the data are only a proxy for turnover) or to a lack of adequate labor turnover information available for potential migrants.

The national migration variable was defined to measure the consistency between regional and national migration trends. For the states studied the results implied that national migration trends do have a strong influence on regional flows, second only to employment opportunities. This suggested that much of the decision to migrate may be influenced by general, rather than specific, regional factors, and in particular how well the national economy is performing vis-à-vis job creation and potential employment opportunities. This is consistent with evidence that suggests that migration is linked primarily with specific age cohorts and may be determined by work-life considerations.

Overall the results of this analysis were quite consistent with previous results: in-migration is a function of economic and social opportunities. It was also shown, however, that in-migration is responsive to short-run (year-to-year) fluctuations, as well as long-run trends in economic activity. Further, it is apparent that the flow of employment opportunities, not simply the stock of jobs at any point in time, is an important determinant (cf. Select Committee on Population 1978). Although many authors have argued that quality-of-life issues are most important for the South and Southwest, our results tend to support earlier claims by Cebula and Vedder (1973) that economic determinants are often stronger than quality-of-life determinants. In this case, the claim is made solely with respect to labor force in-migration.

Having analyzed the relative adaptability of in-migration to changes in economic activity in the first section of that paper, the second step was concerned with analyzing the spatial patterns of the directions and origins of in-migrations. A cross-sectional equation was estimated for each of the 18 years, 1958–1975, and for each state. The model tested, was specified as:

$$M^{i,r} = a + b_1 G^{ir,a} + b_2 E^{i,n} + b_3 X^{i,n} + b_4 C^i + \varepsilon \qquad (3.8)$$

where $M^{i,r}$ was the level of in-migration from region i to region r; $G^{i,r}$ a gravity index relating all other regions (i) to r (the term a referring to the exponent on the distance term and was estimated separately for each region and time period); $E^{i,n}$ the employment growth of region i relative to the nation; $X^{i,n}$ an economic "welfare" index of region i relative to the nation, and C^i a climate dummy (average temperature) of region i. The stochastic error term (ε) and estimated coefficients (b_1–b_4) were also included.

The results of estimating Equation 3.8 demonstrated that the gravity model was universally significant, explaining well over the majority of the migrant locational patterns. There were a number of distinct spatial patterns evident in this context. For instance, the size of the gravity parameter (b_1) varied quite markedly over time and between the four states. In the period 1966–1971, the parameter values are typically large (in-migration from large population centers tends to dominate) while from 1971 the parameter values dropped in size quite considerably. This evidence tended to support Renshaw's (1970) contention that migration is very adaptive in the short run, at least with respect to the spatial distribution of origin population sizes. The evidence in Ballard and Clark (1981) also suggested that economic factors are more important than environmental factors in determining the volume of in-migration to fast growing states. The proposition that the flow characteristics of local labor markets are important determinants of in-migration was also noted. More research is clearly warranted on the role of local turnover and the flow of new jobs in initiating migration. Stock characteristics, such as the levels of employment and unemployment, are unlikely, however, to capture the dynamic or adjustment qualities of labor migration.

This second stage of analysis suggested, however, that migration as a macrospatial labor allocation mechanism may have limited efficiency. Economic opportunity variables were not always significant for the fast growing states. Further, some of the signs on the employment parameters were negative, implying that migrants may come from what are already high relative growth areas in the United States. This result implies that in-migrants do not necessarily come from the correct regions and that interregional migration may not be efficient in allocating labor from depressed to rapidly growing regions.[9]

This conclusion contrasts with evidence presented in the previous section where it was shown that out-migrants from Appalachia do in fact migrate to growing areas. One is left with the suspicion that the flows of labor from already growing areas statistically dominate the flows from depressed regions. Consequently, although workers out- and in-migrate for reasons of economic welfare, there is apparently no symmetry between those workers who out-migrate from depressed regions and those who in-migrate to rapidly growing regions. The evidence also suggested that policy analysts should be wary of assuming that the pattern of in-migration is the same for all southern and southwestern regions of the United States. The evidence suggested that in-migrants to Texas do not come from the same areas, that in-migrants go from the north to Arizona and Florida, Texas on the other hand attracts the bulk of its migrants from comparatively warmer climates (especially California).

LABOR MARKET INTEGRATION AND THE ECONOMY

Before reintroducing the policy context of this study, thereby summarizing the results of evaluating the assumed "facts" of the conservative agenda, I wish to consider the overall geographical volatility of interstate labor migration.[10] That labor is quite mobile and adaptive to short-run economic fluctuations has been clearly demonstrated. Apart from the study by Vining (1974), who used Japanese data, there is little evidence concerning labor-force migration instability in terms of its spatial distribution over time. In this section, I want to reconsider the evidence and accepted views concerning the short-run geographical structure of labor-force migration in the United States. Based on the study by Clark (1982b), two sets of questions will be used to structure our analysis: (a) How volatile are the geographical patterns of interstate migration over the business cycle? In particular, are there variations over time in the significance of different states in the national migration system, and does the structure of the national migration system itself change with fluctuations in economic activity? (b) To what extent are the identified geographical patterns of short-run labor force migration predictable on the basis of the previous year's patterns? These questions were evaluated by means of yearly gross interstate migration data, derived from the Continuous Work History Sample and the Bureau of Economic Analysis, over the period 1958–1975, the data source of previous investigations.

For each year the data were arranged in a 51 × 51 square matrix (the fifty states plus the District of Columbia) analogous to an industry transactions table or commodity flows matrix. Thus, the number and origins of all migrants going to a given state i can be identified as can the destinations of all out-migrants from state i. Following Slater (1975; 1976), an iterative proportional fitting procedure (IPFP) was utilized to standardize each flows matrix so that, for a given year, the matrix possessed equal row and column sums simultaneously ("uniform marginals"). Double standardization removed the confounding effects of origin and destination population sizes which, as implied in the gravity model, suggests that most migrants go to large places. The elements of the standardized matrix can be taken as representing the degree of interstate interaction or linkage as represented by labor-force migration, between states of the national migration system, given the constraint that all row and column sums are equal.

A hierarchical cluster analysis was then performed on each year's standardized flows matrix. The aim was to identify geographical patterns in the migration flows and, in particular, the place of each state in the overall spatial system for each year. This then was the basis for evaluating the volatility of the geographical structure of short-run migration. A series of steps can be identified as forming the basis of the clustering routine. First, the clustering process begins at the level of the nation, where all states together form one group, and it then proceeds to subdivide the nation into groups based upon their power or degree of interaction. The routine thus starts at the *lowest* overall level of interaction and by *stepping down* successively breaks the set into groups of states with higher and higher levels of interaction between the members of each group.

Second, in order to identify subsystems of interstate migration, threshold values of interaction were also specified. Each state had an interaction value, or what Slater (1976) has termed a "strong component value," according to its "place" in the overall interaction system. Since the purpose of the study was to compare the geographical structure of interstate labor migration over time, for each year a

weighted average of all states' interaction values was used to delineate
the threshold. A fixed arbitrary threshold value for all years would
not have reflected the *relative* geographical position of a given state
as overall system-wide interaction varied year to year. As Slater
(1981) noted, it is difficult to be precise as to the statistical significance
of a given cluster, particularly since each cluster is likely to be
composed of other subsets of states. Thus for interpretive purposes,
states were analysed with respect to their cluster groups and relative
"place" in the overall migration system.

Since the threshold value was taken in Clark (1982b) to represent
the average level of interaction between all fifty-one states for a
particular year, a time series of such threshold values was constructed
to represent the changing pattern of overall interaction in the migration
system. It was noted earlier in this chapter that in-migration and
out-migration are particularly sensitive to changing national economic
conditions. Translating this into the context of spatial interaction as
measured by labor-force migration, it was hypothesized that there is
greater interaction between more states in times of economic boom.
Overall interaction may be highest (that is, more people migrate to
and from more varied origin and destination sets) in times of national
economic boom, and lowest (a lower absolute volume of interstate
migration and a more restricted set of origins and destinations) in
times of recession. Of course, system-wide interaction may not
simultaneously adjust to rapid shifts in economic activity. Temporal
lags in adjustment may be reasonably expected.

To investigate this proposition an empirical test was made of a
time-series adjustment model (based upon yearly average threshold
values) of the general form:

$$I_t^{ave} = d_1 + d_2 U_{t \pm j}^N + d_3 P_{t \pm j}^{GN} + \varepsilon_t \qquad (3.9)$$

where I_t^{ave} was defined as the average interaction value for a given
year t; U^N was defined as the national unemployment rate at an
appropriate lag $t \pm j$; and P^{GN} was defined as the gross national product
(GNP) also at some lag $t \pm j$; with the d_1–d_3 being the estimated
coefficients and ε_t the stochastic error term. Multicollinearity exists
between U^N and P^{GN}, thus different forms of Equation 3.9 were
estimated so as to sort out the significance of each explanatory
variable. To give the model a dynamic structure, it was estimated
via a Cochrane-Orcutt (1949) first difference time-series regression
modified by the inclusion of Almon (1965) distributed lags.

Four distinct episodes of national economic activity and change
were identified for the overall period 1958–1975: (a) the 1958–1962
recession and recovery; (b) the 1963–1968 economic boom; (c) the
1969–1971 Nixon policy-administered recession; and (d) stagflation,
1972–1975. The dates of these episodes were derived from analyses

undertaken by the National Bureau of Economic Research and others (*see* Cagan 1979). Although the events of each episode were intertwined with one another, this should not be taken to suggest that each episode was the same. A brief descriptive narrative of the events of each episode was developed based on the Economic Report of the President for each year (U.S. Government, various years) and the results of analysis presented. Emphasis was placed on the major changes in the United States economy and its general character over the short run.

The implications of analysing the geographical patterns of short-run interstate migration over these business-cycle episodes were threefold. First, as suggested in the opening remarks of this section, there was a great deal of volatility in the geographical and temporal structure of short-run interstate migration. Not only did the linkage tree and path of cumulative spatial aggregation of the migration system differ over the business cycle, but the geographical pattern of those states included and excluded at each step of the linkage tree differed over the business cycle, and over successive business cycles. Each phase of boom and recession exhibited marked differences in the geographical patterns of migration and interaction. Second, the identity of those states at the core of the national migration system differed over time as economic conditions changed. Third, there was apparently some stability in the identity of those states added above the average threshold value, if not in their relative rank, at least in terms of their level of addition to the national migration linkage tree.

For example, the economic recovery year of 1962 exhibited a spatial pattern more similar to 1961 than 1960, especially in the West,[11] however, at the first steps of cumulative aggregation there were some similarities to 1960. For example, Rhode Island and Connecticut are added rapidly to the national system at step 2 in 1962 rather than step 9 in 1961, which is more similar to 1960. Few states, however, had the same rankings in terms of the steps at which they were added to national linkage tree over this three year period. Only Maryland retained its place which was, incidentally, in the first core group each year. It was noticeable, however, that in the boom year 1960 there were actually less states in the "major" threshold group than in the recession and recovery years of 1961 and 1962.

Another example was the sustained economic boom of 1964–1969.[12] Although there was no recession in this episode, there was still volatility in the spatial pattern of migration, at least in terms of the relative rankings of most states. On the other hand, membership in the core group did not change dramatically year to year, indicating that the process of interaction and integration was continuing year to year. For example in 1964, 1966, and 1968 nearly all eastern and southeastern states (excluding Florida in every case) appeared in one broad band. Another group, including North and South Dakota,

Nebraska, and Kansas, all appeared together in 1964, 1966, and 1968. The state of Washington appeared in the major system group in all years as did Alaska, North Dakota, and many eastern states. Central group states were also similar, particularly for 1965–1966 where Maine, Massachusetts, Rhode Island, Connecticut, New York, Pennsylvania, New Jersey, Maryland, Delaware, Georgia, North and South Carolina and the District of Columbia figured prominently. Clearly some states grew economically stronger relative to the nation than others. This would account for variations in the rankings of different states. As well, the labor market became distinctly more national in character as there was greater variety in origin and destination sets and each state was tied more strongly than before to the total national migration system. Sustained national economic growth enabled greater choice by migrants.

Finally, another example of the distinctive geography of the business-cycle in terms of interstate migration, is to be found in the 1972–1975 period.[13] In 1972 the major group of states had representatives from the Northwest, Midwest, and Southwest regions of the United States. A number of those states were also in the core group, including the Dakotas and Mississippi. In 1973 a year of strong economic growth, there were some similarities to 1959 and 1964 with a second and third subgroup within the major group. As in those previous years, one of the subgroups was composed of Arizona, New Mexico, and New York, and that subgroup also appeared in 1975. The third subgroup which appeared for the first time in 1973 and 1974 was composed of two states: Alabama and Georgia. The only other significant difference over that episode was the entry of California into the major group at its strongest level of interaction over the total 1958–1975 period. A number of states, including Maine, Massachusetts, and Pennsylvania appeared to be important for the major group over the last three years of the episode. Further, in 1975 the eastern states of Maine, Massachusetts, Rhode Island, Connecticut, Pennsylvania, and Virginia dominated the core group of states. Overall the pattern established in the early 1970s was maintained although there were marked differences between years in the positions of individual states in the overall national migration system.

In analysing the geographical patterns of interstate labor-force migration for the years 1958–1975, it became apparent from the data that there was a strong link between the level of overall spatial interaction (evidenced via interstate labor migration) and the path of the national economy. In recession the range of interaction values tended to increase, particularly towards the higher end of the distribution with the effect being to increase the overall average interaction value. Put simply, the national labor market was regionalized and segmented with small groups of states being relatively more integrated internally than with the rest of the spatial economy. The wide range of interaction values represented heterogeneity within the national labor market. During economic booms, however, the range tended to decline, and the cumulative linkage tree is more compact. Thus the average overall interaction value declined.

The implications for understanding the relationship between short-run geographical integration and national economic fluctuations were twofold. First, greater compactness of the national migration system implies that the geographical system was closer knit and more integrated. Conversely, the greater the range and the more elongated the interaction system, the more likely the overall geographical migration system was less integrated. Second, with less spatial economic integration, subsystems of migration tended to dominate the overall interaction pattern of the national labor-market system. In essence, as economic activity declined, migrants were apparently less willing to consider the widest set of possible destination options and more likely to follow, if migrating at all, conventional and more narrow paths of interstate migration.

The expectation was also that as GNP increases, average overall spatial integration also increases. The results of estimating Equation 3.9 confirmed this expectation. A series of tests were conducted to explore the significance of national unemployment and GNP as determinants of interstate labor-market integration. National unemployment was found to be consistently insignificant as a determinant of average overall interaction. On the other hand, GNP was consistently important in determining average overall interaction with the expected sign (negative) on the Almon distributed lag parameter estimates. All those distributed lag parameters were statistically significant with the largest parameter value being at lag zero, implying that adjustment to changes in GNP, in terms of the spatial adjustment of interstate migration, occurs simultaneously with changes in GNP. Of course, this effect occurred over two years; however, the largest change was within the first year. For a lagged time-series model, the coefficient of determination (R^2) is quite high (cf. Granger and Newbold 1977), and there was no evidence of first-order autoregressive serial autocorrelation.

It was surprising that changes in national unemployment were not significant in determining changes in national labor-market integration. Previous studies reviewed above have, however, shown that interstate unemployment disparities relative to the nation are significant, if not particularly strong, determinants of in-migration and out-migration. Since the crucial issue in Clark (1982b) was the overall spatial arrangement of interstate integration, it may be the case that relative unemployment disparities determine the volume of migration if not the actual spatial distribution of migration. For employed individuals, GNP may more clearly represent changes in aggregate employment opportunities particularly as the volume of voluntary quits (turnover) increases as economic activity increases (Clark 1981b).

As employed individuals are encouraged or discouraged to migrate by unemployment, changes in the total volume of available jobs, linked of course to GNP, may be the crucial decision criteria with respect to the geographical distribution of migration.[14]

SUMMARY

The report of the *UA in the 80s* Panel and the *1982 President's NUPR* concluded that the trends of spatial deconcentration and economic growth are virtually impossible to reverse. Implied was an assumption that these trends have quite long gestation periods; that the structure of the spatial economic system is bound by the chains of inevitability. The evidence presented in this chapter casts considerable doubt upon the plausibility of those assumed facts. In the first instance, it is plain that the volume of interregional labor force migration is sensitive to short-run economic fluctuations. For depressed and growing areas alike, the evidence suggests that the volumes of gross migration (in and out) vary *pro-cyclically* with the path of the national economy. No one would propose at the national level that the path of the economy cannot be influenced by government policies. No one would surely suggest that the aggregate economy is subject to laws of motion that make it impossible to intervene to alter its path so as to achieve social and economic goals. Likewise, once it is accepted (based on the evidence above) that interregional labor migration is an element, albeit spatial, of the national economy, then the notion of inevitability of trends has to be similarly rejected.

Of course, it is true that the tools of intervention in this context are less well developed than macroeconomic policy. Nevertheless, the opportunity of intervention afforded by the temporal and spatial volatility of migration cannot be lightly dismissed or ignored. For example, it was noted that in-migration to growing areas is a function of the relative economic performance of a given area vis-à-vis the nation. To the extent that public policy can alter the relative fortunes of different areas, then the volume and pattern of migration will similarly be altered. Imagine that a depressed area could be stimulated relative to the nation, then the volume of out-migration would decline. The effect would be to initiate a growth process that is both cumulative and multiplicative. By reducing the volume of out-migration through economic growth, population growth would be advanced further ensuring the growth in local demand, thereby stimulating further economic expansion. Trends in this context are neither *irreversible* nor particularly *stable*. What is apparent is that if the relative position of an area can be improved in the short run, then labor migration will adapt. But of course this does not mean that the spatial system itself will be well coordinated in the aggregate!

The evidence summarized in this chapter also implied that there is a very real opportunity for the national government to intervene in directing and coordinating labor migration. It is not obvious that labor comes and goes to and from the correct regions. That is, the targeting of labor migration is not, in the aggregate at least, spatially efficient. If we were to accept the idea that labor migration should be efficient then at the very least, governments could and should intervene to promote allocative efficiency. Moreover, because it is apparent that migration is quite volatile, there are opportunities to shift the overall spatial and temporal patterns of migration.

Even so, for all the evidence on volatility, it is not obvious that labor migration is entirely predictable in its effects upon wages and employment. The evidence presented in this chapter of the impacts of gross migration was, at best, mixed. In some instances, migration causes higher relative wages; in other instances, migration causes lower relative wages. Those inevitable laws of supply and demand, implicit in the conservative urban agenda, are not obviously effective once we consider whether or not, in the aggregate, migration leads to interregional wage equalization. These so-called laws cannot be depended upon to create spatial and economic welfare equalization through efficiency any more than we can depend on the national economy finding its own path to full employment and rising real incomes. Rather, the "free" operation of the spatial economy will likely founder upon an inadequate spatial-temporal coordination and allocation of labor, and structural discontinuities in wages and employment. Until proven (as opposed to asserted) otherwise, the logic and evidence on interregional labor migration supports those who maintain the necessity of government intervention.

Conservative theorists suppose that national economic priorities of growth and stability must take precedence over local concerns. It is argued that interregional migration is a means of facilitating aggregate economic efficiency. Yet the results of empirical analysis reported here provide support for a reversal of their argument: without macroeconomic growth interregional migration will falter and become spatially fragmented. The implications are twofold. First, it cannot be assumed migration is solely a secular and trend-related oriented process separate from the path of the national economy. To think of interregional migration as a separate, somehow isolated, process is to mistake the real process. Second, public policies that depend upon such a supposition will inevitably fail. Migration is not a unique process that can solve problems of deficient demand and national stagnation. There must be jobs for people to migrate, and the structure of spatial activity must be interrelated with the decentralized process of decision making.

The policy problem which these results also emphasize is the consistent geographic separation of employable labor from employment sources by some non-trivial distance—rigidities which stem from the existence of large distances in the marketplace. In essence, the friction of distance and lack of information constitute barriers to inter-local labor market efficiency. Under conditions of perfect competition, these barriers might not exist. As recent job search and labor turnover models have shown, such immobility is thought to be responsible for higher levels of aggregate national unemployment than would otherwise exist (the result of a locational mismatch rather than deficient demand). A remedy for reducing geographic segmentation based on a job search and turnover model would contain two main components. First, better job information pertaining to outside labor markets is required to overcome the lack of communication imposed by geographic distance. Second, financial assistance may be required to enable those with little wealth to afford the investment of moving and to offset the uncertainty that accompanies such movement. The type of worker assisted need not be solely restricted to the unemployed. If an employed worker has a greater prospect of benefiting from moving to another area than an unemployed worker, then he/she could be encouraged to move since his moving will open up a job slot that may be filled by an unemployed worker. These issues are explored in subsequent chapters.

NOTES

1. This section is based upon Clark and Ballard (1981).
2. The relationship tested for each state of the United States over the period 1958–1975 used a time-series testing strategy utilizing either the Cochrane-Orcutt (1949) method of controlling for first-order, autoregressive, serial autocorrelation or the Koyck (1954) arithmetic distributed-lag procedure. Since the Cochrane-Orcutt method involves first differences, the actual relationship tested (a variant of Equation 3.1) was in fact an economic adjustment model wherein response to market changes was the critical measure of wage convergence. Similarly, the Koyck procedure is also a time dependent formulation (also implicitly an adjustment model). Both the employment and migration variables were modified, the former by invoking a Koyck distributed-lag term and the latter by specifying different in- and out-migration variables. The choice between different specifications was based upon the overall fit of each combination of variables and equations.
3. Actually, this is probably the only source for such data in the United States, however, researchers have developed data series on a limited basis from the Internal Revenue Service. The CWHS data file used in this study included those individuals employed and between the ages of 24 and 64, inclusive. Excluded were the unemployed, retired, and student age groups. To enable comparison between states of the significance of migration variables, both in-migration to state i and out-migration from state r were made relative to each state's non-moving work force.
4. This section is based on Clark and Ballard (1980). Pion Ltd. has kindly permitted reproduction of some portions of that paper, which was published in *Environment and Planning A,* 1980, 799–812.
5. The six industry groups used in analyzing out-migration were mining, construction, manufacturing, wholesale/retail trade, finance/insurance/real estate, and other services. The agriculture and government sectors were not included because of problems in data availability and coverage. The equation for each industry was estimated in a time-series ordinary least squares (OLS) regression framework for the years 1958–1975. A system of Koyck distributed-lags (w_j) was used to link current and previous observations. The argument is that individuals make migration decisions only after observing the relative performance of the local economy over a period of time. It was also assumed that there is a time structure to the response or decision making

process rather than an instantaneous response to changes in the determining variables (cf. Bennett 1979).

6. The temporal aspect of migration decision making has been well documented in the literature. Nonetheless, little theoretical work has been done to specify the type of lags implicit in the decision process. For example, it is not clear that lags should be one or five time periods removed, or in fact what scale of weights should be applied to different lags. In many studies, including the ones reported here, the lag structure is often determined empirically. Sims (1974) has noted that economic theory in general is poorly developed in this area. He argued that the use of multiple lags in OLS regression may cause problems of serial autocorrelation or lead to cross-correlation with other variables.

7. New employment growth ($E^{r,n}$) was defined as a Koyck-distributed lag of the growth in regional employment (ΔE^r) minus the share of national growth (ΔE^n) that would go to the region based on its share of national employment (E^r/E^n):

$$E^{r,n} = \Sigma w_i \Delta E^r - \left\{ [\Delta E^n * (E^r/E^n)] \right\}_{t-i}.$$

The rationale for this share transformation was that if the region's employment grew at the same rate as the nation's, there would be no change in relative opportunity and thus no inducement to migrate.

8. To reduce any possible coverage bias, the number of insured unemployed was inflated by the ratio of total labor force (LF^r) to insure labor force ($LF^{r,i}$) in the region. Bias can be expected due to workers too discouraged to look for jobs, and who are thus not counted as unemployed. In addition, workers unemployed for less than two weeks over a specific period (26–65 weeks), or falsifying their unemployment status would bias the turnover indicator.

9. Morrison (1972) found that, in the long run, migrants go to the correct destinations but do not necessarily come from the correct origins. Based on evidence accumulated from migration models, such as Lowry's (1966), this conclusion has been interpreted as meaning that migration from depressed regions is unresponsive to origin characteristics. The degree of responsiveness is, however, a crucial aspect of equilibration models since such theories are of no practical use if it cannot be shown that migration is able to allocate surplus labor to high-demand areas.

10. Thanks to Pion Ltd. for permission to publish portions of a paper by Clark (1982b) that appeared in *Environment and Planning A*, 14, 146–164.

11. From 1958 to 1962, the U.S. economy oscillated, but in a generally downwards direction. Unemployment rates were higher during recession than before and remained higher during fast growth periods. Whenever a recovery began as in 1958 and 1961, interest rates were raised to prevent prices from rising faster than the federal government desired. Recessions were inevitable, but under these policies they became worse and the economy moved from recession to partial recovery to deeper recession. The 1960–1961 recession was particularly important in this context.

12. Economic growth in the United States was continuous from late 1963 to 1968. In 1963, the annual rate of increase in fixed investment advanced sharply, consumer spending increased rapidly, net exports increased, state and local spending increased, although, surprisingly, federal spending slightly declined. In 1964, business fixed investment rose $5.75 billion to $87.5 billion. Again, in 1965, the U.S. economy expanded in all major markets, with increased productivity and capacity and even greater increases in output. The 1964 tax cut stimulated consumer spending and business investment as a cut in corporate taxes at the beginning of 1965 further fueled business spending on plant and equipment. The national unemployment rate fell to 4.6% in 1965 compared to 5.2% in 1964 and 5.7% in 1963. The federal budget ran a $12.5 billion deficit in 1967 compared with a slight surplus in 1966. The shift from surplus to deficit provided a fiscal stimulus that helped to moderate a minor slowdown in the economy. Thus 1968 was again another year of economic expansion. Unemployment dropped to its lowest level in fifteen years and personal income again advanced sharply.

13. After the 1969–1971 recession, inflation only slowly declined. The rate of inflation fell from 6.1% in 1969 to 5.5% in 1970 according to the consumer price index (CPI). After rising at a rate of 3.4% per year during 1971 and 1972, the CPI rose 8.8% in 1973 and 12.2% in 1974. There were several reasons for the rapid rise in inflation. The first was the poor harvests in 1972 and 1973 which forced food prices up 20% in 1973 compared to under 5% in 1972. The second reason for high inflation was OPEC's action of quadrupling oil prices between September 1973 and May 1974. Wage and price controls ended in the spring of 1974, leading to a burst of "catch-up" inflation. In 1973, real GNP rose 5.5% and unemployment fell from 5.6% to 4.9% and production exceeded the Council of Economic Advisors' predictions by $8 billion. Despite these statistics the economy slowed during 1973. After a huge first quarter surge, GNP practically stalled for the rest of the year. In the fourth quarter of 1973 the Arab oil embargo began and the economy declined in 1974. Real GNP fell 1.4%, whereas the last half of the year was worse than the first half. The unemployment rate rose to an average of 5.6% for the year 1974, and reached 7.2% by the end of the year.

14. Some caution should be exercised in interpreting the results reported here. First, by standardizing for population size, the absolute volume of migration between states was conditioned so that a state such as California can appear at the periphery of the national labor market despite being a significant element of gross migration flows. In essence, California dominates the national system by reason of its size, not its relative importance. Second, the link made between integration and changes in the GNP was primarily descriptive. More work on the actual causal links between spatial form and economic processes in the long run and short run is required before more sophisticated analysis can be undertaken. Third, Slater's technique was used here as a means of organizing the massive sets of data and patterns; as such the analysis was not so much a test of the technique's usefulness so much as a means of description. Other techniques may be useful in describing particular gross flows, especially if concern is with the degree of symmetry between in-migration and out-migration.

FOUR

Regional Growth and Migration

INTRODUCTION

Having reviewed the evidence on the aggregate patterns of interregional labor migration, responsiveness to economic determinants and spatial allocative efficiency, the next step is to consider the relationships between labor migration and regional economic growth.[1] To understand the structure of regional net investment we need to understand both the dynamics of gross migration and the patterns of causality between labor migration and capital growth. For example, if it can be shown that capital relocation initiates migration, then to the extent that the location of capital itself is not fixed, policy makers could successfully intervene to direct growth to certain areas of the spatial economy. On the other hand, if migration and regional growth are not immediately linked, then the role of public policy vis-à-vis migration would be much more limited. This is, of course, unlikely given the patterns identified in Chapter 3.

It is also obvious that what we expect in the way of relationships between migration and local capital growth will be largely influenced by our theoretical perspectives. For example, it will be noted here that in neoclassical models, migration and regional capital growth have only weak causal links, while other theories, perhaps less popular in the academic literature, take a more structured view concerning the significance of capital in modern society.

Virtually all theorists agree that labor and capital markets interact in the regional development process. Some theorists, such as Borts and Stein (1964), would suggest that the interaction of these two markets is benign, leading to even regional development, equity, and allocative efficiency. Others, such as Markusen (1978), have argued that their interaction inherently implies exploitation and uneven development. Based on the pioneering work of Greenwood (1981) and Muth (1971), the 1970s was a decade of sustained empirical research on the interrelationships between labor and capital, and especially the interactions between labor migration and regional growth as measured by changes in employment and population. Using quite complex econometric models (*see* Alperovich et al. 1975 for example), researchers have sought to answer a number of relevant questions. Which comes first, economic growth or population in-migration? Are there distinct lags in the adjustment of labor to the growth process (or vice versa)? Does out-migration contribute to economic decline at the origin? Does economic decline precede out-migration? Moreover, a number of academics have sought to determine the lines of causality between growth and migration; although early on, Muth (1971) conceived of the issue as a chicken-or-egg problem, implying that causality on one side or the other is logically misleading and difficult to sustain empirically. A consequence of this type of reasoning has been the proliferation of models which simultaneously determine labor migration and economic growth.

For some, the results of this type of analysis have been satisfactory. And yet, in the realm of public policy analysis and implementation, knowledge of the particular lines of causality between labor migration and regional growth is a fundamental necessity. One way of resolving this apparent gap between empirical aim, theoretical methodology, and policy requirements is to question whether or not the typical empirical testing framework has been adequate to the task. In this context, there are grounds for questioning the adequacy of many empirical models of labor migration and regional growth. Obtaining adequate data on migration and economic growth has been a continuing problem. Census estimates of migration are quite crude in that they lump together employed, unemployed, and those not in the work force. Similarly, indicators of economic growth have rarely, if ever, measured investment directly, relying instead on proxies such as employment and population. Not only have adequate data been a problem, but perhaps more critical has been the lack of time-series data that could *directly* illuminate the dynamic interrelationships between capital growth and labor migration. Comparative statistics can only imply dynamics; yet empirical models have been essentially compromised by the data and their temporal (or should we say, static) character. A further important issue is the continuing use of net migration rather than gross flows; the point is quite simply that empirical models have been rarely equal to the task. This point has been made recently by Casetti (1981).

Essentially, this chapter reports on previous empirical analysis of the temporal relationships between gross in- and out-migration, and between labor mobility and capital growth. In terms of our evaluation of the conservative urban policy agenda, this empirical analysis will deal with two related evaluative criteria. First, we will again consider the match between the "facts," as conceived in the conservative agenda regarding the regional growth process, and the actual empirical evidence. Thus, much of the empirical evidence begins with the problems and concepts of neoclassical economics. To give this evaluation greater critical resolution, my evaluation will also compare contending explanations of the dynamics of regional growth and labor migration. As such, I extend the analysis to an external critique of the conservative position. Second, my evaluation will also be concerned with the hard cases, the ability of the conservative model to comprehensively predict rapid regional economic growth and decline. In this regard, I first begin with univariate statistical models of gross migration and then move on to considering the dynamics of capital and labor migration in relation to one another.

MODELING GROSS MIGRATION

For a variety of reasons, traditional methods of forecasting migration have come under increasing scrutiny. As recent court challenges to the 1980 census have shown, there are instances of incorrect estimates of current population as well as the forecasts made from such data. Researchers, such as Jackson et al. (1981), have claimed that census forecasts of interstate growth and decline have often been wrong. Growing areas that were predicted by the Census Bureau to slow down maintained their growth, and areas that were predicted to grow, did not. Of course, hindsight is far more accurate than forecasts, and it is easy to find fault in the census. Academics and policy makers have, with rare exceptions, been poor judges of likely spatial growth patterns (*see* Zelinsky 1977). Few anticipated the turnaround in migration patterns identified by Vining and Strauss (1977) and others. In fact, early consideration of the reversal of rural to urban migration dismissed the phenomenon as a statistical accident. As the evidence has been collected and evaluated, however, questions have been raised concerning not only the accuracy of data collection and forecasting techniques but our understanding of the migration process itself.

One of the implications of the preceding discussions of labor migration in Chapter 3 was that gross flows can be effectively modeled separately. For example, it was shown that out-migration is related to local (origin) prosperity (wages, employment, and unemployment) relative to national indicators, whether the region is growing or declining. As an area declines (or grows) relative to the nation, the volume of out-migration increases (or decreases). Conversely, it was also shown that in-migration to an area is related to local opportunities weighted by national indicators. The primary issue here is separating out questions of the determinants of migration from questions of the resultant spatial allocation of labor vis-à-vis the pattern and structure of wages and employment. Basically, migrants do not necessarily come from, and go to, the "correct" regions as predicted by conventional policy models of the migration process. This does not mean that gross flows are unrelated to local opportunities. On the contrary, local wages and employment characteristics are key determinants. The point is that once the gross flows of labor migration are modeled separately, the net results of gross migration for the landscape of spatial equilibrium are more problematic: flows may be interrelated in terms of local determinants, but not efficient in allocating labor over space. Once gross flows are recognized as separate behavioral categories, net migration must be consequently recognized as being a purely statistical category.[2]

The focus in this chapter is reserved for analyzing the temporal dynamics of gross migration. However having said that, it is apparent that there has been very little academic research on this topic. There is very little in the way of hypotheses that could give structure to an empirical analysis. Of the few studies on the temporal adjustment properties of gross migration, only Alonso (1980) has attempted to relate the time paths of in- and out-migration. He suggested that in-migrants have a high propensity to out-migrate again, although this propensity is thought by Alonso to decline with length of residence. Presumably, a rapidly growing area with high in-migration will have high out-migration. The question here that, however, remains unresolved is: does out-migration lag in-migration, or is it closely synchronized in time? Implicit in Alonso's argument is a dichotomy between fast growing and slow growing areas. The former type of area is presumably dominated by high rates of migration, the latter type of area is likely to have much less volatility in migration as the proportion of recent arrivals diminish(es) relative to total retained immigration. Less volatility implies different temporal structures in gross flows; thus, it should be possible to distinguish between areas in terms of their underlying temporal properties.

Alonso's argument is not unlike that of others who have argued, at least in effect, that out-migration from economically depressed areas occurs at a constant rate. Lowry (1966) came to that conclusion after finding that origin characteristics were unimportant in "pushing" migration (a conclusion not shared in this book). His alternative explanation was to invoke cohort specific rates of out-migration related to the migration propensities of the population. Less apparent from this discussion is the expected temporal structure of in-migration to slow growth areas. Conventional economic theory assumes in-migration to be negligible compared to out-migration, which is not in fact the case. Presumably, following Alonso's logic, in-migration would not be volatile, perhaps even dominated by long-run return migration by those who left earlier in their lives.[3] In any event, if out-migration is relatively stable, then by implication the rate of in-

Table 4.1 Employment Growth by State and the United States, 1958–1975

State	Growth Rates 1958–1966	(percentages) 1967–1975
Arizona	151.6	162.5
Florida	145.6	150.3
Virginia	132.9	131.9
New Mexico	123.1	133.8
Texas	127.0	135.7
Wyoming	110.8	147.3
Delaware	129.3	114.8
Iowa	124.6	118.7
Kentucky	126.4	124.7
Connecticut	124.4	107.9
Indiana	130.3	108.6
Michigan	129.8	107.7
Illinois	119.5	105.5
New York	111.3	(99.0)
Pennsylvania	111.3	106.0
United States	124.5	116.9

migration must be small relative to those retained in-migrants. What of the degree of temporal synchronization between in- and out-migration to and from slow growth areas? One would expect little synchronization if out-migration is constant and related to the local age structure, and if in-migration is more to do with return migration.

Thus there are two problems associated with understanding the dynamics of gross labor migration. The first is theoretical; it is basically a question of stepping out on the straight jacket of conventional policy models that assume stability where in fact there may be significant temporal discontinuities. The second problem is empirical and it is linked to the initial time-series specification of the process of migration. The approach taken in Clark (1982c) to the latter question was to model gross migration flows using the stochastic time-series techniques made popular by Box and Jenkins (1976).[4] There are many reviews of these techniques and some applications to regional economic phenomena (Bennett 1979). Rather than repeat these extensive reviews, the modeling methodology and conceptual basis of autoregressive integrated moving average (ARIMA) models is outlined in Appendix I.

A set of states were selected for the analysis of their dynamic gross migration structures (*see* Table 4.1). These fifteen states were arranged into five different groups according to their growth of employment over the 1958–1975 period (Bureau of Labor Statistics 1977). Using national growth rates as reference points, the first group was characterized as a *maxigrowth* group. Basically, all three states

Table 4.2   Autocorrelation Models of Gross Migration, by State

| State | Gross Migration | |
	In	Out
Arizona	IMA (1,1)	AR (1)
Florida	ARMA (1,1)	ARI (1,1)
Virginia	IMA (1,1)	ARI (1,1)
New Mexico	ARI (1,1)	ARI (1,1)
Texas	ARI (1,1)	IMA (1,1)
Wyoming	IMA (1,1)	IMA (1,1)
Delaware	AR (1)	AR (1)
Iowa	AR (1)	ARMA (1,1)
Kentucky	ARI (1,1)	MA (2)
Connecticut	AR (1)	ARI (1,1)
Indiana	AR (1)	IMA (1,1)
Michigan	ARI (1,1)	ARMA (1,1)
Illinois	AR (1)	ARIMA (1,1,1)
New York	IMA (1,1)	AR (1)
Pennsylvania	IMA (1,1)	ARI (1,1)

grew very fast over both 1958–1966 and 1967–1975. The second group had average initial growth rates and then took off. It is described here as the *accelerated growth* group. The third group grew in both periods at much the same rate as the nation and were summarized as being the *average growth* group. In contrast to the second group, the fourth was summarily termed the *decelerated growth* group. And, in contrast to the first group, the last group grew, and even declined, very slowly; states that are termed (relative to the nation) as the *maxidecline* group. Consistency and similarity in growth patterns were the primary criteria for the inclusion of any state in a particular group. Not surprisingly the Southwest is represented in the first two groups while the Northeast is represented in the last two groups.

The results of modeling each raw gross flow for each state are summarized in Table 4.2. Taking in-migration first, nine of the fifteen states modeled had identified AR time-series processes, five had MA processes, and one was mixed, ARMA.[5] Of the states requiring differencing to induce stationarity, most were either growing or declining states, indicating the existence of an important trend component. In addition, four of the five states with MA in-migration time-series processes were shared equally between two groups of states: maxigrowth and maxidecline. In-migration to Wyoming, an accelerated growth state, was identified as the other MA process, while in-migration to Florida, a maxigrowth state, was identified as a mixed ARMA process. Implied in a MA(1) process is that the current observation can be best (parsimoniously and accurately) expressed as a function of current and immediately prior random shocks. This would seem to imply that in-migration to these types of states was a quite volatile dynamic process, more vulnerable to exogenous and rapid shocks than to previous patterns of in-migration. In contrast, average and decelerating growth states were better approximated by first order AR processes. Implied in those cases, which constitute the majority of the in-migration series modeled, was that in-migration is a function of previous levels of in-migration plus a random shock.[6]

From the results summarized below it is also clear that out-migration for some states can be best modeled by first order MA processes (Table 4.2). Fewer states, however, are in this category; they are Texas and Wyoming, which were accelerated growth states, and Indiana, a decelerated growth state. Notice that knowing the order and the process of in-migration for any given state was not sufficient to guess the order and process of out-migration from that state. Only three states had the same time-series process for both in- and out-migration. Further, there was no clear pattern with respect to economic growth or decline.

For the most part, the estimated parameters of the in-migration models were statistically significant; the exceptions being found in the states of Virginia, Texas, Wyoming, and New York. (These are not reported in detail here; *see* Clark, 1982c.) All, except Texas, were identified as MA processes. In effect, because the parameter on previous values of in-migration to Texas was insignificantly different from zero. Any current value of in-migration was only significantly dependent upon the current random shock. Again, this was a source of volatility in any estimate of in-migration even though previous values of in-migration do marginally lower the forecast errors. Large and significant in-migration AR parameters were found in both growing and declining states. The lowest parameters were found in the average growth group of states indicating again that in-migration to those states was less volatile than for growing or declining areas— a result that should not come as a surprise to proponents of conservative and radical doctrines.

Some parameter estimates for out-migration time-series processes were found to be not significantly different from zero. This was true for Florida, Virginia, Texas, and Wyoming (maxi- or accelerated growth states); and Indiana, Connecticut, and Pennsylvania (decelerating growth or declining states), although there was a mixture of AR and MA processes involved. The implication was that the current random shocks have an important role in determining current out-migration. Given the conventional assumptions of the long-run stability of out-migration, especially with regard to declining regions, these results indicate that policy models prefaced on such an assumption are likely to be fundamentally compromised.

So far discussion has centered on the particular time-series structures for each gross flow and state.[7] Elsewhere, it has been observed that in- and out-migration appear highly correlated, both in terms of the volume of gross migration and their rates of change (Clark, 1982c). In addition, it was noted that Alonso (1980) among others contended that in-migration can lead to out-migration; that is, in-migration precedes in time and therefore in some sense causes out-migration. The primary question here is then: are in- and out-migration temporally related? I emphasize the phrase *temporally related* because it is very difficult to demonstrate causality in this context. The basic problem is that both gross migration flows are related to the same set of exogenous variables; wages, employment, and unemployment for example (see Appendix I). Consequently, their individual autocorrelation structures are intercorrelated, not independent as required when testing for causality in the time domain. While, according to Granger and Newbold (1977), issues such as lead/lag structures and correlation between gross flows at particular points can be investigated, any argument concerning causality would be simply spurious. In this section we focus upon the cross-correlation functions of gross migration for each state.

All states had very similar cross-correlation functions with the highest cross-correlation estimates being centered around zero lags (Table 4.3). The highly centered character of the cross-correlations and the lack of other significant spikes might well have been expected given that most estimates of their underlying time-series properties were quite simple AR(1) or MA(1) processes. Yet, at the same time, these results are surprising at least in the context of the hypotheses of conventional theory. The Lowry hypothesis holds that in-migration responds to differential shifts in local economic activity while out-migration is a longer-run phenomenon. If this was true, one might expect to see quite long leads/lags reflected in the data. Also, Alonso's (1980) argument that in-migration *causes* (in the sense that knowledge of the former improves the forecasts of the latter) out-migration implies some type of lag structure, but again the evidence does not directly support his hypothesis. After all, if the highest cross correlation is at the zero lag, then both gross flows adjust coincidently in time, although separately. Only Delaware and New Mexico had cross-correlations below the 0.800 level. Moreover, in all but two cases the highest correlation was centered around the zero lag. Florida's highest correlation is centered on one year, indicating that in-migration may lag out-migration, while for Delaware the results imply that in-migration may lead out-migration by one year.

From these results we can speculate as to the role of U.S. interstate labor migration vis-à-vis regional economic growth and decline. It is hard to escape the conclusion that gross migration has very similar (even mirror-imaged) dynamic properties in Texas and Pennsylvania, two archetypical economically growing and declining states, although in Texas, migration may be more volatile. This suggests that the migration data file used here (CWHS) measures labor turnover, that is, job switching. It is well known that job switching is highest among younger workers, and this is consistent with the age profiles of

Table 4.3   Cross-Correlations for Gross Migration by State

State	Gross Migration	
	lag$_k$	r$_k$
Arizona	0	0.872
Florida	1	0.951
Virginia	0	0.965
New Mexico	0	0.728
Texas	0	0.972
Wyoming	0	0.903
Delaware	−1	0.743
Iowa	0	0.901
Kentucky	0	0.913
Connecticut	0	0.940
Indiana	0	0.949
Michigan	0	0.840
Illinois	0	0.961
New York	0	0.928
Pennsylvania	0	0.969

employed migrants. It is also well known that job switching typically involves promotion and higher pay (Bartel 1979). Thus at the micro-level, job switching carries obvious rewards, whether the job is located in a growing or declining state. How might this explain the higher rates of gross migration in growing areas and net in and out migration?

First, the question of the rate of gross migration. Growing areas are characterized by high labor turnover; quitting is more prevalent and can be shown to be positively linked to the rate of local wage inflation (Clark 1981b). Turnover is associated with the level of economic opportunities, and in growing areas labor turnover is a means of gaining rapid job promotion and higher salaries. Thus, to the extent that labor turnover involves relocation across state boundaries, the actual rate of gross migration will reflect this particular kind of labor mobility. Elsewhere, it has been observed that interstate migration in the South and the Southwest is highest among rapid growth states, and is, therefore, indirect evidence for this hypothesis.

Why then the difference in net migration between growing and declining areas? I would contend that there are simply not enough job opportunities in slow growth states. Voluntary turnover is significantly lower in these types of states. Job switching that involves out migration can, of course, occur with relative ease. On the other hand, job switching that involves in-migration is less likely because of the more limited set of destination opportunities. In addition, declining industries in low growth states do not provide the same number of middle-level jobs that are accessible for younger workers. Consequently, younger workers are lost to the region (through turnover) and not completely replaced.

This interpretation will be explored in more detail in the subsequent section, where two contending schools of thought will be compared and contrasted. The first is termed the capital-logic school, which is based upon the idea that capital through ownership retains the initiative in location and relocation. The second school of thought is termed the competitive market school. This latter school is implicit in the conservative urban agenda, and it assumes simultaneously equilibrating regional capital and labor markets. From these two perspectives, the conservative agenda will be evaluated for its relative *internal* and *external* coherence and comprehensiveness.

THEORIES OF MIGRATION AND CAPITAL

The capital-logic school focuses on the social relations of production and especially the strategies of domination and exploitation used by firms to control labor. Firms are viewed as being more mobile than labor, if not in terms of the physical stock of production, then at least in terms of their financial assets. The case studies of the New England economy by Bluestone and Harrison (1982) have gone some way toward confirming this proposition. Because of the interdependent nature of production, firms need labor and labor needs firms if both are to survive, and because of the fact that surplus value is a function of the amount of labor embodied in the production process, firms necessarily attempt to control and exploit labor. The central problem for labor is its dependence, its lack of ownership of the means of production, and its reliance on firms for jobs. More bluntly, firms own the jobs, have the power of hiring and firing, and ultimately the right of initiating and terminating employment. Power in the employment relation is unevenly distributed unless labor can constrain the actions of firms through tactics, such as unionization, and the use of state apparatus, such as the courts, to prohibit runaway plants. To the extent that capital is not dependent on a limited geographical set of locations for resources and markets, firms will locate so as to avoid entrapment by labor.

Given these assumptions, a series of scenarios can be identified so as to represent the interrelationships between labor migration and capital growth. First, imagine that a firm has the choice of a wide number of locations for production (as, for example, an electronics firm may have when assembling transistor radios; *see* Clark 1981c). Walker (1978) and Gertler and Whiteman (1982) have suggested that such a firm will locate so as to use a relatively immobile and vulnerable labor force. Two sets of variables will dominate the choice of location: the degree of local worker organization and labor costs. Meyer et al. (1980) similarly argued that these two variables are crucial locational criteria.[8] To manage, organize, and control this work force, a technocratic class loyal to the firm and not tied to any location may be required. In addition, uniquely skilled workers may be needed. In this context the local labor market may not be completely adequate; labor, as a floating technocratic class, follows capital. Employment is initiated by the firm for local labor and outside workers. Thus, it is hypothesized that there would be an empirically observable lag between capital growth and in-migration. Also, this scenario suggests that as labor begins to exert power over the firm, the relocation of capital will occur, thereby initiating an out-migration of its technocratic elite. Again, change in the capital stock (in this instance, decline) initiates migration, but of course only for a narrow portion of all employees—the balance would become unemployed.

A parallel argument has been made by Massey (1978) and Massey and Meegan (1982) in their studies of capital restructuring, relocation, and the economic crisis of Great Britain. Their evidence, and that of Bluestone and Harrison (1982) for New England, suggests that restructuring has a significant spatial component. Relocation enables firms to leave behind old forms of organization (technocratic and social) and out-moded capital stock. The consequences of relocation are a decline of local employment and the selective out-migration of certain primary workers. Often coupled with this process is a second sequence of events: selective centralization and decentralization of corporate control functions and production facilities. Accompanying this scenario is a clear spatial division of labor. To the extent that corporate control functions require a technocratic elite, then capital growth and labor migration are likely to be closely related with small temporal lags in adjustment.[9] At the other end of the division of labor, however, decentralized production may require few outside workers, implying that capital investment may not be related at all to labor migration. By decentralizing production, firms may be able to invade existing and vulnerable local labor markets and thus maintain their exploitation of labor. Again capital retains the initiative and more technically (empirically) provides the underlying rationale for assuming labor migration to be dependent on capital growth (although, of course, there may not be a strong relationship).

A third scenario has been suggested by Markusen (1978) who emphasized how labor reserves can be manipulated in mediating the powers of labor. For firms that are geographically bound by reason of resources or markets, for example, a way of maintaining control over wages and the conditions of work is to import labor to the region. In contrast to the scenarios suggested above, the type of labor that is imported may be unskilled. Individual firms may arrange to import this type of labor (as suggested by Piore 1979), although it is clearly possible for the state to encourage labor migration through policies such as guest worker visas. This latter approach has been quite popular in western Europe (Fielding 1982) and less so in the United States, although it could be argued that the massive, and largely uncontained, volume of illegal immigration is a tacit "reserve army" policy. Clearly labor migration in this context is dependent on demand and the level of investment. It is also possible that among larger multilocational firms there will be firm-initiated labor migration that is unrelated to demand (labor transfer within the internal labor market).

The neoclassical theory of factor mobility and regional growth is well known and it has been the subject of considerable debate concerning its theoretical propositions (*see,* for example, Miernyk 1979 and 1982) and empirical relevance (Clark and Ballard 1981). It is hardly necessary at this point to review at length its intricacies. At the minimum, its principal assumptions regarding the relationship between labor mobility and capital growth need to be explicitly noted in order to facilitate empirical analysis and comparison with the capital-logic school. The neoclassical model and its variants derived from international trade theory have been characterized as the competitive market school for two reasons. First, since it is assumed that workers and firms independently pursue goals of utility and income maximization within the structure of market opportunities, it is obvious that the manner in which labor and capital markets function and intersect with each other determines the relationship between labor migration and capital growth.

Second, because it is the operation of the market that provides rewards, this approach quintessentially applies the rules of supply and demand to labor and capital as if they were solely exchange commodities. The market conceptualization is used by neoclassical theory to provide an institutional order to the exchange process. Very simply, labor is assumed to migrate in response to geographical variations in wages, climate, and job opportunities. These types of variables are assumed to figure prominently in an individual's utility function. Moreover, it is implicitly assumed that the individual initiated migration in accordance with the spatial distribution of these economic variables, producing an outcome which is optimal both for individuals and the broader regional economic system alike. By migrating to a high-wage area, the individual benefits *and* labor is allocated more efficiently with regard to the spatial configuration of the demand and supply of labor. Consequently, as labor migrates to high-wage areas the supply of labor is increased at the destination and decreased at the origin so that, over time, following a sequence of such moves, wages will be equalized between all regions of the spatial economic system. For the labor market, migration has two virtues. It rewards individuals in the sense that their welfare increases, and it efficiently allocates labor between areas so that factor price equalization is achieved. This school of thought is clearly the basis of conservative theorizing concerning the proper national urban policy. In this context the "free market" is thought to be the ultimately efficient and fair allocator of resources (Chapter 2).

From the perspective of capital, it is apparent that the spatial configuration of labor costs (i.e., wages) will structure capital mobility.

Following Romans (1965) and others, capital is presumed to migrate from high-wage to low-wage areas. Holding the location of labor constant (no migration), the result will be an increase in labor demand in low-wage areas and a decline in labor demand in high-wage areas. Consequently, wage equalization should occur between the regions of the economy. Assuming perfect information of all wages and prices, capital and labor adjustment in the form of migration should occur simultaneously. This is the basis for assertions by members of the competitive market school that economic and demographic variables are mutually interdependent in the regional growth process. Muth's (1971) chicken-or-egg problem (which comes first, labor migration or capital growth?) is an instance of partial equilibrium analysis. The challenge is simply to designate the point or stage in the interdependent process at which to begin analysis. Following this logic, an obvious solution (and one promoted by Greenwood 1981, ch. 6) is to model the system as a simultaneous process.[10] The problems of designating causality are circumvented, and thus the assumptions of non-contingent individual optimizing behavior can be maintained.

Imagine that labor is not as fast as capital in adapting (that is, migrating) to the map of economic opportunities (surely, a realistic hypothesis); the result would be that labor migration would lag capital growth. Labor might in-migrate to a once high-wage and high-employment region not knowing that the reason for high economic growth (previously strong capital growth) had since moved. To correctly specify an empirical model of the simultaneous relationship between migration and capital, such a possibility in the form of leads and lags would have to be taken into account. Because the competitive market school has no *a priori* expectation of whether or not (and by how much) labor lags capital, extensive empirical analysis has to be undertaken prior to simultaneously modeling these two markets, in order to correctly specify the adjustment characteristics. But what if lags were found? Could their existence be explained? The most obvious response would be that the initial assumptions were not met. Information about competing opportunities is not complete nor is it uniformly available (Rogerson and MacKinnon 1982). Most empirical models deal with this problem in a pragmatic manner and, depending on the situation (typically what the data indicates), leads and lags are introduced to improve the model's predictive performance. Causality in this context (that is, labor migration causing regional capital growth or vice versa) results from an ad hoc examination of reality, rather than a theoretical proposition.

The issue is then more than empirical. It involves us in understanding the *nature* of adjustment assumed in the competitive market model of regional growth. Put simply, this model assumes that labor and capital adjust to the landscape of opportunities in a logical sequence. It is inherently weak with respect to questions of temporal adjustment. The implied Walrasian recontracting process is ahistorical and instantaneous, and it describes a system that "moves" from one equilibrium to another. The parameters that describe the system remain the same; the problem is simply deriving the optimal spatial allocation of resources. Inherent in Greenwood's simultaneous approach is an unstated assumption that the temporal lead-lag issue is only one of mechanical coordination. For instance, in our earlier imagined case of labor adapting more slowly than capital, not only is there a lag between capital growth and labor migration, but the actual economic system becomes transformed in response. Thus, not only are labor and capital out of sequence, but they each face markedly different current and historical conditions. As Iwai (1981) has recently demonstrated, short-run disequilibrium accumulates over *time* into the long-run wherein real events and actions, and their locations in time and space, determine cause and outcomes.

What then should we expect to see in any empirical analysis of the temporal characteristics of migration and capital? The capital-logic school clearly suggests that capital has the advantage of initiation—of ownership of the jobs. Thus, to the extent that labor is required outside the local labor market, whether of the technocratic elite or of the reserve army of the unemployed, capital growth should lead migration. Presumably, the lags should be shorter when technocratic labor is involved compared with the reserve army. It is also plausible that once initiated, migration and capital growth may become a simultaneous process, especially if the region is large and economically diverse. In effect, the reserve army model has a similar causal predictive power with Kaldor's (1970) price model. At the same time, it is also clear that the capital-logic school predicts that a certain portion of labor will migrate regardless of demand, primarily for discipline-related purposes. If all the assumptions of the competitive school are met then presumably there would be no leads or lags between labor migration and capital growth—the markets of labor and capital would operate and intersect simultaneously.

MODELING CAPITAL AND MIGRATION

The study by Clark and Gertler (1983a) was based on interstate labor movements and changes in the capital stock data for a set of states. Using again the Continuous Work History Sample (CWHS) of the Social Security Administration and the Bureau of Economic Analysis, yearly estimates of interstate gross in- and out-migration were collected for the period 1958 to 1975. Data on capital stocks at the regional level are, however, not routinely collected and they must be inferred or estimated from estimates of gross investment. For their study, Clark and Gertler collected yearly data on state capital growth that were made available by the Federal Reserve Bank of Boston.

This latter data set is unique both for its annual time-series nature and its level of spatial disaggregation. The study utilized total state level manufacturing capital estimates, although the same types of estimates are available for a number of two digit SIC industries (the basis for a forthcoming study by Gertler 1983). It is a relatively easy matter to measure firms' new investment each year, and this has been reported regularly in the Census of Manufactures and Annual Survey of Manufactures at the two-digit SIC level on a statewide basis since 1954. At any one time, however, the total productive stock of capital in a region is the source of the current year's investment plus a portion (depending on depreciation) of investment in previous years. The major challenge in constructing capital stock figures from gross investment is the estimation of the productive life of a given piece of machinery and the temporal profile of depreciation (in its productive rather than financial value).

The capital stock estimates for the study by Clark and Gertler (1983a) were based on new capital expenditure data for plant and equipment reported in the Census and Annual Survey of Manufactures. To account for the age of existing capital stock, it was necessary to consider past investments dating back to 1921 for equipment and 1904 for plant. Industry-specific rates of technological depreciation (incorporating physical decay, declining productivity, and technological obsolescence) were obtained from the Bureau of Labor Statistics, and were applied separately to plant and equipment series for each industry so as to derive annual capital stock estimates for each state. (For an extended treatment of the steps in constructing these data, the reader is referred to the seminal study by Browne et al, 1980). These data represent a considerable improvement over previous studies, which typically rely on financial or "book value" measures of capital stock.

To enable comparisons across states experiencing different rates of economic growth, analysis was based upon the set of fifteen U.S. states introduced in the previous section. To remind the reader: the first group, including Arizona, Florida, and Virginia, was representative of rapid and sustained growth. The second group, including New Mexico, Texas, and Wyoming, was designated as the accelerated group. The third group, including Delaware, Iowa, and Kentucky, was designated as stable or average (in relation to overall U.S. trends). The fourth group, including Connecticut, Indiana, and Michigan, was designated as the accelerated decline group. And, the fifth group, including Illinois, New York, and Pennsylvania, was designated as the maxidecline group.

The first step of the analysis was to estimate the temporal pattern of cross correlation between capital formation and gross migration (the methodology of this chapter is based on Tiao et al. undated). Selected results from this analysis are presented in detail in Table 4.4. It was clear that when cross correlated with capital growth, both in- and out-migration have very similar cross-correlation functions.

Table 4.4 Cross-Correlation Functions between Capital Growth and In- and Out-Migration

State	Capital and In-Migration		Capital and Out-Migration	
	Maximum CCF	lag b	Maximum CCF	lag b
Arizona	0.845	+1	0.873	+1
Florida	0.875	0	0.882	0
Virginia	0.719	+1	0.753	+2
New Mexico	0.719	+1	0.760	0
Texas	0.783	0	0.715	0
Wyoming	0.268[a]	+10	0.295[a]	+10
Delaware	0.518[a]	+9	0.607[a]	+8
Iowa	0.872	0	0.875	0
Kentucky	0.648	+2	0.674	+2
Connecticut	0.617[a]	+8	0.556[a]	+8
Indiana	0.502[a]	+5	0.601	+6
Michigan	0.798	+1	0.627	+2
Illinois	0.471[a]	+2	0.539[a]	+6
New York	0.590	+2	0.608	+6
Pennsylvania	0.550[a]	+7	0.579[a]	+7

[a]Not significantly different from zero at the 95% confidence level.

For each pair of functions there is a similar symmetry on either side of the peak cross-correlation value. For Arizona, the peak cross-correlation value between capital growth and in- and out-migration occurs at plus one lag. That is, both gross migration flows lag capital growth by one year. Only rarely are there differences between the pairs of cross correlation functions in terms of their peak values or lags. The most obvious examples were for the states of Illinois and New York. For both states, in-migration lags capital growth by two years and out-migration lags capital growth by six years. But it is also clear that these results are the exception, not the rule.

In relation to the standard literature on interstate migration a number of surprising contrasts deserve mention. First, supposed differences between in- and out-migration in their responsiveness to economic variables must be questioned. Both gross flows are temporally interrelated with capital growth for growing *and* declining states. It cannot be assumed, as Lowry (1966) would have it, that out-migration is unrelated to economic change. Moreover, the symmetry between in- and out-migration in this context has gone largely unrecognized in the literature. Second, these results provide weak evidence for the question of whether or not migration and capital act simultaneously with respect to one another. The strongest claim of the competitive market school is simultaneity, and should be reflected in zero lags between capital and migration. Yet, this was hardly the case for the majority of states analyzed here (Table 4.4). Only in a few cases, notably strongly growing states, were there zero lags between migration and capital. Most states ranged between one and two year lags. As was noted previously, writers of the competitive school such as Greenwood (1981) are clearly aware of this issue. Nevertheless, the evidence is systematic enough to suggest that lags (non-simultaneity) are the rule, not the exception.

CAUSALITY ANALYSIS

What cannot be directly ascertained from cross-correlation functions are the directions and strengths of relationships between variables. To accomplish this task, capital growth and gross migration were modeled in a time-series framework, concentrating on establishing causality and the estimates of structural parameters. The first step in this process was to model their joint error structures so as to provide a preliminary guide to the underlying time-series properties (see Appendix I). An incorrect assumption of the process or its order can, as noted above, lead to spurious and misleading conclusions vis-à-vis causality and the significance of parameter estimates. Many states had autoregressive (AR) processes of low orders, and there are two key implications which followed from these results. First, the histories (or previous values) of each variable, capital formation and migration, are obviously important in *conjunction with one another* in determining current and future levels of capital growth and migration. As Granger and Newbold (1975) have noted, this need not be the case as many economic processes can be best characterized as stochastic random-walk time-series processes. Notice in this context that Wyoming was resistant to process and order identification and that the relationship between capital growth and in-migration for a set of slower growth states may have a significant stochastic component (Table 4.5).

Second, the relatively low orders of the underlying time-series [e.g., AR (1)] suggested that time lags are limited between capital and in-migration; a proposition entirely consistent with the cross-correlation functions. But the implications of this observation are more important than the simple question of consistency. In essence, the fact that most time series are autoregressive of order one or two indicates that the distributed lag between capital growth and in-migration may be only of one or two years. Some writers such as Moriarty (1976) have suggested that the distributed lags are in the order of five, even ten years. Thus, these results are of crucial significance because they enable a *direct* evaluation of previous studies' assumptions regarding the nature of lags. Obviously, these results are a product of the data; its time-series as opposed to cross-sectional character. These results were direct, however, and not simply inferred.

The results of causality tests between capital growth and in-

Table 4.5   Preliminary Time-Series Order Identification for Capital and In-Migration

State	Process and Order[a]
Arizona	AR(1)
Florida	AR(1)
Virginia	AR(1)
New Mexico	AR(1)
Texas	ARMA(1,1)
Wyoming	—
Delaware	AR(1)
Iowa	AR(1)
Kentucky	AR(1)
Connecticut	AR(1) or ARMA(1)
Indiana	AR(1 and 5) or ARMA(1,5)
Michigan	AR(2)
Illinois	AR(1 and 2) or AR(1 and 2 and 4)
New York	AR(1)
Pennsylvania	AR(1) or ARMA(1)

[a]When the parenthesis includes "and—", this refers to order plus significant lags. AR indicates autoregressive and ARMA refers to autoregressive and moving average.

migration are shown in Table 4.6. Unidirectional causality dominated the first two groups of growth-oriented states. For Arizona, Virginia, and New Mexico the evidence suggested that in-migration at time t is a function of previous years' capital growth. As suggested by the capital-logic school, capital growth determines migration. Within this group the exceptions were Florida and Texas. In the former case, the result was not unexpected; previous in-migration of even employed individuals (not retirees) determined capital growth in Florida. A simple characterization of the differences between Arizona and Florida might be that in the first case, autonomous investment determines migration; while, in the second case, demand initiates investment. For Texas, however, the process is simultaneous and jointly determined with no apparent time lags. In this instance in-migration and capital growth are mutually interdependent *and*, most importantly, behave coincidentally in time. Given that the data are yearly, there may of course be within-year time lags. Even so, this result tends to provide the strongest support for the case made by the competitive market school.

Of the remaining average- and declining-growth states, only Iowa has a similar causal framework to that of Texas. All other states are characterized by time lags in their adjustment to changes in in-migration and capital growth. Like Texas however many average-growth states had simultaneous processes; in-migration causes capital growth as capital growth causes in-migration. The autoregressive nature of this process is evident in the time lags associated with both capital and migration. Again, however, this evidence tended to

Table 4.6 Results of Tests for Causality: Capital and In-Migration

State	Functional form
Arizona	$IM_t = f(K_t)$*
Florida	$K_t = f(IM_t)$
Virginia	$IM_t = f(K_t)$
New Mexico	$IM_t = f(K_t)$
Texas	$IM_t = f(K_t)$ and $K_t = f(IM_t)$†
Wyoming	—
Delaware	$IM_t = f(K_t)$ and $K_t = f(IM_t)$
Iowa	$IM_t = f(K_t)$ and $K_t = f(IM_t)$
Kentucky	—
Connecticut	$IM_t = f(K_t)$ and $K_t = f(IM_t)$
Indiana	$IM_t = f(K_t)$ and $K_t = f(IM_t)$
Michigan	$IM_t = f(K_t)$
Illinois	$IM_t = f(K_t)$ or $K_t = f(IM_t)$
New York	$IM_t = f(K_t)$
Pennsylvania	$IM_t = f(K_t)$ and $K_t = f(IM_t)$

*K_t indicates that the determining variable is lagged over time.

†Combination indicates that capital and in-migration are determined simultaneously.

support the competitive market school rather than the capital-logic school because of the implied multidirectional simultaneous temporal structure of economic change. The exceptions to this were Michigan and New York where lagged capital growth caused in-migration. Perhaps one consolation for the capital-logic school is that where it really matters (strong-growth states; the "hard" cases), capital determined in-migration. The competitive market school was surely compromised by its inability to correctly predict the patterns of causality among these types of states. The growth process and its relationship to in-migration is obviously simpler and more direct than it would contend, *but* the middle order—of average growth or decline—is much more complex.

What of the parameter estimates and the actual functional forms of the relationships implied by these tests of causality? (*See,* for more detail, Clark and Gertler 1983a.) The only surprises in this context came from slow growth or declining states, such as Connecticut, Indiana, and Pennsylvania, which had lags of eight, five, and seven years respectively on both migration and capital (some of which were insignificant due to the shortness of the series). When compared with the results derived from their cross-correlation functions, it is apparent that there was some consistency here. Delaware was also noticeable in this regard, although it is not a declining state. Finally, it should be acknowledged that the underlying error structures of a number of the states with simultaneous equation systems are quite complex and interdependent (see Texas and Iowa).

Table 4.7   Preliminary Time-Series Order Identification for Capital and Out-Migration

State	Process and order[a]
Arizona	AR(1)
Florida	AR(1)
Virginia	AR(1)
New Mexico	AR(1)
Texas	AR(1)
Wyoming	—
Delaware	AR(1)
Iowa	AR(1)
Kentucky	AR(1)
Connecticut	AR(1)
Indiana	AR(1 and 5)
Michigan	AR(1)
Illinois	AR(1)
New York	AR(1 and 5)
Pennsylvania	AR(1)

[a]When the parenthesis includes "and—", this refers to order plus significant lag. AR indicates autoregressive.

To establish the lines of causality between out-migration and capital growth the first step was to model their joint error structures. Table 4.7 reports the results of these analyses, indicating that all processes were identified as autoregressive (AR) of very low orders. When we considered capital and in-migration, most states were found to have AR(1) structures, but a few also had more complex ARMA structures. In this instance, it was clear that the past histories of each variable interact in determining present and future levels of capital growth and out-migration. Also consistent with the previous results was the fact that the time lags implicit in an AR(1) process are small, indicating that the interaction between capital growth and out-migration is quite dynamic. This is an important implication once we remember that many authors, including Lowry (1966), have assumed out-migration to be unaffected by short-run economic variables, and that it is a product of very long-run changes in age composition. Again, in relation to the previous results, Wyoming proved resistant to ready identification. Apparently, all three series—capital growth, in- and out-migration—for that state approximate random noise.

The results of testing for causality between capital growth and out-migration are summarized in Table 4.8. When compared with Table 4.6, it is immediately apparent that the states with simple unidirectional relationships have switched from the fast-growth (as in capital and in-migration) to the very slow-growth instances. Those

Table 4.8 Results of Tests for Causality: Capital and Out-Migration

State	Functional form
Arizona	$EM_t = f(K_t)$ and $K_t = f(EM_t)$
Florida	$EM_t = f(K_t)$ and $K_t = f(EM_t)$
Virginia	$EM_t = f(K_t)$
New Mexico	$EM_t = f(K_t)$ and $K_t = f(EM_t)$
Texas	—
Wyoming	—
Delaware	$EM_t = f(K_t)$ and $K_t = f(EM_t)$
Iowa	$EM_t = f(K_t)$ and $K_t = f(EM_t)$
Kentucky	$EM_t = f(K_t)$
Connecticut	$EM_t = f(K_t)$ and $K_t = f(EM_t)$
Indiana	$EM_t = f(K_t)$ and $K_t = f(EM_t)$
Michigan	$EM_t = f(K_t)$
Illinois	$K_t = f(K_t)$
New York	$EM_t = f(K_t)$
Pennsylvania	$K_t = f(EM_t)$

states were, moreover, split evenly between those that were found to have capital growth causing out-migration (Michigan and New York) and those that were found to have out-migration causing capital growth. All four states were found to have lagged exogenous variables. When we look for other examples of unidirectionality, only two other states were found—Kentucky and Virginia. In these two states capital growth again causes out-migration. For the capital-logic school, these results are of some significance. Capital growth obviously plays a significant determining role vis-à-vis out-migration. Yet, in two instances the converse was true. How can this be explained? One possibility is that out-migration causes a change in the capital investment due to a shift in demand. It is plausible, for example, that as the population of a state declines due to autonomous out-migration, capital investment declines in response. Of course, this explanation begs the question of what causes out-migration from depressed areas (but, *see* Clark and Ballard 1980).

No functional or causal relationships were found for Texas and Wyoming, which should not be surprising at least in the latter case. With reference to the remaining states it is clear that simultaneity is a strong characteristic for fast- and medium-growth states. In some cases, capital growth and out-migration are interdependent and coincident in time; in other instances, there are time lags involved. There are no clear patterns with regard to the rate of growth of the states concerned; it should be noted that very fast-growth and average-growth states are found to have causal relationships with no evidence of lags. Again, this is evidence of temporal adjustment that is much faster than commonly supposed in the policy literature. An assumption of five- or even ten-year distributed lags would be clearly difficult to sustain in the face of this evidence. For the competitive market school, of course, the simultaneity of capital growth and out-migration for seven of the fifteen states must be counted as evidence for their propositions regarding adjustment. At the same time, the evidence is hardly cause for rejoicing; unidirectional causality dominates the slow-growth states and tends to support the capital-logic school's notion of capital determinancy.

Consistent with the evidence suggested in the cross-correlation analysis, most studied states had quite small lags between capital growth and out-migration. Only Indiana and New York had significant lags beyond one year, and both Delaware and Connecticut had results similar to those obtained for estimating the relationship between capital growth and in-migration for those states on these terms. This suggests a consistency between in- and out-migration and their relationships with capital growth—an issue worthy of greater study! Again the error structures of each equation or set of equations were quite complex, requiring in some instances significant lag parameters (for example, Delaware).

SUMMARY

In this chapter, I was concerned to document the relationships between in- and out-migration and between capital growth and labor migration. The capital-logic school argues that capital determines migration primarily because of rights of ownership and the power of initiation. In some instances, where a floating technocratic elite cadre of workers is involved, the time lags between capital growth and migration are presumed to be quite small. In other instances, perhaps where the reserve army of the unemployed is concerned, the time lags are presumed to be quite large. On the other hand, the competitive market school (the basis of conservative urban policy) argues that migration and capital growth are initiated separately but in reaction to similar macroeconomic variables. The result for the competitive market school should be an intersecting and interdependent set of labor and capital markets that, in the absence of market imperfections, should behave coincidental in time without lags. In such a system, migration causes capital which causes migration; it is a simultaneous process. Lags can only be identified in an ad hoc manner because they are determined by particular causes. The goal of this chapter was to establish the direction of causality, of determinancy between these variables in the context of two contending schools of thought.

To establish causality and the relationships between capital and migration, the analytical framework was based on recent developments in time-series analysis. Tests of causality, Box and Jenkins (1976) transfer function models, and evaluations of cross-correlation functions were the basis of this framework. In using these techniques, I departed from conventional empirical models of regional growth.

Rather than base the analysis on comparative statics, these models were dynamic. Rather than prior specification of leads and lags, these models derived these relationships from the actual observations. Rather than implicitly accepting the contaminating effects of autocorrelation, these models explicitly sought to model the underlying autocorrelation structures. And, rather than presuming a certain pattern of causality, even simultaneity, we directly tested for the direction and strengths of causality between capital and migration. In these ways, the methodology differed from others who apply simultaneous equation models to regional growth without first checking for the temporal structure between capital and migration. It was noted, moreover, that many models of regional growth are unable to deal with these questions because they are not even conceived in the time domain; they are not dynamic.

The results of analysis provide two general conclusions. First, the temporal dynamics of the relationships between in- and out-migration and between capital growth and in-migration and capital growth and out-migration are quite similar at least in terms of their patterns of adjustment, underlying temporal processes, and relatively short time lags. This conclusion directly contradicts those authors, including Lowry (1966), who have maintained that in- and out-migration react to different determinants over different time scales. Second, neither the capital-logic nor the competitive market school completely dominate the other in terms of their predictive or comprehensive abilities vis-à-vis causality. It is clear that in some instances, notably fast-growing states for in-migration, and slow-growing states for out-migration, the capital-logic school can provide a convincing theoretical and empirical exposition of the determining role of capital. In these instances, and some other exceptions, capital deformation determines migration. This result is of major importance, especially since the capital-logic school is so adept at explaining and predicting the hard cases of rapid economic growth and decline. By itself, this conclusion has a great deal of force since it is those instances wherein economic events rapidly shift and change that provide the major challenges to the design of public policy. Thus the empirical case for the capital-logic school is quite strong. But also important is the consistency of the initial assumptions regarding the determining influence of capital. The competitive market school, and thus the conservative agenda which is based on this model, is extremely weak at this level, and must be viewed with a great deal of caution regarding the reliability of its predictions regarding causality and timing. Of course, it is true that middle-order growth states are best modeled via a simultaneous framework (causality cannot always be uniquely determined), but this result hardly compensates for its dismal failure to deal with the hard cases.

What does this imply about labor migration and its determinants? At one end of the spectrum, capital initiates migration; at the other end, migration and capital apparently adjust in time in relation to one another. Only very rarely does prior migration initiate a spatial flow of capital (*see,* for example, the case of Florida). Thus, at one end of the spectrum, labor has no free will; it depends on capital for employment and for the opportunities that come with capital investment. At the other end, migration and capital are interdependent. To capture this conception of the relations between labor migration and capital growth a more explicit model is required that can account for the shifts in the power of initiation. It is also clear that the competitive market school is patently unable to help in this regard because of the assumptions of free will and independence that characterize the implied behavior of labor and capital. The logic of the capital-logic school is more developed in that it can be made contingent on specific events and the actual underlying structure of ownership and control. It is this aspect that gives it strength. Inevitably, however, this model is not a general theory that encompasses all economic systems.

These results also reintroduce the importance of bringing jobs-to-people as an *empirically* obvious and necessary policy option. In brief, the programs of the Economic Development Administration (EDA) assume greater significance than recognized in the conservative urban agenda. EDA, unlike other federal programs of labor market intervention, has had the mandate to directly influence the location of long-term jobs in distressed areas of the nation. Its programs are delivered through a network of regional offices which receive applications for funding from local government and business entities located in one of a number of specifically designated areas.

EDA's basic approach has been to engender economic development through the attraction of employment opportunities and the improvement of public works and infrastructure. For example, Title I furnishes grants to governmental units for the construction and renovation of public works and facilities. Title II, on the other hand, provides loans and loan guarantees to businesses wishing to locate or expand in a designated local labor market based on satisfactory assurances that a predetermined quantity of jobs will be created in the area. Title III makes grants to cities, states, and distressed areas so that they can obtain technical assistance in economic planning. And, Title IX is intended to aid areas experiencing either slow, steady deterioration or "sudden and severe economic dislocations" by offering the same assistance available through Titles I, II, and III, plus special measures such as temporary public job creation, revolving business development loans and unemployment compensation.

NOTES

1. This chapter is based upon Clark (1982c) and Clark and Gertler (1983a). The Association of American Geographers kindly consented to republishing some portions of those two papers.
2. The relative simplicity of modeling each gross flow is not reflected in net

migration; because of the mixture of processes implied above, net migration cannot be an MA (moving average) or markovian (AR, autoregressive) process. This can be easily demonstrated either by manipulating the estimated equations for gross migration or by actually analyzing the autocorrelation functions of net migration time series. Net migration time series are at best random noise, and at worst have very complex nonautocorrelated error structure.

3. The Select Committee on Population (1978, p. 6) argued that return migration is particularly important for those unemployed workers who out-migrate from depressed areas. Their temporal frame is somewhat different from Alonso's; they argued that return migration occurs very quickly for the unemployed. The evidence for this proposition is weak at the very best of times. For the Select Committee, the evidence was produced in the form of assertions!

4. As in the previous chapter, the data for this analysis was taken from the Continuous Work History Sample (CWHS) of the Bureau of Economic Analysis and the Social Security Administration. This data set has been subject to some criticism. Plane (1981), for example, suggested that there is significant overcounting, and Renshaw (1978) has questioned its reliability, given that the data are reported by place of work, not place of residence. Even so, the Bureau of Economic Analysis has spent a considerable amount of effort in ensuring the accuracy of the data, especially with regard to the overcounting problem. If we were using small contiguous units as the geographical basis of analysis, then the cross-boundary problem (an employer moving from one location to another within commuting distance) might be an issue. Here, as in previous studies (Clark and Ballard 1980), the analytical unit is the state. It should also be recognized that time-series analysis is not sensitive to the levels so much as to changes in migration. It is the consistency of the data, year to year, that is the crucial issue.

5. An AR time-series process is usefully considered to be an economic process of continuous and cumulative growth/decline. Put another way, economic change is relatively smooth and linked to previous patterns of economic change. On the other hand, an MA process could be thought of as an economic process of discontinuous change wherein past patterns of growth/decline are not as important as rapid and unanticipated shifts in economic activity. For example, imagine what would happen to local employment if a large manufacturing plant moved in from out of state.

6. The reader may wonder about the accuracy of time-series models which have been estimated on the basis of only eighteen annual observations. This poses no problem if the time-series and the models fitted to them exhibit relatively simple (low-order) autocorrelation structures. Most of the models identified and estimated in this analysis are of order one. In those cases in which higher-order lags are found to be significant, however, the high-order components of these models are to be interpreted with caution, pending further investigation with parallel data or longer series. In any event, the standard errors of the parameters would have indicated the existence of any estimation problems.

7. No attempt is made here to model the possible spatial interdependencies which might exist between states, in the manner suggested by Bennett (1979). While this may ultimately prove to be a fruitful exercise, its omission did not introduce any bias or inefficiency into the derived parameters, did not inflate the observed coefficients of determination, and did not render any confidence intervals or tests of significance invalid. These assertions are made on the basis of the decisions in Clark (1982c) and Clark and Gertler (1983a) to estimate the models in time-series rather than spatial cross-section. The implication of restricting investigation to the time domain is that the serial autocorrelation properties of the models (a task for which the Box-Jenkins techniques are admirably suited) must be fully evaluated even though there need not be any consideration of spatial autocorrelation.

8. Meyer, Schmenner, and Meyer (1980) have argued a similar case. They noted that, based upon employer interviews, "labor costs and the level of workforce organizations are key variables in making location decisions. Giving a union a new workforce that is nearly impossible to organize is perhaps the most prized side benefit of a new plant site, and for many companies it becomes a controlling consideration"

(p. 15). Note that these conditions can also be found in inner-city locations where the traditional work force has been supplanted by Hispanic and other minority groups who do not have the same "history" concerning labor-capital relations.

9.   John McKay of Monash University has noted in conversation that many larger multinational firms deliberately seek to separate the technocratic elite from where they live because this class often has to perform functions that conflict with local economic interests. For example, in Australia, savings banks are state and nationwide with no responsibility for investing locally. Bank managers are often moved to maintain their allegiance to the bank rather than to local entrepreneurs.

10.   Unfortunately much of the data used in simultaneous models have been cross-sectional. The problems of this type of strategy are twofold. First, the dynamics of migration and capital adjustment can only imply dynamics through estimated elasticities, and are not considered directly. Thus, there is no evidence on real trajectories of economic change, only on ahistorical generalizations of possibilities. Second, simultaneous models beg the question of causality itself—the framework is not sensitive to actual patterns of causality, an a priori decision is made that is a veritable straightjacket upon subsequent enquiry. After nearly a decade of simultaneous-type models we are really not any closer to knowing the causes of regional growth.

FIVE

Search Behavior and Labor Markets

INTRODUCTION

In the previous chapters of this monograph, recent research on U.S. interregional migration was reviewed for insights concerning the macroeconomic spatial and temporal efficiency of labor migration, and the structure of causality between labor migration and regional capital growth. In the first instance, the patterns of migration and the significance of various determinants, like employment and wages, were considered in a choice-oriented framework. That is, I assumed that people seek better jobs, and that they respond (albeit "inefficiently") to the spatial arrangement of opportunities.[1] This conventional choice-oriented model was then subject to greater scrutiny in Chapter 4 wherein, through advanced time-series techniques, it was shown that it is regional capital growth and decline that *initiates* labor migration in many instances. If individuals wish to obtain better jobs, or even jobs in their own right, they necessarily have to respond to the locational preferences of capital. Thus, internally and externally, the conservative urban agenda can be subjected to fundamental questions concerning its coherence and ability to deal with the hardest of cases. Furthermore, the "free" market of conservative ideology apparently severely structures individuals' options and ultimately the overall spatial pattern of labor migration.

As a means of expanding the external critique of the conservative agenda, in this chapter I want to consider the hardest case—why people do not migrate even though local economic conditions are incredibly harsh and unrewarding. By doing so I wish to demonstrate in the strongest possible theoretical terms that the conservative agenda for minimal government intervention is thoroughly misplaced. As long as the discussion remained concerned with documenting and interpreting interregional migration patterns, the conservative agenda's logic was at least partially legitimized. That is, even if migration can be shown to be poorly coordinated in space and time, and even if the causal links between migration and regional growth are poorly articulated, even completely inadequate for the task of prediction, some might suggest (such as Mueller 1981a) that the underlying logic of the competitive market model of migration remains viable: people still migrate for economic rewards, and the system still rewards those individuals despite imperfections.

Spatial coordination of the demand and supply of labor is not a problem for labor markets in equilibrium. The stocks of employment, unemployment, and job vacancies would be simultaneously adjusted in such a system so that a balance was achieved, at a particular wage, between the demand and supply of labor. The fact is, however, that labor markets typically function out of equilibrium (Pissarides 1976). The job coordination process is a very real problem for individual employers and workers and for the spatial labor market system as a whole. Factors such as the distance between workers and potential employers, imperfect information of job opportunities and worker characteristics, and the heterogeneity of worker skills and job skill requirements all contribute to a situation whereby local labor markets function in dynamic disequilibrium. In essence, the market is in continual flux with flows between the stocks of employed and unemployed being the crucial elements or mechanisms of adjustment and response.

My purpose is to examine the market pressures that drive and preserve a wedge between one place and another inhibiting aggregate short-run labor market adjustment and full employment equilibrium over space. I wish to demonstrate that separate sets of labor market conditions can coexist affecting the lives and job prospects of people located in contiguous places. And, rather than placing responsibility for labor market disequilibrium on supposed irrational individual behavior, it is argued that it is precisely those individual rational decisions in the face of varying spatial labor market conditions that preserve geographical inequalities in employment opportunities and local labor market disequilibrium.

JOB SEARCHING AND THE SUPPLY OF LABOR

Schultz (1980) argued in his Nobel lecture on global poverty that the microeconomics of being poor are no different from the microeconomics of being rich. Poor people, he argued, are as competent as rich people in adjusting their preferences or choices to match their resources and particular scarcity constraints. A part of what makes poor people different from rich people, then, must be the macro-economics of the situations that the two groups face, and the imperatives of the situations to which they must respond (Schelling 1978). That the parameters defining the economic environment within which individual decisions are made differ for rich and poor people is the central theme of this analysis. Instead of being concerned with mass rural poverty my focus is with the rigidities of geographical labor market adjustment.[2]

Wage-labor, not land, represents the primary source of local household income. Therefore, the processes that match people to jobs are the crucial determinants of local welfare and structure. In this analysis, labor—the commodity that employers buy from workers—is not, however, the standard homogeneous good as assumed in the neoclassical model. Here labor is characterized by differences in skills, education, and training that are often job specific (Williamson 1975). The labor market itself is given a distinct geographical configuration. For labor to be traded between workers and employers, a fundamental requirement is for such an exchange to take place at a specific location. The spatial scale of this location may vary considerably, particularly with respect to the skills required and where they are located. The market for academics, for example, is a national one, perhaps even international. This wide reach is clearly a function of the uniqueness of skill and of the institutional structure of the university system, and especially the associated social networks.

Where uniqueness of skill and wide-ranging networks are lacking, the labor market process is likely to be more localized, perhaps limited to a few towns.[3] Such localization is especially typical of low-wage jobs and of workers who are typically defined as lacking skills and can be characterized as being in the "secondary" labor market. A choice of spatial scale then is a choice of market. This chapter investigates the labor market at the inter-metropolitan level, and it is therefore more concerned with average and low-wage jobs and low-skill workers than it is with highly skilled managers.[4]

In decentralized local labor markets of low-wage jobs, a special trading arrangement exists that reflects both the "quality" (skill) of labor and the relative scarcity of desirable jobs—workers have to search out firms to find job vacancies for which they qualify. Workers have to discover the wages offered, and they must assess the risk of layoff implicit in any job. Also required is some assessment of the likely implications of a particular job for their future careers (although all too often in the case of low-skill secondary jobs, the implications are zero; *see* Piore, 1979a). If offered a job, workers have a choice of taking it or leaving it, knowing that in accepting the job they will be constrained to certain working conditions, such as a fixed number of hours per week at a given wage rate, set by the employer.

Coordination between workers and employers in this situation carries with it a requirement for both parties to meet. Their employment relationships are characterized by a high degree of interdependence. This process can be expensive in time and money for prospective employees. Moreover, these expenses are not often reimbursed in low-wage jobs, and the costs of search, including travel expenses, lost earnings, and "finders" fees, must be borne by the worker. Such costs reinforce the local character of the low-wage labor market, since the costs of searching are clearly less for jobs closer to home. Given workers' experience in the labor market concerning the distribution of job/wage offers, there will be a point where a wide spatial search will incur greater costs than the likely return in wage offers, thus perpetuating the spatial segmentation of the low-wage and low-skill labor market.

Here, theoretically, the supply of labor is determined by workers' job-searching behavior.[5] The demand for labor, on the other hand, is assumed to be a derived demand—derived, that is, from the uncertain demand for firms' output (assuming for the moment that as demand for output changes firms adjust the quantity of labor employed rather than changing their products' prices; *see* Barro and Grossman, 1976). Firms advertise their demand for labor informally by making job offers and sometimes formally by placing job-wanted advertisements in the media. The job offer is actually a total package of wage rates, layoff risks, working hours, and working conditions. Essentially, the demand for labor implies an implicit contract that is likely to be more favorable for high-skill/high-demand workers than for secondary workers (Williamson 1975). The searching worker must locate an offer, assess it, and decide whether he or she is willing to accept the conditions implicit (or, in fact, explicit if unions are involved) in the employment contract.

Thinking of the supply of labor as the result of a job search (even migration) has the advantage of being realistic. It tells a story with which many of us are familiar (*see* Hall 1980). Much of the elegant internal coherence of job search models, however, comes only at the expense of some crucial limiting assumptions about the real world of the labor market. The most important assumptions concern the volume of information in the job market and the sources of labor market information. Workers of the conventional job search models of McCall (1970) and others are assumed to know the mean wage in "their" labor market, and often the dispersion of wage offers around that mean. These models also limit the degree of uncertainty involved in looking for a job. For example, the actual job offer is often thought to contain complete information about layoff risks, career prospects, working conditions, and so forth (Burdett and Mortensen 1980). This is clearly an oversimplification: full information is only revealed with on-the-job experience.

Some proponents of job search models have argued, as well, that they "explain" current high levels of unemployment, more so than

Keynesian theories of deficient demand. That is, the volume of labor turnover may explain high levels of unemployment. According to Feldstein (1975), the stock of unemployment at any point in time is a function of many people entering and leaving the pool of unemployment relatively often and for relatively short intervals. This view is in direct contrast to the notion that most people are involuntarily unemployed for long periods of time. Although not disagreeing with the conceptualization of the labor market in terms of dynamic flows, recent evidence has suggested that recurrent turnover may not contribute as largely to the level of unemployment as initially thought. Clark and Summers (1979, p. 14) found that "most unemployment, even in tight labor markets, is characterized by relatively few persons who are out of work a large part of the time." They concluded that recurrent turnover "can account for only a small part of measured unemployment." In fact, it was shown that the extent and duration of long-term unemployment are much more significant than initially thought. The Job Search and Relocation Assistance demonstration project conducted by the U.S. Department of Labor also concluded that the duration of unemployment varies with age, education, and race for both the control and experiment groups (*see* Lilien 1980, for a related analysis of Feldstein's position).

Although the simplified treatment of information and uncertainty is a crucial failure of job search theories, it does not render them useless. Similarly, one does not have to agree with Feldstein (1975) to explore the ramifications of search theories. Such theories provide useful starting points for describing and analyzing how workers go about finding jobs in a system of local labor markets.

In summary terms (see Appendix II) a worker will not accept a job if its value is less than that achievable by further search. The value of a job to the individual is defined with reference to a "reservation" utility below which the worker is not willing to drop. In essence, the workers' decision rule is to set a reservation wage and search for appropriate job offers. The issue is complicated by the fact that search can be costly both in terms of out-of-pocket expenses (travel, etc.) but more importantly in terms of foregone income. In effect, these costs make the worker less adventurous and ambitious than he or she might be in a frictionless world. These costs act as a discouragement on the amount of time and geographical extent that the worker is willing to spend searching for a job. Workers whose hopes start out high but who receive no equivalently high offers, will have to settle for less than had been hoped for (of course, the reverse may also be true). The problem, however, is to understand the process by which workers locate job offers and to establish a relationship between this process and workers' reservation utility levels (and, hence, their reservation wages).

In the first instance, workers who are employed face a decision: whether or not to quit and then search for a job either locally or in another labor market. Generally, economic conditions and expectations of future conditions are the determinants of job search behavior. In a local labor market characterized by less than perfect information, there are clearly risks associated with job searching. All potential job and wage offers involve significant risks, particularly if information of current economic conditions is incomplete or distorted by distance and by the behavior of complementary agents. Under these conditions, quitting to search for a job involves significant costs and potential risks: lost wages, job instability, and the prospect of making a wrong decision. In deciding whether or not to quit, workers consider a number of decision variables including wages, unemployment, and the flow of new hires. If wages increase in other firms for similar jobs or job functions, but remain stable in the individual worker's firm, relative wage disparities will increase, leading at a certain point to workers searching for better wage offers (Hicks 1932). This case presumes that skill requirements remain constant for particular jobs and that the firm is unresponsive to interfirm wage disparities.

Wage opportunities could also change, however, as skill requirements change. For example, if skill requirements were to decline for a set of job types, vertical or occupational mobility within and between firms would become possible for individual workers seeking to improve their wages and job conditions. If skill requirements were to increase, however, the potential for vertical mobility could decline. In essence, quits are a function of relative wages and the general temporal pattern of wage rate changes. Notice that wage rate changes could either induce the worker to quit to search or to quit to directly accept another job offer found through on-the-job searching. Quits are also likely to increase if the temporal pattern of wage offers is more stable over time. The costs of making an incorrect quit decision are such that impulsive quit/search decisions are unlikely to be a large proportion of total quits.

Two other variables are important in determining the volume of quits. Hires by firms represent an important element in the individual decision-making process. Simply, the number of job offers in the local labor market may induce workers to change jobs (or quit) or risk being unemployed in order to conduct a wide search for all available job/wage options. In a region with little wage competition between firms and workers (presumably a depressed or declining region, such as Philadelphia), this variable may be very important as a means for workers to improve their job and wage status without having to bargain directly with employers for increased wages.

Similarly, the state of the labor market itself may be an important determinant of the volume of quits, as a high level of unemployment could discourage workers from "testing" other job-wage offers. Clark and Ballard (1980) argued, in the context of the decision to migrate, that the level of unemployment represents implicitly the uncertainty of finding a job. The implication that as unemployment increases in the local labor market, the ratio of quits to search will decline. Even the worker who quits to take another job directly faces the prospect of losing seniority and his experience rating and thus increasing the vulnerability to being laid of in subsequent recessions.

Once workers begin the search process, different issues come into play. Some authors have suggested that workers collect job offers in a specified time period and over a particular search horizon. David (1973), for example, has argued that this is analogous to drawing a random sample from a set whose distribution is known. Others have argued that workers must decide whether to accept or to reject an offer before receiving another one (this is defined as a sequential model). Reality is probably a mixture of the two models with workers feverishly trying to locate better offers before they have to say yes or no to the offer they have already received. This suggests a hybrid model. After locating the first acceptable offer, given a specified reply time, the worker sequentially searches for better offers, using the utility expected from the latest job offer as the new (and higher) reservation wage. If a worker fails to locate a better job offer in time, he or she must accept the one in hand. If successful, however, the worker can gamble once again with a new reply time and with a new and even higher reservation wage. The fact that searching is costly in terms of out-of-pocket expenses and foregone earnings will provide an upper limit on the time workers can spend looking for jobs and, consequently, on the number of times they can afford to gamble in searching for other offers.

Jobs themselves can, of course, be described by a variety of dimensions, including wage rates and layoff risks. Working hours and working conditions are not considered in most job search models. Thus, the link between utility and income is actually weaker than is often supposed. Nor is the process made explicit whereby workers evaluate the career paths inherent in any job. This is usually collapsed into one variable called the "expected discounted lifetime income of a job with characteristics (wages, layoff risks) that are accepted for at least one period" (Burdett and Mortensen 1980). Since individuals are not all the same, it should be expected a priori that reservation wages (the acceptable policies of workers) would vary from individual to individual. Some people are, and can afford to be, higher risk takers than others. Logically, risk takers will have higher reservation wages than risk averters (Rothschild and Stiglitz 1970). Variations in initial wealth and in "tastes" (caused, for example, by having children or not) will also generate variations in workers' reservation wages. Reservation wages, however, are also responsive to factors in the job search process that lie outside the workers' control. Some of these will apply uniformly to all individuals, and will not affect the distribution of reservation wages. Others will apply unevenly, and will therefore change that distribution.

Consider the possibility that the distribution of wage offers for a given job type changes. For example, an increase in the mean wage may increase the expected return to search and, hence, the reservation wage. This may affect all individuals, but not uniformly, because increases in the mean wage change the risk associated with job searching. Increasing the mean wage may result in a greater than proportional risk in the reservation wage of risk averters. A change in the distribution of wages about the mean also changes the distribution of reservation wages. The higher the maximum wage offer in the job market, for example, the greater the possible return of continuing to search. The bigger risk taker might, therefore, set a higher reservation wage. Conversely, the lower the minimum wage offer, the lower the wage a risk averter will settle for (mitigated, obviously, but the existence of minimum wage laws and other institutional factors. *See* Burdett and Hool 1982).

Layoff risks can also be independent of the individual and be associated with the type of job.[6] Burdett and Mortensen (1980) argued that these risks would not affect the reservation wage because a marginally acceptable job has the same payoff as that associated with continuing to search. Thus, for any given layoff risk, the reservation wage cannot therefore be an increasing function of that layoff risk. For this to be true, however, the layoff risk and wage would have to be independent. This may be plausible over very long time periods, however, overall annual income (or "short" time period) must depend upon both wage and job stability. Clearly it is entirely possible that wages and layoff risks are strongly associated. Hall (1980), for example, argued that jobs with high layoff risks can only attract workers if wages are paid to compensate for this possibility. Implicit employment contracts typically include wages and layoff risks. Other means of risk compensation are also possible, including unemployment insurance. Annual income directly affects the value of search, and so the reservation wage (itself a function of the value of search) will change in response to changes in layoff risk.

A worker accepts a job only if its utility is greater than the expected value of continued search. The reservation utility which defines the acceptable jobs level at any time during search is a combination of the utility of either accepting or rejecting the present situation. The utility of accepting the present situation is given by the utility of the pre-search situation (both are defined net of search costs). In addition, the utility of rejecting a current job offer/position situation is the expected value of continued search (less search costs). Thus, a worker will quit searching if his or her evaluation of a continued search falls below the value of the present situation.

The time path of an individual's reservation utility level during search, therefore, depends upon the path of the expected value of continued search. Based upon Pissarides (1976, ch. 9), the expected value of search V_t, follows a simple recursive relation. Essentially, the difference in an individual's expected value of search between two elementary search periods (t and t–1) is thought to be equal to the average utility of acceptable jobs minus the expected value of continued search in the later time period. If the set of acceptable jobs in period t, is not "empty," then it follows that $V_{t-1} > V_t$. On the other hand, if the set is empty, $V_{t-1} = V_t$. Since job searching is, however, costly and because the job searcher will not find any acceptable job offers, no job searching will be undertaken. Moreover, if the set is not "empty," the expected value of continued search will fall over time, and thus the reservation utility level (and hence reservation wage) of the disappointed job seeker will also fall over time.

A further consideration is that since job search is costly, workers will contact their most promising employer contacts first. The risks associated with such behavior are lower at the start of searching because of the greater information available. Over time, however, as information sources become exhausted, the search process becomes more random and consequently more risky. It could be hypothesized then that the volume and quality of job offers will deteriorate over time, leading to a steeper reduction in workers' reservation wages than initially supposed, although the exact fall-off in reservation wages will depend upon the individual's ability to absorb the costs associated with increasing risks. The worker will stop searching when the expected value of continued search in period t becomes equal to the worker's reservation utility level. The dependence of reservation wages on offered wages is shown analytically in the Appendix II.

These speculations on the behavior of the individual worker job searching have been made under certain restrictive assumptions. Workers were assumed to be equally well informed about job offers and wages, etc. Also, for the sake of simplicity, I have limited the extent of uncertainty in the process to not knowing *when* a job will be found, or what kind of job will be found. Once located, everything relevant about the job is assumed to be known. The implications of relaxing these restrictive assumptions of uncertainty are complex. Perhaps they hint at the use of adaptive choice models in the sequential process (Viscusi 1976). For present purposes, the results derived from these assumptions will be utilized to develop my argument concerning individual mobility and possible strategies of adaptation to a system of local labor markets.

Assumptions about the nature of information of job opportunities, however, pose a different problem altogether. These conclusions do not hold for all individuals alike, since every individual is not necessarily equally well informed. Leads to possible jobs are found through social networks, especially by knowing somebody already working in the firm. In this context, Burdett and Mortensen (1980), have suggested that the probability that an individual worker will receive an offer from firm i can be approximated by n_i/N where n_i

is the number of workers in firm i, and N the total number of workers in the labor market. This is a stochastic representation from an aggregate perspective of what is in part a deterministic process at the level of the individual. Both the location of employers and the spatial patterns of informal job networks play a vital part in the informational process. The implications of relaxing these assumptions are explored in a later section, especially with reference to the significance of reservation wages and the path of the expected value of searching.

DEMAND FOR LABOR AND EMPLOYMENT CONTRACTS

Workers supply their labor to firms by searching for the jobs that are offered. There is nothing in this process that determines the number of jobs available. As noted briefly above, in fact the demand for labor is derived from the uncertain demand for firms' products. Given that workers are typically employed by firms before changes in demand are recognized, this presents the firm with a problem—rapid shifts in the level of employed labor represent costs to the firm because the mobility of labor is imperfect. On the supply side, mobility is restricted because search is costly and because skills are not necessarily directly transferable. On the demand side, because of separation payments, recruitment costs, lost production, and training costs firms may attempt to hoard their labor (Oi 1962). Moreover, high labor turnover may mean that the firm will be unable to attract the type and quality of labor it requires for efficient production (*see* Iwai, 1981 for further details).

For many firms, technical staff are significantly different from production employees on a number of counts. Most importantly, R/D workers, for example, generally perform highly detailed and technically demanding tasks. Williamson (1975) and Doeringer and Piore (1971) have identified four sources of such task idiosyncracies. First, equipment used in R/D innovation and development may be so unique or at least non-standard that particular experienced workers are required for efficient operation. Second, actual operating procedures may be developed by workers themselves either because equipment is made by those workers for a specific, nonrepeatable task or because interface procedures are determined by the background and experience of each worker. Third, tasks may require other workers to operate as a team. Personalities and common experiences may not be interchangeable without restructuring the teams and their composition (what Piore [1979a] termed "socialization"). Finally, unique information that is only available through repeated on-the-job experience may be required to undertake a task. In contrast, production workers perform specific tasks that are so standardized and routine that workers and labor in general may be completely interchangeable. Craft-type skills are often redundant, with the only requirement being manipulative dexterity.

A possible response by firms to such labor specificity may be to offer employment contracts.[7] These are the job offers that workers seek out. In reality such contracts can be implicit or explicit containing complex packages of wages, layoff risks, working hours, and working conditions. But, in theory, contracts are often considered only as combinations of wages and layoff risks. The firm's problem is to ensure a labor force that is neither too big nor too small to meet the demand for its output that it knows only *after* it makes job offers and hires workers. Consequently, a firm must have an active employment policy in three areas: a policy for the retention of its existing labor force; a layoff policy when necessary; and, a recruitment policy to fill vacancies. These policies are designed to ensure that the firm's desired labor force is ex ante chosen to balance the expected loss associated with not having a large enough labor force ex post with the additional cost of having another employee.

In order to retain its workers, a firm must offer a wage that is greater than that which a worker could expect from searching, net of search costs. Given a certain level of labor demand and an areawide money wage, any reduction in wages paid by an individual firm to its workers is likely to result in increased labor quits. If labor quality is important to a firm's production process a firm would have to initiate a search process for labor replacements. Hicks (1932) argued that "he (the employer) might succeed in getting men of as good quality as those he lost; but even so, these in their turn are likely to drift away. By reducing wages, he has reduced his chance of getting good workmen" (pp. 45–46). The implication of reducing wages for the volume of labor turnover is clear—workers will quit to search for other jobs, offering at least the average going wage. The quit decision is, of course, dependent upon the likelihood that the individual worker will be able to find alternative work and wage offers.

This offered wage will, of course, vary with the layoff risk and tenure possibilities. In essence, the firm has to offer the individual worker his or her reservation wage or at least be close enough so that the wage offer does not induce the worker to search for another job, assuming profit maximization by the firm. On the other hand, a worker will search for a job if the value of search exceeds the average value of existing conditions of tenure and layoff weighted by their respective probabilities. Under relatively restrictive assumptions concerning complete information and perfect competition, it can be shown that firms will act non-cooperatively to retain their labor force. Even if these conditions do not exist, it could be argued that the particular firm specific skills learned while on the job will encourage firms to compete with other firms to retain their labor (through higher reservation wages) in the fear that such labor could not be replaced in the short run.

Retention in this sense does not mean that workers are always employed by the firm, merely that they are not working for anybody else. In low-wage jobs, the phenomenon of temporary layoffs is common. The optimal policy for the firm is to ensure that "its" labor force, when laid off, does not find, or is encouraged to find, a better job elsewhere. This may mean paying higher wages to workers when they are actually working or making agreements with unemployment compensation agencies to maintain institutional links to particular labor groups. In the short run, therefore, Burdett and Mortensen's (1980) conclusions may be a little tenuous. Their assumptions of marginal productivity and a uniform value of worker time being the primary determinants of wages ignores a wage setting process that in the short run has a strong social content. Hicks (1932), for example, argued that wages are set by comparison across "equal" workers and by comparison and differentiation between "unequal" workers (cf. Dunlop 1950).

Imagine that two firms pay the same average wage over the period t to t+n ($W^i = W^j$) but that one varies its wage over the period according to unemployment conditions such that $\sigma_w^i > \sigma_w^j$. The result might be that workers would quit firm i for firm j. Hicks (1932) concluded that "if a firm varies its [wage] rates, that means that the terms it offers to permanent employees are, on a long view, rather less attractive; and it might find that, as a consequence, it gets less good workmen than it would get if it paid the same average wage" (p. 47). The implications of the Hicksian model of wage determination for how the labor market is viewed as operating are twofold. First, although firms are assumed to be profit maximizers, they may have little individual ability to affect the going, area wage rate. Thus, firms compete (hire and lay off) for a given quantity and quality of workers rather than discriminating amongst potential employees solely on the basis of price. Second, the ability of workers to quit is dependent upon other job and wage offer combinations. It is not clear that all workers need have specific skills vital to the firm. For instance, dual labor market theory suggests that some workers are "captured" by firms because of their lack of skill and their inability to find other offers.

The firm has an alternative retention policy. It could locate in a place that limits the employment alternatives available to workers. This would make comparison difficult between different sets of workers and different firms' retention policies, thus increasing the bargaining power of the firm. Moreover, such a strategy would reduce the expected value of search for all workers. The firm could then spatially separate workers whom it wishes to retain in full employment from those for whom it has only irregular and temporary demand. This would effectively prevent workers from demanding equal contracts and perpetuate for the existence of a segmented local labor market. Of course, if different types of workers were segmented spatially and functionally according to their different retention contracts, the firm would be in an even more powerful position to carry out its optimal contract policy.

Spatial segmentation of production by relocation to peripheral areas may cause, greater employment instability in the destination regions although total numbers employed may actually increase; higher regional hourly wages, but greater instability of income—possibly lower average yearly incomes; and, greater mobility in firm location patterns. Taking the first point, relocation may contribute to a net increase of employment, but in doing so the firm may be able to reassert its preferred external employment relation—that is, little internal promotion, and minimal on-the-job training. Compared to previous locations, job security may be eschewed in favor of flexibility in production and hiring. The implication could be that the rate of hiring/layoffs may increase relative to the turnover practices it previously maintained. Depending on previous local turnover levels, relocation may actually increase overall job instability while providing a net increase in the total available jobs.

The same argument could be made concerning wages. Hourly wage rates may be similar, but greater instability in employment may reduce the total overall wage per worker and the total wage bill. This coupled with lower or nonexistent layoff benefits, for example, could lead to the paradoxical position where the local hourly wage rate increases but local yearly incomes per worker decrease. The advantage of relocation is not simply lower wage rates. Firms are as interested in more traditional local labor market structures that place much of the burden of the labor market instability upon the worker. Consequently, local right-to-work legislation and an antiunion philosophy are attractive because they reinforce the strength of the employer in the employment relation—authority, discipline, and control. At the same time, they enforce the dominance of external labor market conditions. Public policies that bear the costs of providing semi-skilled labor, training, and reinforcement of work habits similarly externalize the costs of the labor market for the firm.

Layoffs can be assumed to be a function of the uncertain demand for firms' output.[8] This assumption is prefaced upon the notion, introduced above, that the demand for labor is a derived demand. Of course, this is only plausible if money wages are "sticky" downwards. If wages could be decreased in line with decreases in output and product prices, then a firm's labor force would likely be retained. As Hall (1980) has shown, however, wages are quite stable over the business-cycle—especially when compared with fluctuations in output. Thus, layoffs are the firm's only alternative if it decides not to hoard its labor in the short run. In theory at least, one might expect firms to lay off either their most costly workers or their least productive workers. Practically, however, differences in contracts between higher-paid management types of workers and assembly-line workers will likely mean that the latter group will experience more layoffs (Hall 1980). According to Hicks (1932), those more likely to be laid off are also those who can be more easily replaced in the short run.

Pissarides (1976, ch. 3) distinguished between recruitment policies that operate under fix-wage and flex-wage conditions. In a fix-wage world the firm can control the supply of its labor by varying its requirement standard. The trade-off, however, is between hiring a less efficient worker sooner and a more efficient one later. This, of course, depends upon how quickly the firm requires added labor, and upon the existing supply of (searching) labor given a set of general skill requirements and efficiency standards. Under these conditions, the firm is certain of the wage but not of worker productivity. In a flex-wage world, the firm controls its supply of labor by varying the wage rate. The trade-off in this case is between a higher wage that may be needed to attract labor quickly and foregone production because of the unwillingness of workers to accept a low wage. Under these conditions, however, the firm sets a particular recruitment standard, but it is uncertain of the wage that it will have to offer. Both of these policies have implications for the time path of recruitment. If a vacancy goes unfilled, then in the flex-wage situation a firm has to increase the wage rate offered for that particular job. On the other hand, if it is flooded with applications, the firm could afford to lower its subsequent wage offers. Note that it is this process of sequential wage offers that establishes the appropriate wage offer: a process located in time and space that is bound by the external local labor market environment (including other firms). In the fix-wage situation, if a vacancy goes unfilled, the firm will have to lower its recruitment standard. Firms have a choice over adopting a fix-wage or a flex-wage policy. The possibility of choice leads to variable wage offers and recruitment standards and is a source of monopoly power for firms over labor (Clark 1981c).

The supply of labor in the local labor market has been described as the process of job searching. Demand for labor, on the other hand, was described as a process in which firms offer explicit or implicit contracts. Coordination of such trading arrangements depends upon the extent of worker mobility between firms and on the existence of wage variability. It was noted that inter-firm mobility of workers is restricted on the supply side by search costs (Keeley 1977), including the problems of risks, information on and the spatial configuration of the local labor market, and the uniqueness of job skills. On the demand side, inter-firm labor mobility is restricted by a whole host of items including separation, recruitment, and retaining costs.

Imperfect worker mobility between firms ensures the existence of variable wages for a given job in the local labor market without all workers instantaneously seeking jobs with the best-paying firms, and without lower-paying firms losing their labor force overnight. Moreover, inter-firm labor mobility is also limited by a wide distribution of worker reservation wages: a product of worker risk characteristics as well as the environment in which workers have to respond. Wage variability exists and will persist because of the ability of firms to choose recruitment policies as in the choice between fixed- and flex-wages. Wages will also vary because of technological differences between firms. The optimal technology may not be unique with varying labor requirements in terms of skill. Finally, because wage offering is a sequential process and that firms may have imperfect and particular information of local and alternative labor market conditions (the supply of searching workers and their reservation wages), there will be a distribution of wage offers in the labor market system.

Variations in wage levels will also cause variations in the reservation wages of workers by changing the value of search and risk behavior. This further limits inter-firm labor mobility. Hence, in the short run recurrent exchange relations will persist between local labor markets, and as a consequence they will not be at equilibrium (Pissarides 1976). Market interaction is then bound by the search behavior of workers and the hiring practices of firms. Both aspects imply wage distributions. In the case of workers the wage distribution is determined by their estimates of their appropriate reservation wages. Firms' wage distributions are determined by what they believe to be the minimal necessary wage offers. It is the intersection of these wage distributions that is market interaction.

WHY POOR PEOPLE DO NOT MOVE

To give the previous theoretical analysis greater specificity, this section considers an hypothetical example of two towns located close together, Poortown and Richtown. This example remains theoretical because of the principles I wish to illustrate concerning the rigidities of labor migration. But in doing so I hope to demonstrate that the reasons for low mobility in the face of depressed local economic conditions are entirely rational. Consequently, the presumption of veracity extended to the conservative urban policy agenda, given its underlying logic, if not its practical usefulness, will be directly challenged.

Poortown was once a healthy manufacturing town, selling many of its products to a thriving textile industry; however, it is now a morgue of idle lathes. Richtown, on the other hand, is located near a new interstate highway in a peripheral area of the region, and the town has been able to capture a large portion of the growing electronics industry of the region. Richtown's success is now hailed as the model of economic recovery for many northeastern cities from their declining nineteenth-century manufacturing industries. The loss of jobs from the center city and increasing spatial employment specialization in the metropolitan area have affected the two cities in very different ways. Poortown's unemployment rate is high, but has not been particularly concentrated in its black population because Poortown has been predominately white (more than 85%) over the past century.

There is increasing immigration of Hispanics into Poortown. Its residents have been filling fewer and fewer jobs in the adjacent center city. Through the growth of the service sector, jobs have been provided, but mainly to commuters who live in suburbs such as Richtown. Low per capita income in Poortown (the lowest in the state) is attributable in part to unemployment, but mainly to the concentration of its residents in low-paying jobs. Economic decline has also taken its toll; large plots of land lie vacant awaiting re-use and low-income residents live with a legacy of high assessed house values and consequently high property taxes. Poortown can do little to lower tax rates as increasing demands for welfare and public services have exacerbated its fiscal plight. Richtown has none of these problems. As with its wealthy commuters, many of its residents are employed by the newer electronics firms. A high proportion of housewives there can easily find temporary and permanent jobs as production workers.

The contact network for jobs operates well in Richtown. Residents often hear about jobs from a friend "who knows someone who heard." Simply because of the number of jobs in Richtown, these clues are often frutiful. Further, because of the relatively high demand for labor, firms actively seek labor through advertising and their own networking.

Consequently, for Richtown residents the process of searching for jobs provides a very different experience than it does for Poortown residents. First of all, the expected value of search is higher in Richtown. This is due not only to higher wage levels but also because the distribution in wage offers is more extended on the high side. This maximum is higher because of Richtown's tight labor market and a trend toward lower recruitment standards; both conditions thus allow for greater upward mobility. Wide variability in wages encourages further job switching, especially as the "downside" risk can be protected somewhat by searching while on the job. Jobs in Richtown are also characterized by a lower layoff risk.

Because of the structural differences in jobs between the two towns, Richtown jobs often demand higher education and skill levels and the implicit contracts offered by employers promise better tenure. Besides, the economy is so much healthier (and protected from short run fluctuations by relatively inelastic product demand) that there is less need to lay off even production workers. Employers are concerned to hold onto their labor in the short run for fear of being unable to replace scarce labor supplies. This allows for even higher reservation wages for risk takers, and in general these conditions have prompted a high volume of voluntary job quitting as worker's reservation wages continue to increase and their searching is rewarded.

Searching for jobs in Poortown is naturally a much more difficult task. To begin with there are fewer jobs available. Many jobs pay a wage that is barely above welfare and the minimum wage levels deemed appropriate by the government. Consequently, the value of searching is lower. This means that there will be fewer workers searching. Because there are fewer job openings the worker must spend more time looking for a job—searching many fruitless leads. Thus, since the costs associated with searching are much higher than in Richtown, Poortown workers will only accept new offers if the new wage offer is significantly higher in proportion to their current wages compared with Richtown workers' reservation wages. Note, however, that the informational issue may be less important in determining the mean wage than the actual distribution of low-wage and high-wage jobs in an urban area. Here, it is assumed that Poortown jobs are lower wage jobs compared with the distribution of jobs in Richtown. Thus, in analytical terms, this simultaneously lowers the expected value of search in Poortown and the reservation wage. Further, because of the higher layoff risks associated with Poortown jobs, to change jobs without a significant increase in wages would be an irrational move. Thus Poortown workers are likely to be less mobile than Richtown workers despite their obvious relatively greater need for high-paying employment!

Employers in both towns are indifferent as to whether a job applicant lives in Richtown or Poortown, and they both pursue a variety of recruitment policies (fix-wage and flex-wage). Because jobs are scarce in Poortown, firms located there feel confident that they will be searched more often. The risk of lost production in holding out for a more efficient worker or a worker who will accept a lower wage is therefore lower than in Richtown. Consequently, there is lower variability in wage offers and there are more stable recruitment standards in Poortown. This then limits the expected value of search by lowering the maximum and mean wage offer in the city. Employers in Richtown however act to retain their workers, especially their most skilled workers. Because job networks are so good in the town, they have to offer competitive employment contracts with higher wages and/or lower layoff risks compared with even similar jobs in Poortown. And because of "fuzzy" skill level differentiation in the tight local labor market, this effect even spills over and benefits ordinary production workers who live and work in Richtown. Employers in Poortown also act to retain their workers who live there. They have an advantage, however, in that Poortown residents have fewer alternatives. Employers can confidently lay off workers when necessary, and still expect to rehire those workers or equivalent workers when necessary.

Cyclical fluctuations in aggregate demand also affect Richtown's employers differently than Poortown's employers. In slack times, they tend to maintain their employment levels by hoarding their labor because they cannot be sure that they will be able to rehire when demand increases. In the short run, Richtown employers cannot relocate production facilities to low-wage and low-labor-demand areas so as to reduce costs by temporary layoffs. Consequently, some firms have attempted to meet shortages of labor in boomtimes by inducing in-migration. Thus, the actual labor market area tends to expand and contract cyclically. Finally, employers in the two towns have different attitudes to employment histories. In Poortown, being laid off is a fact of life, a product of the employment policies of firms. Thus few employers, if any, ask for extended work histories upon job application. In Richtown a history of being laid off is frowned upon; it signals incompetence to the prospective employer.

From this hypothetical example, there are two implications for public policy, and especially for the conservative urban policy agenda. First, whatever the imperfections of local labor markets, a case can be made that discontinuities are structured, not accidental. That is, even if both firms and workers act rationally, there are imperatives of risk avoidance and utility maximization that sustain disequilibrium. Second, workers are clearly at a disadvantage when bilaterally negotiating with employers if the structure of opportunities are unfavorable. The process is cumulative and tends to inequality rather than equality. Thus, faith in the market as a means of creating just and efficient outcomes is misplaced and this may be true even if we begin with assumptions common to the competitive market model.

SUMMARY

Pissarides (1976) stated that the problem of economics is to "study the actions of individuals, . . . in relation to social rather than individual life." Instead of supposing a rational individual and then deriving a collective result—the traditional approach of economics—this chapter considered the converse case. I have taken an aggregate result and have speculated upon its implications for the rational behavior of individuals. Following research initiated by job search and implicit contract theorists, a model of labor market mobility was constructed and justified. Speculations, consistent with both the model and the context, were then made about the implications for individual behavior. It can be shown, albeit theoretically, that interlocal labor market adjustment and systemwide equilibrium is unlikely because of the rational behavior of individuals responding to particular environments.

My results (theoretically based, of course) were then inconsistent with more orthodox neoclassical models of jobs search behavior. Instead of implicating misinformed and irrational job seekers as the cause of aggregate disequilibrium (and even the slope and position of the Phillips curve), I argued that the economic environment in which individuals act must bear much of the responsibility for non-equilibrium solutions. Furthermore, rather than concluding that low mobility propensities and inequality are the result of poor individual motivations or some "suboptimal" social attachment to a particular community, my model suggests that *place* characteristics are very important in determining the behavioral responses of individuals. The local environment in which job searching occurs for many people is as important as the job seeking skills of workers themselves, in terms of identifying the appropriate policy variables.

It seems that, in the short run at least, space (masquerading as a whole series of variables including economic history, cost of distance, information networks, etc.) has a number of effects that severely limit inter-local labor market adjustment. Given that the long run is derived from just a series of short short runs (Kalecki 1971), there is cause for concern. The unemployed isolated in areas throughout the country are not going to move because there are no advantages for them to do so. In this context, the conservative urban policy agenda is completely inadequate. Policies may have to be developed to give the residents of Poortowns the chance to fully search out opportunities in other local labor markets.[9] Direct subsidies that shift the slope of the reservation wage curve and remove the significance of the reservation wage threshold are obviously vital. Moreover, better informational networks that would minimize risks may also be important. It should also be recognized, however, that before these types of policies are tried, a more general approach may need to be undertaken: one oriented toward changing the local economic environment rather than supposed individual irrational behavior. This may mean increasing the total supply of jobs in poor communities.

The types of policies most appropriate here are then those that are both *locationally* and *individually* targeted. A good example of the types of policies appropriate in this context, could be found in the Comprehensive Employment and Training Act (CETA), although it has become a prime target of budget and program cutting under the Reagan Administration.[10] Its basic goal is to improve employment opportunities for identified segments of the "economically disadvantaged," through a variety of training, public service employment and placement programs. Unlike EDA, it does not have the mandate to increase labor demand by inducing new private sector job creation. In this regard CETA assumes a passive posture, depending on matching its clients to job opportunities generated independently by the private sector. Thus retraining and job opportunity identification are key avenues for CETA, in an overall program cluster that is aimed at improving the quantity and quality of labor supply and at facilitating the labor placement (exchange) process in the labor market (Clark and Gertler 1983b).

A major characteristic of CETA is its decentralized administrative structure and its reliance upon specific geographically-defined labor markets. All services are planned and delivered at the state and local level by "prime sponsors" (usually political jurisdictions or combinations thereof possessing populations in excess of 100,000). CETA's clients reside within the administrative jurisdiction of the prime sponsor, although they were eligible (through counseling, placement, and training) for jobs identified by their CETA office within the entire metropolitan labor market. Assistance to local labor markets is targeted according to two general criteria: first, funds were apportioned to local areas on the basis of their aggregate economic conditions, measured by indicators such as the level of unemployment, the proportion of population below the poverty line, and the proportion of the population belonging to a defined minority group. Having apportioned funds to areas, the second criterion focused on those "significant segments" of the area's population most in need.

For example, Title II-B provides a broad range of services to particular segments of the economically disadvantaged, including minorities, the unemployed, veterans, displaced homemakers, youth and welfare recipients. These services include classroom instruction, on-the-job training (OJT), counseling and other support functions. Title II-C includes provisions for skills upgrading for those currently employed who were skilled or semi-skilled and lacking in the normal opportunities for advancement. CETA also provides retraining to laid-off workers who were deemed to possess little chance to be re-employed. Title II-D provided, before it was eliminated, transitional public service employment (PSE) for the economically disadvantaged, a program intended to combat cyclical unemployment.

NOTES

1. This paper is based upon Clark and Whiteman (1983) which was published in *Environment and Planning A*. Pion Ltd. kindly gave permission for reproducing some sections of that paper. Dr. Chris Pissarides of the London School of Economics provided comments on a previous draft.

2. Despite the heavy investment in local labor market planning by the federal government over the past decade, there has been surprisingly little academic interest shown in the structure of local labor markets (*see* Oi 1976; and Rees and Shultz 1970 as exceptions).

3. There are some noteworthy exceptions, like the "van system" of Boston's Chinatown. That system, which is privately organized, dispenses restaurant workers throughout the whole metropolitan area, far beyond what one would otherwise expect given the skills of those involved. A distinction can also be drawn between labor market matching in the short- and medium-run. In the short-run, residence of labor is presumed to be constant. The matching efficiency of the spatial labor market in this instance will depend, in part, on the patterns of commuting of labor. On the other hand, the medium run (between 3 and 5 years) is presumably a time-span in which residential location adjusts to workplace location.

4. The actual geographical scale of labor markets is an important policy issue, not only a functional question. For example, SMSAs have been used by the courts as the bases for evaluating affirmative action and employment discrimination under Title VII of the Civil Rights Act of 1964. A key issue in litigation has been determining labor availability in a spatial context. For example in *EEOC v. Dupont Co.*, 16 FEP 847 (D. Del. 1978), the U.S. District Court noted that commuting patterns have been good and reliable indicators of available labor. Of course, for some occupations the appropriate labor market scale may be national (e.g., computer engineers) and thus some courts have related the spatial scale of analysis (SMSAs) to particular occupations; see, for example, *EEOC v. Radiator Specialty Co.*, 21 FEP 351 (4th Cir. 1979).

5. The radius of the spatial market is likely to vary from individual to individual, according to their occupation, socioeconomic status, and the surrounding "density" of potential employment opportunities for which the individual is eligible. To the extent that the same characteristic can be associated with groups of individuals, a commonality of spatial labor markets can be said to exist.

6. Here I assume a continuum of jobs from unskilled to skilled, essentially a queue. More formally, the conception of a job queue implies a single ladder on which all workers in a given area are ordinally and hierarchically ranked, according to their individual productivity. Three implications arise from viewing the local labor market in these terms. First, a worker can only move up the employment queue by receiving training and education. Second, employment vacancies which occur in the queue are likely to be filled in the short-run by those positioned on the rungs directly above or below the vacancy. Third, given the first two conditions, any member of the local labor force in the long run may, through self-improvement, legitimately compete for *any* job in the market. Notice as well, however, that in the complete absence of skills, individuals will not even make it onto the bottom rung of the ladder.

7. Brechling (1977) has also suggested that there may be institutional reasons for a firm to hoard its labor. Firms are required by law in virtually all states of the United States to pay a portion of the unemployment insurance payments to workers they fire. Consequently, there are strong inducements for the firm to maintain its work force despite short-term variations in local labor market conditions. Thus, the impact of local labor market conditions on firm layoff behavior may be quite variable. As in the case of quits, the decision mechanism taken by firms implies a temporal distribution of cause and effect. Trends in economic activity are important decision criteria in themselves as in fact are the contract and employment practices of individual firms.

8. According to Parsons (1977), the existence of layoffs represents a puzzle in and of itself. In a flex-wage labor market there would be no layoffs since firms could continuously revise, upwards and downwards, wage offers in response to labor and commodity demand and supply conditions. Job separations in such a labor market system would all be voluntary quits. Realistically, however, wage offers tend to increase, not decrease (Keynes' 1936, "sticky wage" phenomena).

9. I do not wish to suggest that workers necessarily move to be nearer to their workplace, although this is quite possible. Rather, with greater affluence they are likely to change neighborhood or residence. Empirical evidence with respect to retraining and search assistance and their impact on residential mobility is still however scant and as yet anecdotal. It is worth pointing out here that "distant placement" and ensuring residential mobility are unlikely fates for the more seriously disadvantaged segments of society, who are unlikely to be placed in a primary/suburban job due to the barriers enumerated earlier. Any "placements" they do attain are more likely to be in low-wage, high-turnover positions in central cities—enough perhaps to be counted as a "success" as far as some agencies are concerned but promising few real prospects for the client.

10. The Reagan administration has planned significant reductions in employment and training budget allocations over the next few years. Public service employment programs were cut entirely from the 1981 budget, with planned reductions in outlays of the order of $3.6 billion in 1982. Consolidation of various CETA titles and the expiration of a number of other programs (youth employment and training) have also led to further planned reductions in outlays. The net effect is to drastically cut CETA funding in real terms from the levels reached in the Carter administration (Office of Management and Budget 1981)

SIX

Community Development and Mobility

INTRODUCTION

Previous chapters of this book demonstrated that the conservative urban policy agenda is fundamentally compromised in terms of its *internal* and *external* logic. The internal coherence of both the 1982 *President's National Urban Policy Report* and the panel report *Urban America in the Eighties* collapses once we destroy their arguments and conceptual frameworks. Both emphasized the primacy of national economic growth and allocative efficiency, but failed to substantiate a viable and unambiguous interpretation of these concepts. As I noted in Chapter 2, the internal coherence of their conception of the national urban problem collapses under the weight of their inability to fashion a logical argument. Even if we take seriously the conservative propositions regarding the processes of regional economic growth and decline, empirical evidence directly contradicts their assumptions. For example, in Chapters 3 and 4, interregional migration was shown to be quite volatile, spatially and temporally, evidence which directly contradicts the conservative agenda's assertions that such patterns are dominated by long-run trends which cannot be manipulated by government policy. Similarly, their frequently asserted claims for the spatial allocative efficiency of interregional labor migration cannot be justified once direct empirical evidence is introduced. Again, the internal coherence of the conservative position is extremely questionable, especially on empirical grounds.

It is not surprising that the conservative agenda also failed to sustain its efficacy when more difficult tests of analytical coherence were introduced. For example, in Chapter 4 it was shown that the conservative agenda is unable to deal with the "hard cases"—the patterns and processes of rapid regional growth and decline. Its lack of internal comprehensiveness was contrasted with the power of an alternative and competing conceptualization of migration and regional capital growth. Using the same data, a radically different interpretation of rapid regional growth and decline was developed which had greater flexibility and interpretive strength in dealing with these "hard cases." This *external* test of the conservative position was probably fairer to its underlying logic than to the competing conceptualization, because the "facts" employed in this analysis were based upon the former paradigm. External analysis of the coherence of the conservative agenda extended into Chapter 5 with a more theoretical evaluation of why people do not migrate even though the local economic conditions may be quite disastrous. It was demonstrated that reasons for the immobility of labor can be entirely logical and rational. Thus, even the underlying conception of the utility optimizing individual migration decision, so central to the conservative model, can be shown to create markedly different results than those assumed by conservative theorists—disequilibrium and inequality rather than equilibrium and spatial economic justice.

Failure of the conservative agenda to sustain a viable and coherent case for their urban policy prescriptions re-opens for debate the larger question of the proper national urban policy. What the role of public policy should be is obviously a normative question and, as noted before, a question that cannot be resolved by simply appealing to "facts." And, because the problems of regional growth and decline are so often related to specific contexts, the design of policy must be related *both* to broad policy objectives and the reality of specific instances. In this penultimate chapter, and the next one, I set out a framework for national urban policy that attempts to relate to both dimensions of policy design. Because of the specific concern of this monograph with questions of interregional migration and regional growth and decline, the focus of these two chapters is on questions of regional welfare and social justice. To give a particular context to this discussion, I deal specifically with the crisis of midwestern auto manufacturing cities, notably Flint, Michigan.

ECONOMIC CRISIS AND DISLOCATION

Flint, Michigan, is undergoing a profound economic crisis. Unemployment is endemic to the city and surrounding county, and is reaching the proportions not seen since the 1930s depression.[1] Over 15,000 General Motors (GM) employees have been laid off, nearly 25% of the local GM workforce. The massive slowdown in auto production has drastically affected the many smaller supply firms,

causing innumerable business failures and lay-offs. Adult unemployment for the city is at least 25% and youth unemployment is well
over 60%. Not only is the auto industry faltering, but construction
and retailing are also experiencing tremendous pressures to rationalize,
consolidate, and shrink. One estimate has placed unemployment in
the local construction industry at about 80%, spread evenly among
job categories such as unskilled laborers, journeymen, and skilled
craftsmen. One has only to walk through the downtown shopping
center to see the ravages that this local economic depression has
wrought on the commercial sector of the city. Even the newer shopping
malls have vacant stores, unused parking lots, and failing businesses.
This economic crisis has been gathering momentum over the past
five years, threatening the long-run viability of the whole regional
economy.

Unemployment has meant for many people the collapse of their
dreams of a secure economic future. Defaults on home mortgages,
auto loans, even month-to-month expenses, such as telephones, are
at record levels. Independent young workers have been forced to
move back in with parents, while the resulting pressures of looking
for employment, maintaining a reasonable standard of living, and
coping with extraordinary changes in social status have drastically
increased voluntary and involuntary hospital admissions.[2] A way of
life, a standard of living, and a community are being fundamentally
threatened.

As the economic crisis has developed over time, laid-off workers
have exhausted their unemployment insurance benefits plus their
associated GM lay-off benefits. Some younger GM workers stand to
lose, if they have not already, their eligibility for recall in the unlikely
event of rehiring. Some workers have been unemployed longer than
their original length of employment with GM. The prospect of large
numbers of workers going on welfare has prompted many older
residents to draw parallels with their experiences of the 1930s Great
Depression. In essence, Flint is in the grips of a new economic
depression.

The effects of unemployment and economic dislocation have,
however, been spread quite unevenly. Because of the seniority clauses
in the GM-UAW contract, younger, less experienced workers have
been laid off first. The lines of unemployed at the local Michigan
Employment Security Center (MESC) illustrate in graphic detail the
selectivity of layoffs. Younger men and women and, as often as not,
minority workers dominate the queues for unemployment insurance.
The advances made in the 1970s concerning equal opportunity and
affirmative action had a perverse side effect. Those younger minority
and less-skilled workers with proportionately fewer years of job tenure
have consequently borne much of the layoffs. For the local black
community these layoffs have drastically affected the prospects of
black businesses and the overall economic viability of a community

already the victim of years of discrimination and neglect. Not only have individuals been affected, but specific segments of the community have been more affected than others, as have been the public policies of advancement and integration that depend on a healthy and robust local economy.

A legacy of the 1930s was a folk law, a story of subsequent expansion and sustained economic growth during the 1940s, 1950s, and 1960s. Those who remember the 1930s in Flint recount the economic disaster and the events that led to the city's revival. Defense expenditures, rising real incomes, and a comparative advantage all contributed to an unparalleled boom in Flint in the 1960s. There is, however, cause for long-run pessimism that this recovery will not be repeated. The UAW predicts, and GM privately admits, that at least 10,000 of those GM workers already unemployed in Flint will likely not be rehired even if the national economy rebounds in the next few years. Since 1945, after each economic slowdown, less workers have been employed in GM plants in Flint than at the previous peak. Rationalization has gone on during economic recessions leading to net job losses over the past thirty-five years. Although this process has been gradual, the next phase of economic growth (when, or if, it comes) will leave behind it a massive problem of redundancy and permanent unemployment. In many analysts' views, the past will not be Flint's future. The economic crisis of today will not be nearly compensated for by any future success.

This pessimistic scenario for the future is not unique to Flint. Michigan, and the Midwest more generally, is dotted with cities facing very similar problems and prospects. Bay City, Pontiac, Lansing, and even Detroit are experiencing massive economic dislocation of similar magnitudes. The unifying factor in these cities, and other similar cities throughout the United States, is their dependence on the auto industry and heavy manufacturing in general. For cities such as Flint, they have had no other history than the development of the auto industry. Moreover, GM was born in Flint, and it built Flint by providing housing for its employees, and by recruiting employees to its Flint plants from the South of the United States and from Europe. The causes of local economic crisis are then embodied in the very fabric of the industry and community. Of course, part of the explanation for current record layoffs in the auto industry lies in the economic health of the nation as a whole. Extremely high interest rates over the past few years have drastically stifled consumer expenditures. Even rebate periods for buying new cars have met with successively smaller and smaller levels of consumer enthusiasm. Many durable and investment goods industries are suffering under the Fed's regime of tight money supply, restricted credit, and high interest rates.[3] When these factors are coupled with overall declining national real wages, it is little wonder that the economies of areas such as Flint are faltering.

The long-term nature of the crisis in the American automobile industry should also be recognized. The switch in consumer preferences from large to small cars during the mid-1970s found the industry unprepared and ill-equipped, technologically and in terms of actual products. Subsequent attempts to recapture part of the market have taken enormous amounts of capital investment and transformation of the technologies of production. At the same time, the market for autos has become more volatile, swamped with overseas competition, and, recently, very restricted in terms of quality of product and price, that was not even contemplated ten years ago. In response, manufacturers like GM have attempted to cut the costs of production by reducing the quantity and quality of labor input, and rationalizing their organization of production by phasing out older plants and building newer ones in areas of lower labor costs. Thus, not only are there fewer autos produced in Flint, but the actual methods of production are changing rapidly, leading to higher capital/labor ratios and ultimately fewer jobs.[4]

Low labor productivity and relatively higher labor costs have been significant impediments to meeting overseas competition. But it has also been contended that the problems of the American auto industry are due to management shortcomings. A recent example was the decision of GM to invest $120 million in the Flint Buick plant for a return of only a 1% increase in labor productivity. A local management consultant noted than an investment of $100,000 in the same plant for improved management skills resulted in a 7% increase in labor productivity. Lester Thurow, among others, has claimed that less than one-third of the cost differential between American cars and Japanese cars is due to labor costs. The rest, by implication, is a product of management style and organization. The problems of GM and its attempts at reorganizing, investing, and adaption are having massive impacts on the local economies of many cities throughout the United States. As capital intensification continues, automation and robotics take the place of workers.[5] Older plants are left behind for more modern and efficient plants. What we are witnessing, then, is the destruction of whole communities and, given labor's dependence on the location of capital, the geographical dislocation of workers and their industry.[6]

Attempts at restoring the economic vitality of the Flint-area economy have been, and are continuing to be, made. For example, a leading bank, a retail chain, the Mott Foundation, and the city of Flint are attempting to revitalize the downtown. A new Hyatt-Regency hotel has been built, the bank has built a new building (connected to the hotel), a university campus has opened nearby, and plans are going ahead for a $60 million tourist center to be called Auto-World. The aim of this activity, according to the Flint Area Conference Inc. (FACI), is to make the downtown a tourist attraction for the whole Michigan population. It is projected that Auto-World will employ some 400 people, mainly as concessionaires, food sellers and attendants. Retail stores, amusements, and educational facilities will be provided. It is being funded by a UDAG grant, industrial revenue bonds, tax abatements, and grants from Mott. Because of the UDAG component it will seek to employ minorities, youth, and (by implication) the unskilled. Yet by itself, this project is hardly likely to make inroads into the numbers unemployed or lead to a revitalization beyond those retail stores directly involved.

Another project being considered by the Mott Foundation is a small business, hi-tech–oriented, venture capital assistance scheme. The goal is to finance innovative entrepreneurs on the assumptions that small businesses create the most jobs in any given year, small businesses are very innovative, and small businesses will provide a way of "growing" Michigan-based industry rather than "stealing" other localities employment and firms.[7] The focus on hi-tech firms in the University of Michigan–Ann Arbor region presumes that geographical trickle-down effects will help Flint area workers in the long run by providing relatively lower skilled employment. The likely match between the employment effects of these firms and the characteristics of the Flint (or, for that matter, the Detroit) workforce, remains quite problematic. Skilled male auto assembly workers may not be appropriate for hi-tech firms. More likely, those firms will employ either recent science graduates or unskilled women and minorities (Clark 1981c). Moreover, given the tremendous failure rate of small businesses in recent years it is difficult to imagine that these firms will provide, *on net,* more jobs in the immediate future. If one was to be cynical about this project, one could describe it as a reinvention of the American entrepreneur, not a concerted attempt to improve the employment chances of laid-off auto workers.

The city of Flint, like many others in the region, has attempted to deal both with the local unemployed and the generation of new jobs; however, their various programs have met with mixed success. Retraining schemes, run in conjunction with the local Private Industry Council (PIC), depend on jobs at the end of training for success. All the same, the enthusiasm for hi-tech training has not been met with the necessary jobs at the end of training. Retraining requires supporting the income of those undergoing training; at present, support for trainees has become difficult to secure as UI benefits become exhausted. Moreover, the restricted length of current training schemes may only create a semi-skilled worker who, in relation to other similarly trained workers throughout the U.S., may not attract hi-tech firms to the area. The city of Flint also offers tax abatements, industrial revenue bonds, and other inducements to outside firms to relocate in Flint. But again, this policy has not met with a great deal of success and is, in any event, simply a "beggar-thy-neighbor" type of policy. There are some moves to use the Community Development Corporation model to create *new* firms and to encourage self-sufficiency. These programs are, however, small given the dimensions of current and forecast unemployment problems.

The dimensions of unemployment and the paucity of current public and private responses, has been amply reflected in the attitudes and actions of the UAW local in Flint. Its crisis center counsels members and the community-at-large on ways of finding employment, dealing with unemployment, and maintaining rehiring eligibility. In addition, the UAW provides advice on moving out of Flint to other areas of the U.S. to search for jobs. This has included transfer within GM under Paragraph 95 of the UAW-GM collective agreement, use of MESC job-bank information on alternative jobs in the Southwest, and how to actually search/move for/to other jobs outside Michigan. For the UAW such advice is a difficult policy to justify in terms of their organization—a worker who goes elsewhere is a lost member for the union local. On the other hand, given their expressed concern for the welfare of their members, mobility may be the only way to give a worker a new life or chance at employment. Since many of the GM unemployed workers are young, this policy may be more reasonable than expecting older workers to move. However, as we have seen (Chapter 5) workers face large barriers to mobility.

These policy responses and projects are largely ad hoc, uncoordinated, fundamentally inadequate, and reflect a diverse set of agendas and motives. The commercial sector of Flint is loath to encourage out-migration, but at the same time cannot realistically provide more than a fraction of the jobs needed to sustain the unemployed. The Mott Foundation sees the solution in venture capital and small business which may have only a negligible effect on local employment. Although not stated as such, one might suspect the Mott Foundation of having no interest in the problems of unionized workers. The city of Flint has attempted all kinds of policies but is simply unable to cope with the magnitude of the problem. With increasing welfare problems and the costs of sustaining a growing welfare population, the city of Flint faces bankruptcy if the auto industry does not recover. And, finally, the UAW provides advice and counseling, but it is obviously ill-equipped to deal with these issues in the long run.

Given the dimensions of this problem, what should be the role of public policy? What levels of government should be involved? What types of policies might be implemented? The answers to these questions obviously will reflect our previous discussion concerning interregional migration in the U.S. as well as the notions of aggregate efficiency and social justice. I begin by an assumption that some kind of public policy is needed. The question is what kind.

THE ROLE OF PUBLIC POLICY: THE COASE OPTION

The use of UDAG grants for initiating the Auto-World project in Flint, job training through the local PIC organizations, and industrial revenue bonds for local economic development indicates that the federal government is involved in Flint, if not in a consistent way, at least as a primary source of "seed" money for projects. There are many other roles that the federal government plays. If, however, we are to understand the basic choices before the current Republican administration, and other administrations in the future, a more general way of classifying policy options is needed. Two broad models of public policy intervention will be considered here. The first will be referred to as the Coase Option, wherein government intervention is conceived to be at the very minimum and limited to facilitating market transactions (as in the competitive market model of the conservative agenda). The second model of public policy intervention will be referred to as the Rawls Option, wherein government intervention is thought necessary to ensure the individual and collective welfare or justice of society.

The *Coase Option* should be immediately recognized by the reader as a close relative of the Coase Theorem (Coase 1960). There are two elements of this theorem. The first is quite specific in that it deals with the determination of liabilities for externalities. The second is more general in that it deals with the economics of market transactions. Coase (1960) argued that in an economy characterized by no transaction costs (where the price mechanism is "super" efficient), rational decision making, and no legal impediments to bargaining, the market will efficiently allocate all resources to those who desire them the most. It is then tautological that the only transactions that will occur under these conditions will be those which are *Pareto superior.* This means that individuals will only trade if they are not made worse off, and preferably if they are better off; a product of the rational decision making assumption and an implied "free will" clause that would invalidate any transactions that would occur under conditions of duress. In aggregate, the sum of these transactions imply the wealth of society which is itself dependent upon the degree of specialization and exchange, and, broadly, the efficient use and allocation of resources.

Demonstrations of this theorem are usually based on an example. Thus, imagine that a steel mill and laundry are located near each other. The social, as opposed to the private, cost of producing steel in that location is the reduction in the value of the laundry's products. That is, I am assuming that the steel mill pollutes the water and the air that the laundry uses to clean fabrics thereby leading to higher costs in producing clean fabrics. Conventionally, these *social costs* of production are termed externalities. Coase goes on to demonstrate that in a world of no transaction costs, the steel mill will bribe the laundry to use the polluted water up until the point where the mill's costs of bribing the laundry will equal the costs of instituting a pollution abatement scheme. Of course, it may be that the laundry values clean water less than the mill's costs of investing in pollution controls—thus a bargain will be struck that benefits both parties. This example assumes that the laundry is entitled to clean water, but it also demonstrates that without transaction costs there will be an efficient allocation of resources despite an initial definition of entitlements (however conceived). Notice also that the Coase Theorem is not concerned with absolute costs, but rather with comparative or opportunity costs. While there may still be some pollution, the bargain struck between the two parties will ensure a relatively efficient allocation of resources.

If there are no liabilities involved, if the steel mill is not liable for pollution, the theorem implies that the laundry would bribe the mill to produce less pollution. This is a crucial point because Coase uses it to demonstrate that confounding the *cause* of an externality with liability can lead to faulty law and economics. In terms of the *aggregate* allocation of resources it makes no difference who subsidizes whom in mitigating the pollution problem as long as the *joint* costs are minimized. Coase also attempted to show, that in terms of the aggregate allocation of resources, in a world of no transaction costs and no liabilities, the comparative costs of this arrangement would be less than if liabilities were assigned to the steel mill. The implications for the design of public policy of this theorem are twofold. First, the government should not intervene to assign liabilities (or, at the very least, be very careful) because inefficiently assigned liabilities would create a misallocation of resources. Second, to the extent that there are transactions costs and bargaining under duress, the government should ensure that these perversities are minimized. It was Calabresi (1968) who noted the second conclusion which compromises Coase's underlying argument that governments should not interfere in the market, and that even if it does, it will inevitably cause more harm than good.

It is this last two-part argument of Coase's which dominated the conservative agenda as represented by the *UA in the 80s* Panel report and the 1982 *President's NUPR*. Although unstated as such, it is obvious that both reports used this theorem to argue that government intervention in the spatial economy *inevitably* creates less efficient allocations of resources. Accordingly, the social costs of production are higher, and aggregate welfare (or wealth, in Posner's 1981 terms) lower. Notice also that our earlier argument that the *distributional* issues of such non-policies are ignored by the reports has been vindicated. The question of distribution for Coase is irrelevant in the sense that he was only concerned with minimizing the social costs of production—he neither recognized nor allowed for the fact that the underlying distribution can have a determinant effect on the actual allocation of resources and the efficiency of production itself (Kelman 1979). Moreover, others have noted that for Coase, distributional issues are outside the proper realm of economic theory— such issues, according to this logic, are political and should be set aside for others (Stigler 1972).

Plant closing legislation has been vociferously criticized by many conservatives, including the *UA in the 80s* panel. They argued that by attaching liabilities to firms who wish to relocate, aggregate welfare is ultimately compromised. The opportunity costs of such policies were suggested to be higher than the costs of relocation and dislocation. Again, the methodology is comparative in that one allocation of resources is compared to another although, as noted earlier, there was no evidence presented to support this supposition as true. Similarly, the report criticized public policy that intervened in the market to reorder the spatial map of economic opportunity costs. For example, the use of industrial revenue bonds, local tax abatements, and the like were considered to be inefficient in the sense that the social costs of production are increased relative to market conditions (assuming rational, transaction costless bargains). And, there may be some truth in the assertion that these instruments do not increase the *aggregate* wealth, rather simply redistribute income (from tax-payers to firms). Therefore, the assertion that tax abatements increase the social costs of production by spatially misallocating resources is questionable.

The *Coase Option* as a public policy model is then subject to many of the criticisms raised earlier, of the Posner-type of maximum national wealth model. Exactly what is implied in efficiency-oriented social goals remains very much in doubt. If we take the Coase position literally, minimum social costs of production is a value in its own right. And yet, as we noted earlier, this position is hardly adequate. We still require rules of discrimination between aggregate allocations of resources that equally minimize the social costs of production. These rules would inevitably acquire a higher order of importance, and they would also require an underlying theory of social justice. Otherwise, we must explore the Coase theorem for the implied values that the minimum social cost option serves or achieves. There is no evidence that interregional migration necessarily increases local welfare or that the market allocates resources efficiently. In fact, the evidence noted in Chapter 3 suggested that migrants do not always go to the "correct" destinations. While we may be very critical of this policy model in terms of its substantive values and assumptions we should also recognize a more subtle version of the Coase formulation: a blue-print for market efficiency.

Coase has been quite impatient with attempts to analyze his theorem in terms of its *ideal-world* implications. That is, he rightly noted that the more interesting questions relate to the real world of transaction costs, bargaining under duress and, more generally, uncertainty. It is the existence of these attributes that has led Williamson (1979), among others, to investigate the economics of transaction costs. Furthermore, it was in this context that Calabresi (1968) argued that the Coase theorem implies an important role for public policy in facilitating the functioning of the market—in brief, minimizing transaction costs. Both conservative urban reports failed to adequately recognize this subsidiary role for public policy even though the existence of transaction costs fundamentally compromises the possibility of achieving their market solutions to urban problems. Maximum wealth is only possible through transactions, according to Posner (1981), and so any policy that facilitates transactions by reducing the costs associated with market trading would increase the possibilities (if not the realities) of greater aggregate welfare.

There are three kinds of transaction costs:[8] those that are a function of the means of exchange (Type I); those that are a function of the organization of production (Type II); and those that are a function of uncertainty (Type III). Type I transaction costs result from the existence of inefficiencies in exchange. For example, transportation between buyers and sellers might neither be cheap nor quick. Innovations such as electronic mail could speed transactions (although it may not actually cheapen them) compared to normal surface mail. In addition, the dispersion of production may also figure in the costs of transactions even though trade may be costless. An appropriate policy in this regard may be to centralize production, spatially and sectorally. Note that minimizing transaction costs in this instance, could be equivalent to sustaining urban agglomeration economies. Coase was primarily concerned with Type III transaction costs, those that are a function of uncertainty. Within this type we can identify three interrelated costs of transaction. First, there are costs that result from discovering who it is that one wishes to exchange with and then informing them of the terms (search and information costs; *see* Bebchuk 1982). Second, there are costs inherent in conducting negotiations and initiating contracts (bargaining and decision costs). And, third, there are costs in ensuring compliance (policing and enforcement costs). Generally, these costs occur whatever the methods of exchange and organization of production.

Public policy according to this view should then be primarily concerned with the procedural efficiency of transactions, not with particular outcomes. To the extent that public policy can improve transactional efficiency, then the social costs of production would presumably decline. There is, however, no absolute measure of a *good* level of social costs. Lower social costs of production are measured by comparison with previous social costs—the measure is empirical, and neither ethical nor moral. Similarly, a policy of reducing transaction costs is judged according to its relative performance vis-à-vis other policies of reducing transaction costs. If this means that there are two policies that equally reduce transaction costs, then there can be no way to discriminate between their desirability. For example, we could imagine that transaction costs are equally minimized, either through absolute centralization (agglomeration) or absolute decentralization (self-sufficiency). Which then would be the desired *map* of economic activity is problematic. And, because social and transaction costs are measured empirically, there is no implied view of a *good* spatial distribution of economic activity; moral values are eschewed in favor of prices that inevitably take as given the existing social-political character of the economy.

Consequently, the overriding substantive values that are inherent in the *Coase Option* must be those that reflect the market itself—that is, freedom of contract, freedom of choice, and freedom of exchange. Duress or unconscionability would threaten the very fabric of the market and implies that writers such as Coase and the authors of the conservative urban agenda view society simply as a market. Assuming rationality, the implied policy of the *Coase Option* would then be to facilitate mobility (to enable people to live where they choose) by reducing transaction costs. This option is incredibly optimistic and naive concerning contemporary society. We must assume that transactions are mutually beneficial (not a zero-sum game), that duress does not exist (either ownership of the means of production is evenly distributed or that owners and workers need one another to the same extent), that choice exists (not coercion of limited means and limited abilities), and that the economy itself is self-regulating. I would suggest that these assumptions stretch reality far beyond what is credible.

THE ROLE OF PUBLIC POLICY: THE RAWLS OPTION

The alternative public policy model is what I have termed as the *Rawls Option*. To paraphrase Hobbes's *Leviathan,* without the direct intervention of the government "life would be nasty, brutish, and short" (Cooter 1982).[9] A more circumspect way of putting this claim is that "justice is the first virtue of social institutions" (Rawls 1971, p. 3). The legitimacy of governments and their functions must then satisfy the aspirations of its citizens for justice (however defined). This model is in obvious opposition to the model that dominates public finance, and that is inherent in the work of Coase. Public finance economists argue that the state should only intervene in certain technical situations. That is, where the market fails—whether by virtue of nonpriced (negative) externalities—or where collective social goods are required but which do not have a private market. Coase would argue of course that the externality issue is a function of transaction costs, and that collective social goods can in fact be provided by the market *if allowed to do so!* (*see* his discussion of the provision of lighthouses: Coase 1974).[10] At the same time, it should also be acknowledged that Coase and others do not deny the importance of justice, rather they prefer to dismiss this issue as being outside the science of economics (Stigler 1972).

The role of the state, in Rawls's view, is as a positive agent of social change, a role we recognized in Chapter 2 as being at the center of more liberal national policy since the New Deal era. As will become clear it is a model that I certainly prefer when compared to the *Coase Option*. However, it would be inaccurate to simply note this model as my preference; the achievement of social justice is actually the *only* true rationale for the state.

To some extent, I agree with Coase (1974) in assuming that the existence of externalities is not a necessary condition for state intervention. To demonstrate the veracity of this proposition, I will consider an analogy dealing with state autonomy and its bases for legitimacy-claims. Based upon Clark and Dear (1984), it runs as follows: If the state is in fact autonomous, if it can create its own legitimacy through clientism and control of the interpretive organs of society, and if it has its own agendas of reproduction and power, how is it different from organized crime?

Functionalist descriptions of the state often dwell on collectivist roles that presumably cannot be undertaken by society at large. In these terms, the state is often described as the provider of public goods and services. The rationale goes as follows. First, it is noted that the market system may not be efficient. The costs of pollution, to quote the favorite example, are not adequately priced so that true costs are accounted for in the costs of production. The market system may not be able to solve problems of underconsumption, economic crisis, or reproduction. The state's function in these terms is to act as the market regulator. Second, it is also noted in the public finance literature that the market may be far too cruel in distributing rewards. That is, the market may reinforce inequality, create poverty and disproportionate wealth when compared with social standards of equity and justice. The function of the state in this model is to redistribute wealth in accordance with social goals. Both functions, derived from the public finance literature, assume the state exists only as a social instrument.

Another functionalist model, this time derived from the political science literature, emphasizes the role of the state as the guarantor of the rules of the game, the procedures that enable social intercourse and individual freedom. People have to be protected from one another; they must be assured that their commitments are undertaken freely and without duress, and can be depended upon in the future. The classic restatement of this model is by Nozick (1974), who emphasized American values of natural order coupled with the theory of a minimalist state. Yet another functionalist model can be derived from the sociological literature on conflict and antagonist interests. Here, the state acts as an umpire or arbiter of conflict in this type of model. A more general functionalist description would, of course, include all these functions plus many others. But when this functionalist model of the state is coupled with realist notions of relative state autonomy and hidden agendas of power and continuity, the state may become a quite ominous institution. Despite nominal democratic control, it becomes difficult to separate the actions of the state from those of any other organization that purposely seeks to maintain its power and at the same time ensure external support through specific client groups.

In these terms, organized crime and the state have some similarities. For example, imagine the state ensures orderly trading in goods and services. Organized crime might do the same—perhaps for a more limited set of goods (drugs such as heroin), but nevertheless for a rationale not so different from that of the state. Orderly trading facilitates the generation of a social surplus, it benefits those who control the production of goods, and it *creates* support for organizations that guarantee trading standards. These organizations garner external support (perhaps even legitimacy) for their actions, appropriate revenue through taxing the social surplus, and are able to ensure their continuity with respect to power and relative autonomy. Just because the state provides and is sustained by these actions in a legally sanctioned market economy, the state is not any different in effect from organized crime that runs illegal markets. At this point, it could be protested that my characterization of the state ignores the democratic electoral system. Perhaps so; however, it is important to distinguish between the potential of democratic action from its reality. I think it is difficult to sustain an argument that democracy determines the *actions* of the national or local governments.

Extending this analogy further, it is also true that the state and organized crime have supporters outside their institutional membership. These groups are termed interest groups or client groups in the conventional political science literature. We can also imagine interest groups that support the actions of organized crime, for example, money lenders, prostitutes, and drug traffickers and addicts. What are the differences between these client groups? At first sight, it is obvious that they are *often* different people. But, let us assume that they are different people. On closer inspection, however, it should be obvious that they do have some things in common. They are often consumers of "public" goods, they often depend upon the "state" for their livelihood, and they have a vested interest in the continued existence of the "state" despite the threats and extortion that may be inherent in any similar relationship. The point is that in all these circumstances, legal or illegal, the relationships between clients and institutions are coercive, based upon power and autonomy. Nevertheless, they may entail returns for those involved.

There are many other state functions that could be thought to be equivalent with the functions of organized crime. Policing intergroup conflicts is an obvious function shared by both. Guaranteeing rights and contractual agreements is a similar function for the state and organized crime, even though in abstract some theories of rights are ahistorical, natural rather than social. Even capital infrastructure, such as roads, railways, and other physical social goods could be provided by organized crime *if* such functions contributed to its power and longevity. By analogy, the state is often argued to be dependent upon the economic system for the generation of wealth. To the extent that social capital goods facilitate maximum economic growth, the state can then sustain its own activities by "skimming off," through taxes, income and, at the same time, *creating* external support for its actions in the benefits that accrue to certain privileged groups (e.g., capitalists). And, more recently, we have seen the state become highly involved in creating its own wealth through its ownership of production facilities. Again, it should be emphasized that organized crime has very similar functions.

The point in exploring this analogy is not to suggest that the state is simply a bandit. Obviously, it can be interpreted as such in specific circumstances; however, more generally it should be noted that many different types of social institutions could provide its functions, whether coercive or non-coercive. Functionalist, even realist, descriptions of the state describe situations wherein an organization like the state, may be necessary. The state need not provide marketing boards; collective capitalist agencies could as easily function in the same manner. So, if it isn't the functions that distinguish the state from other social (legal or illegal) institutions, what are the specific characteristics that could provide a unique rationale for the state and distinguish if from other social institutions? The only plausible answer is one that does not deny the functions of the state, but also provides an *intent,* a reason for action that exists outside itself. The only answer that could possibly accommodate these requirements has to be normative and essentially altruistic. So as to distinguish the state from organized crime and *its* own agendas, the state *must* act through its many functions to provide for the welfare of its citizens, and not itself. And the one goal that would command legitimacy and support from society, in general and not just in client groups, is social justice.

For Rawls (1971), a well-ordered society is one which is "designed to advance the good of its members and [is] effectively regulated by a public conception of justice" (p. 14). Note that the exact definition of what is good is left open, as are the specific procedures by which the good is to be achieved. The abstractness of this model is evidenced in Rawls's (1971) attempts to conceive of rights that are neutral with respect to the definition of what is *good.* As in Dworkin's (1978) model of rights, however, Rawls is concerned to establish basic conditions and procedures for action. In essence, society is designed, not left anarchical, and it is given a fundamental moral goal, not left amoral. This well-ordered society is democratic in the sense that it is "effectively regulated by a public conception of justice," and its institutions are centered upon society for legitimacy. In consequence, the role of government is to be responsive to public conceptions of justice, and to implement those policies that would achieve goals of justice and fairness. Thus, government intervention is not simply a function of empirical rules of efficiency. Rather more specifically, governments intervene to bring about social transformation. Moral principles guide its actions.

The *Rawls Option* takes as its theoretical basis the Rawlsian vision of a well-ordered society. Moreover, it assumes the existence of a set of conditions or a reality that threatens the basic welfare of many of its citizens. In this respect, the *Rawls Option* is based on specific historical circumstances and inequalities. Contrasted with the *Coase Option,* it is obvious that it presumes the existence of exploitation, dependency, duress, and unconscionability. The conservative agenda takes issue with the *Rawls Option* in its attack on the possibility of government intervention. It is an extreme version of Coase, going far beyond a belief in government inefficiency to a *distrust* of government. Its case is extremely weak, morally and empirically. It presumes to invalidate democratic aspirations of justice and equity by asserting that "people should be left alone," and confounds the question of policy efficiency and design with intent and goals. That is, while it may be true that some policies are poorly designed, their intent, being based upon community visions of justice, cannot be faulted. To do so is to deny the democratic system itself.[11] Thus, we have to be very wary of blanket assertions of *good* or *bad* policy that imply different visions of real conditions and real social goals.

In the following sections, I reconsider public policies that encourage mobility (people-to-jobs) and community integrity (jobs-to-people) in terms of the *Coase* and *Rawls Options.* My goal is to separate out the basic objectives of each policy option and its basis in social values. By doing so, I hope to provide support of those who question the veracity and appropriateness of Coasian economic efficiency arguments. I want, as well, to reconsider the adequacy (not the intent) of many community economic development policies.

COMMUNITY INTEGRITY

Maintaining community integrity is a very strong policy goal when compared to policy alternatives that stress labor and capital mobility. It involves taking jobs to people, thereby building the economy in terms of the locational preferences of residents, not firms. Before the reader dismisses its importance out of hand, we would do well to recognize an implied strong social value that goes to the heart of this policy option—the right of individuals to choose where to live and, once a choice has been made, the requirement that governments support this choice by providing for residents' welfare wherever they live. This particular goal combines at least three statements of moral importance: (a) that individuals should have a *free* choice in where they live; (b) governments must respond to the preference of their citizens (Rawls's good-society rule); and, (c) governments must provide for the welfare of their citizens as embodied in societal conceptions of justice. These last two statements are clearly related to a Rawlsian vision of the proper role of public policy, where the first statement is clearly more generally accepted as a basic moral principle in the United States, whatever the form of government policy.

All three principles have some role in current public policies. Geographical mobility is enshrined in the Constitution and has been a major issue before the Supreme Court over many years (Clark 1981b). It is thought of as a *right,* and is of great consequence when deciding the constitutionality of entitlements that have a residency requirement. Similarly, job creation programs that have a quota for local residents are also highly irregular. All this is well known and hardly controversial.

It is also the case that governments provide for the welfare of citizens according to where they live. In terms of the economic problems of Flint, two programs can be interpreted as maintaining community integrity: unemployment insurance (UI), and welfare payments. The former is funded by employer contributions, state, and federal funds; the latter, by state and federal funds, subject to restrictions. Employees are entitled to UI if they are laid off and may continue for up to one year in Michigan. We might term this type of support as *no-fault* insurance in that public policy attempts to mitigate the worst effects of job loss that occurred through no fault of the employee. Given the level of benefits, and the eligibility of GM workers for GM benefits, this policy has sustained the residence preferences of Flint workers. In the past, this policy has benefited workers and GM alike in that the local work force was maintained in periods of recession, and was then available for rehire during boom periods. Although public policy in the past was closely "dovetailed" with GM labor requirements, this aspect is not the principal goal of UI, compared to maintaining workers at their choice of location. When we couple this policy with the stated objective of the Michigan Employment Security Center (MESC) to secure jobs for local residents in Flint, then the importance placed on this option by the community should be appreciated.

Given this UI policy, it is then just a small (conceptual) step to bring jobs for residents. Public service employment is one possible policy, as are training and education for local jobs that require specific and different skills. In these terms *community integrity* is the product of the choices of individuals. To the extent that individuals wish to remain in Flint, then the *Rawls Option* would suggest that the government should support their welfare. This can be accomplished through direct transfer payments, or through the provision of jobs assuming an inability of the private market to provide suitable and/ or enough local employment. A second major support mechanism is welfare. But, this is qualitatively different from UI in that it supports the income of those who do not work (for reasons of choice, incapacity, and so forth), and is quantitatively different in that the level of support is significantly less than UI. Implied in the funding and the structure of welfare is a *weaker* conception of the role of public policy. That is (to paraphrase what is only hinted at by policy makers), if people are unwilling to work or relocate to take employment elsewhere—for whatever reason—the government will support their welfare to the extent that *basic* needs are met, at a level commensurate with local and national standards.

It is then a fine line between coercion—reducing benefits so that people are forced to relocate or gain employment against their preferences—and "good" public policy. For individuals it is their subjective choice to accept reduced benefits or relocate, and yet if the benefits are too low—below *basic needs* (which can only be defined by a combination of objective and subjective assessments)— their right to free choice would be violated. This issue is further complicated by the question of which government level is responsible for welfare benefits and the actual level of benefits. Traditionally the federal government has intervened directly with certain classes of welfare recipients such as in the AFDC program. State and local governments have decided the levels of support for local residents. Although some basic standards exist, a number of states maintain very low welfare benefit levels and have, over time, been thought to force out their dependent populations. At this level, community integrity is a function of how much local taxpayers are willing to pay to support their fellow dependent citizens *and* what level of moral responsibility they feel towards their fellow citizens—their public conception of justice.

Flint is extraordinary on two counts. First, it is apparent to any visitor that there is a very strong sense of community identity that links all workers and citizens whether direct GM employees or not. Second, it is also apparent that many of the unemployed do not wish to relocate. Community integrity is an explicitly desired goal for many of its citizens. Thus, it should not come as a surprise that many government agencies are actively seeking ways to improve local employment opportunities. The Community Development Department of the city of Flint has been seeking outside employers, using tax rebates, Industrial Revenue Bonds, self-help programs and the like. The MESC provides a great deal of support for the unemployed—including UI, but also techniques for job searching, resume writing, and counselling. This agency does not list outside job opportunities unless asked by clients. Even the Mott Foundation has attempted to improve the employment climate. And, yet all these policies are not enough.

Whether or not the federal government should intervene to save Flint is actually a somewhat redundant question. In point of fact, policies such as UI maintain community integrity in the short run, and allow individuals to choose to live in an area despite hardships imposed by loss of employment. Since this policy is very much a product of underlying social values, of equity and justice with respect to facilitating individual free choices, the Coasian doctrine espoused by the conservative urban policy agenda is largely irrelevant. As Rawls (1971) and others have noted, justice is the primary principle for government policy. But in sustaining such policies, the federal government has to decide two questions: (a) what is the minimum level of welfare support that is commensurate with individual freedom of choice? and (b) to what extent can the federal government afford to bolster the integrity of the Flint economy beyond the minimal support level? As noted earlier, both questions are political. In the first instance, it depends upon a subjective evaluation of the conditions of choice. In the second instance, the degree of support is a function of the political agendas of the federal government. President Reagan has shown a marked dislike for community assistance, perhaps in the future a Democratic president might be more supportive. Otherwise, the destruction of Flint is inexorable.

In this context perhaps we should look again at policies of the previous Carter administration, especially those that sought to coordinate EDA and CETA programs. While EDA has measured its program impact in terms of the total new permanent jobs created, without regard for the number of disadvantaged local residents who receive these jobs, CETA has attempted to improve its clients' employability without regard for the number of jobs created in depressed communities. Differences in purposes and goals have led the programs to work at cross-purposes. For example, firms attracted by EDA into a community could fill their labor needs entirely with non-disadvantaged local residents and commuters from other areas of the wider labor market. Meanwhile, individuals trained through local CETA programs, denied opportunities in development projects, might remain unemployed or move to other local labor markets. With no coordination between EDA and CETA programs, both policies might succeed at the expense of local residents and perhaps even at the expense of each other's programs' goals.

Formal coordination between EDA programs and CETA was promoted by the Carter Administration through the Employment Initiatives Program (EIP), which was developed by the President's Interagency Coordinating Council for Urban Policy. Bringing together representatives of Department of Labor's Employment and Training Administration, the Department of Transportation, and the President's Reorganization Project, EIP required each participating agency to set aside a portion of jobs created through each project for CETA-eligible individuals. It also required coordination with local CETA prime sponsors to establish subsidized training programs (both classroom and on-the-job) to equip potential employees with appropriate job skills. EDA for example, set aside 10%–15% of the permanent jobs created by its business development program, and HUD similarly earmarked 10% of the permanent jobs generated through Urban Development Action Grants. These standards were set nationally. The set-aside provision of a particular project could have been higher or lower than these levels according to local labor market conditions.

As a similar policy mechanism for coordinating economic development and manpower programs, the Massachusetts cities of Boston and Cambridge have enacted "first source agreements" over the past two years as a vehicle for targeting jobs to local residents. These agreements, between the city and private companies receiving government economic development assistance within that city, were intended to ensure that local residents would comprise the "first source" of labor for the firm, and would have the first opportunity for jobs resulting from development expenditures. Such agreements typically require the firm to set aside a fixed proportion of its jobs for city residents, and other fixed proportions for local disadvantaged groups. For example, labor forces for assisted firms in Boston must include at least 50% Boston residents, 25% minorities and 10% women; Cambridge firms must hire at least 25% Cambridge residents and 15% Cambridge residents with twelve years of education or less (Clark and Gertler 1983b).

The EIP and first source agreements both require economic development and local labor market agencies to look beyond the raw numbers of new jobs created and place constraints on the characteristics of people who actually fill these jobs. Moreover, Boston has used its first source agreements as a means of implementing EIP requirements. Note, however, that whereas EIP sets hiring requirements according to the "employment disadvantage" characteristics of the individual (a set of attributes which determine CETA eligibility), the recent first source agreements have established local residency as the most important employee attribute. While EIP may bring changes in the job mixes offered by economic development projects, first source agreements may significantly affect the spatial distribution of employment opportunities within local labor markets. The efforts to link EDA and CETA through EIP of first source agreements only reached the experimental stages, and deserve greater appreciation, given an inherent legitimacy of the community integrity goal.

Generally, the conception of community integrity sketched above depends upon a moral or normative vision of the proper role of urban policy in the United States. In these terms, it directly contradicts the conservative agenda, both at the level of moral intent (the sustenance of individual choice vis-à-vis their locational preferences) and at the level of intervention in the economy (obviously an active, interventionist stance). I should emphasize that my prescription is normative and moral, and it is based nevertheless on strands of moral values important in America as a whole.[12] I should also emphasize that, at this level, the issue is *normative* not *positivistic*— empiricism cannot discriminate between alternative beliefs.

MOBILITY SOLUTIONS

Although no national mobility assistance program has actually been adopted in the United States, the idea of publicly assisting workers to relocate to jobs in other areas has received periodic attention. Over forty years ago, the Committee on Population Redistribution (the report was reissued in 1970) concluded in their examination of the occurrence of geographic migration from depressed areas to urban centers that:

> citywide migration has coincided with a steadily rising level of living, and our analysis has shown that we cannot hope to reduce even measurably the tremendous inequalities between regions, or to effect any appreciable improvement in the distribution of the national work force, unless we can count on migratory movements better sustained and no less rapid than those of the past. It should therefore be the concern of the Government to ease and facilitate the necessarily difficult processes of adjustment [p. 15].

Thus the development of experimental mobility assistance projects has had a long history. In the 1960s, consideration of a national mobility assistance program progressed from mere policy debate to the operation of experimental mobility assistance projects. Between 1965 and 1972 a total of 29 different small-scale experimental mobility projects were operated under the auspices of the Manpower Development and Training Act (MDTA), the forerunner to CETA (O'Neill 1973). The Jobs Search Relocation Assistance Project was an outgrowth of these small-scale experimental projects. This pilot project involved eight southern states (Region IV) and included forty local employment service offices. Although the experiences of the previous experimental projects were used to help develop JSRA, two significant departures from the program design of its predecessors were apparent. First, previous relocation assistance projects were often initiated in response to the problems of economically depressed areas such as Appalachia and to the problems of workers displaced by permanent plant shutdowns. Such policies targeted mobility assistance to depressed areas and to permanently laid-off workers, with generally good success. In contrast, JSRA was designed to deal with no specific labor market problem of local unemployment or underemployment and it is not targeted to specific areas or workers. John Herzog (1979), the program contractor for JSRA, described the purpose of JSRA as assisting all those workers who are "in the wrong place at the right time." Thus, the major goal was not interregional or class equity but inter-market allocative efficiency. In this regard, it resembles the Canadian regional labor mobility programs of assisted migration.

A second difference is to be found in the types of services provided by JSRA. It offered job search information, job search grants and relocation grants. Under previous mobility assistance projects a diversified mix of supportive services including social adjustment counseling and orientation accompanied by informational and financial assistance provided by JSRA. These supportive services were provided both before and after the relocation, and were found to be essential program components for successfully relocating disadvantaged workers. Furthermore, previous projects were sometimes linked to retraining programs offered under MDTA, and this formed an effective strategy for relocating workers. In contrast, JSRA was solely concerned with helping those able to move—that is, those already possessing skills which were marketable somewhere—and to speed their locational match with existing demand. Thus, the goal was to reduce geographically based frictional unemployment.

These divergences in the program design of JSRA from those of previous mobility programs denote a significant shift in the perceived role of relocation assistance programs. In short, it was an overriding concern for improving macroeconomic efficiency at the expense of the regional justice, objectives that motivated and guided the formulation of previous experimental projects. This bias in favor of macroeconomic efficiency, and the special emphasis given to improving the equilibrating movements of labor, suggest a theoretical lineage stemming from the neoclassical competitive market model and *Coase Option* noted above.

The Department of Labor's Job Search Relocation Assistance project is evidence of how labor mobility policies might be designed. The firm that ran the experiment closely followed the Canadian policy which is administered by Immigration and Employment Canada (IEC).[13] Briefly, Canadian mobility policy has the following characteristics. Unemployed workers must register at the local office of the IEC (termed, in this chapter, Canada Manpower Centers, CMCs) to collect unemployment insurance. As a condition for UI, the unemployed must look for work in the local labor market. Available to counselors and registrants are job-bank lists of job vacancies in the local areas, as well as outside the local labor market. Clients can ask to see these outside lists, which are also available on computer for the national CMC system—over 500 offices across Canada. And if they find a relevant job which matches their skills and experience, they are eligible for grants for interviews and relocation expenses if they are subsequently hired. For a number of the Maritime Provinces (including Newfoundland, for example), this system has been well used by individuals to find and locate to jobs in the west (Economic Council of Canada 1977, p. 181).

Inevitably the jobs listed with the CMC job-bank system are relatively difficult to fill.[14] Employers go to the CMC when they have trouble filling the job through ordinary channels, or when the skills are so specific as to require expert screening of qualified applicants. Typically the jobs listed with the CMC are semi-skilled, craft-oriented trades occupations, as well as more skilled jobs that cover most job categories. The CMC system also provides job training (if appropriate) and job counseling—job search skills, aptitude testing, screening applicants with respect to specific skill demands, and even attitude screening. For an individual client, the local CMC is both a resource for UI as well as a place to search for local and inter-local labor market jobs. For employers, the local CMC is a means of finding qualified employees without having to advertise locally or outside the area, or screen potential employees, or even provide relocation expenses if the *best* employee comes from outside the local area. Recently, the CMC has placed computerized job-bank modules in shopping centers throughout Canada to allow clients and non-clients alike to use at their discretion. By all accounts these modules have been very popular, creating queues to use them in many localities.

The guiding principles behind this system are twofold. The primary principle is that clients should choose whether or not to relocate. Local CMCs are reluctant to encourage clients to consider outside listings, and they will only provide that information upon request. Of course, for those unemployed in the Maritime Provinces, which have very high levels of unemployment, this notion of choice may be problematic. Although UI is provided, with extended benefits associated with the level of local unemployment, and welfare is also provided, the reality is that in many situations there are few jobs available locally (King and Clark 1978). And, while the Canadian government has attempted a program of job creation, many of the unemployed face the prospect of no employment for very long periods of time. By force of circumstances, many have had to look elsewhere for jobs, and the CMC has played an important role in helping these individuals once the decision has been made to relocate (even if temporarily). Like the United States, relocation expenses incurred by individuals can be claimed on federal taxes. Thus, the Canadian government facilitates relocation decisions directly and indirectly, a level of commitment unknown in the U.S.[15]

The second organizing principle of this system is distinctly Coasian in that it seeks to improve the efficiency of labor market transactions (Economic Council of Canada 1977). Officials of the CMC quite directly argue that improved efficiency reduces the social costs of potential market misallocations. By improving the match between employees and employers, the market is more responsive to geographical frictions.[16] Incidently, the costs of shifting an individual across country to a new job are very small compared to the social costs of supporting that individual and family on unemployment. The key objective function of the system is to minimize the transaction costs of a dispersed and heterogeneous national labor market. In doing so, all three types of transaction costs are attacked. For example, the costs of the means of exchange (Type I) have been minimized through the use of computer technology. Second, the costs of the organization of production (Type II) are also important aspects of CMC policy. Mining towns that have unique locations away from centers of industry and trade have been integrated into the national labor market network through both the listing of job vacancies *and* the use of relocation grants. Plant closings have also been considered an integral responsibility of this system, with cooperative tripartite agreements between companies, unions, and the government facilitating the transition from employment to unemployment to employment.

But most importantly the costs of uncertainty in labor market transactions (Type III in the Coasian model) have been directly addressed. Search and informational costs have been minimized— the job-bank finds workers and employers and transmits the terms of employment. The costs of negotiation and contracting have also been lessened—the job-bank allows comparisons between job offers and terms and conditions, and interview grants speed face-to-face contracting—and through screening, the CMCs are able to reduce potential problems of employee compliance (like absenteeism). The key issue for the Canadian government is the procedural efficiency of the labor market system. For employers and employees, this matching process is able to deal with a number of different types of labor market transactions—where employers and employees are indifferent with respect to their identities so that it is a simple price (quantity non-specific transaction); where employers may require specific skills related either to their industry and/or particular modes of operation (mixed transactions); and, where there may be unique skill/personal requirements between employers and employees either in production teams or research and development.

Since unemployment is very high in Canada and in most local labor markets, the crucial transactions are of the last kind, and they are represented in high numbers in the CMC system. Opportunities exist for unemployed workers to relocate across the nation. Assisted by the federal government, workers are helped to take new jobs and hence to reduce their dependence upon welfare. By linking mobility assistance to the unemployed, the Canadian government is able to speed the efficiency of market allocations of excess suppliers of labor to demand for labor (Manpower and Immigration 1975).[17] The policy assumes that the initiation must, however, come from the individual. It is choice-oriented, non-conditional, and it seeks to be non-coercive. For American policy makers this kind of policy represents an important new way of facilitating individual choice and, by implication, of reducing the social costs of market transactions. Tax deductions for moving expenses have been important for many years. It is time, however, that the federal government took a more active role in coordinating the *geographical* character of the labor market.

SUMMARY

The argument in this chapter began with the claim that the federal government must ensure the basic welfare of its citizens, allowing wherever possible individual choice to dictate where people live.

This is what I termed the *Rawls Option.* Evidence presented here, and elsewhere, has demonstrated that community integrity is a desirable goal, at least as represented by the actions of the citizens of cities such as Flint: if given a choice, many GM workers would stay in the Flint area. Forced relocation, either by drastic reductions in local welfare or by government policy that links assistance levels to relocation, is inherently coercive. If society values individual choice above other moral norms, the coercion of circumstances and policies should be regarded as a denial of the basic moral virtue of American society. Furthermore, the *Rawls Option* claims a necessary role for public policy because the spatial market system is neither capable nor designed to ensure the basic welfare of society. This issue is ethical and distributional, and not concerned with efficiency. In these terms, we should accept Coase's argument that due recognition must be given to basic substantive values.

On the other hand, we should not automatically accept idealist versions of community integrity that place primary importance on maintaining the status quo. For some individuals trapped in places like Flint, the status quo may not be their choice. As we have seen in Chapter 5, many poorer people do not move because of the structure of local labor markets—endemic informational costs and search costs. Thus, the second argument of this chapter was still Rawlsian but also, to an extent, Coasian—individuals who wish to relocate to a new job or search elsewhere for better opportunities should be helped. The *Coase Option* may facilitate the practical achievement of two basic social values: individual choice and social justice. Moreover, by facilitating the market, the inadequacies and inefficiencies of the labor market, identified in previous chapters, could be alleviated. In these terms, the *Coase Option* should be thought of as an instrument for achieving wider social objectives. As we have seen previously, market efficiency can hardly be the central social goal in its own right. At this level then, the *Rawls* and *Coase Options* are not exclusive of one another. It would be entirely consistent to ensure community integrity and maximum mobility— after all, it is assumed that the notion of individual choice is the central social goal.

Just as we should be wary of policies that make people hostage to their communities, it should also be recognized that the Coase Option noted here, is a more particular argument for government intervention than Coase (1960) might allow. That is, as with Calabresi (1968), it is argued in this chapter that public policies which facilitate market transactions benefit both individuals and the economic system. The notion that government policy is doomed to failure is rejected here, as is the 1982 *President's NUPR,* as an excessively narrow reading of Coase's argument. The Canadian government's mobility policies have demonstrated that market intervention can be quite consistent with efficiency claims for reducing transaction costs. These policies also demonstrate the necessary responsibility of the federal government in ensuring the welfare of its citizens *and* the underlying principles of free choice and social justice.

NOTES

1. In what follows, the dimensions of Flint's economic crisis are based on interviews with union and community leaders in late April 1982. Thanks to Jack Lietzenburg, Director of the City's Community Development department; Tom Tomaskovich, Manager of the local Michigan Employment Service Center; Dan Sain of the United Auto Workers Union; Frank Zerby of the building trades sections of the American Federation of Labor; Robin Wigery of the General Motors Institute; and representatives of the Mott Foundation and FAC Inc. They are not responsible for any views expressed here.

2. This is consistent with Brenner's (1973) study which linked macroeconomic indicators with mental health, and who argued that there is a strong cyclical (time-series) effect in hospital admissions.

3. Even though interest rates declined in late 1982, the Congressional Budget Office (1982) has remained pessimistic regarding the economic vitality of the American economy through to 1985. Chronic budget deficits, weak consumer spending, and historically high levels of unemployment promise an immediate future of sluggish national economic performance, albeit relieved to a limited extent by a nascent economic recovery. More alarmist prognosis of future economic trends have claimed that a national unemployment rate of 12%–13% is not out of the question.

4. *Business Week* (June 1, 1981) concluded that many "old-line" industries, such as steel and autos face an extraordinarily hostile environment. The high cost of capital, poor returns on invested capital, and corporate strategies of following profits rather than sustaining older divisions will all contribute to a massive disinvestment in American industry. *Business Week* (p. 59) concluded that the "accelerated erosion of the economic base of have-not regions threatens the companies still situated in them with further decay in regional economic infra-structures or with higher state and local taxes [inevitable]."

5. We must be careful not to overemphasize the importance of robotics and high-technology–based automation. In many respects, the auto industry is relatively underdeveloped in these areas. Yet, the rapid development of robotics has meant that each succeeding generation of robots are able to do tasks only dimly conceived five years ago. Ayres and Miller (1981) have noted the exponential growth in the use of robots in American industry, and the General Accounting Office (1982) has suggested that increasing automation will affect many sectors, not only manufacturing. Even so, at present the evidence is incomplete and ambiguous in terms of the displacement effects of robotics on employment.

6. Garnick (1981) has suggested that the prospects for the Midwest are bleak as rationalization of industry continues to increase dislocation of labor and community. In fact, he has suggested that recent forecasts of regional and state employment to the year 2000 may understate the dimensions of contraction in this region over the next two decades (*see* Bureau of Economic Analysis 1980).

7. See Birch (1981) on the job-generation process. But also see the recent report by the General Accounting Office (1981) that severely questions the innovative potential of small businesses.

8. See Dahlman (1979) for the more general discussion of transaction costs, and a critique by Kennedy (1981) on the theorem itself.

9. Cooter (1982) developed a similar analysis to that presented here, using the Coasian model in contrast to what he termed the Hobbesian option. His use of Hobbes to represent the alternative vision was unfortunate for two reasons. First, Hobbes was hardly a democrat, much less a philosopher concerned with the social character of voluntary association. In his vision, the sovereign had absolute powers,

derived from control of police power. Although there may be good and bad sovereigns, the vision is one of totalitarianism. Second, social choice as opposed to paternalism is non-existent in a Hobbesian world. Instead of defining the social "good" through the aspirations of the mass of people, the social "good" is imposed (Berns 1981). In these terms, the Rawlsian notion is clearly more compatible to the issues under analysis.

10.   Coase (1974) noted an important issue in that paper; the difficulty that economists have in demonstrating that public goods *cannot* be provided by the market. It may be true that the market extracts high costs for such functions, critical analysis of these costs however tend to relate, however, to equity questions, and not to efficiency questions per se.

11.   See Paul Samuelson's critique of the ideological content of Reagan's policies in the *Boston Globe* (May 10, 1982). He argued that Reagan is pursuing an ideological agenda that was neither democratically mandated nor discussed under the guise of restructuring the economy through "new" economic policy.

12.   Interestingly enough, both radicals and conservatives alike place a great deal of importance on non-coercive individual choice. For example, in the former instance, Putnam (1981 pp. 146–47) argues against authoritarianism and for political pluralism (but not consensualism). Olson (1965), according to a much more conservative logic, also argues for a choice theoretic scheme. Of course, once we deal with the details of each vision, we immediately confront many dissimilarities and irreconcilabilities. In the former instance, individual choice evolves out of social conceptions of justice and rights. In the latter instance, choice is the basic building block of society itself; it assumes the importance of a *natural* right. My opinion parallels Putnam's (1981) in that I believe society to be the source of social rules like individual choice. Thus, I assume a political theory of rights (*see* Chapter 7).

13.   The following discussion and description of the Canadian policy was based on a series of interviews conducted with Canadian government officials in late April 1982. Thanks to David Neuman, Ian Midgelee, Joe Johnson, George Jackson and Gene Malone. All comments and opinions are not theirs, but the author's.

14.   The Canadian economy is characterized by high levels of national unemployment over 10% during 1982) concentrated in the eastern provinces (particularly, Quebec and the Atlantic provinces of Nova Scotia and New Brunswick). Recent trends also indicate that long-term unemployment is an increasing problem where, for example, over 50% of those unemployed in Quebec have been unemployed for more than three months. Yet, at the same time, there are marked shortages of skilled labor, especially in machining and product fabricating. These shortages are also highly specific to industries and regions (gas exploration in the west, for example) (Economic Council of Canada 1982).

15.   Saunders (1981) has noted however that job training programs are significant impediments to mobility; federal funds limit mobility as much as encourage mobility. The crucial issue is, of course, facilitating individual choice concerning whether or not to remain or to move. Both options are supported in the Canadian system. Given the priority accorded to such a choice, such policies are not contradictory except at a superficial level.

16.   Spatial coordination of the Canadian economy has been a central policy concern of the Canadian government for many years. It has been argued that geographically, the economy is only poorly integrated, and it is a social cost borne by all members of society in terms of the lost efficiency (Safarian 1980). In a study of the regional dimensions of macroeconomic policy, the Economic Council of Canada (1977, p. 120) concluded that a "regionalized stabilization policy to reduce regional differences in unemployment rates would seem to be both desirable and feasible."

17.   Provincial governments have also become involved in intraprovincial training and relocation schemes, mostly orientated towards the needs of private investors (*see* Ministry of Treasury and Economics 1982 for details of Ontario policies).

SEVEN

A Framework for Urban Policy

INTRODUCTION

The mechanics of two competing national urban policy options, termed "community integrity" and "maximum mobility," were set out in some detail in the previous chapter. I dealt primarily with the instruments of policy, with their detailed character, and with their relevance to a specific context—Flint, Michigan. This specificity was in accordance with a basic assumption of this study; that interregional migration is highly specific to events and places. Both the macroeconomic structure of migration, its dependence and association with local capital growth, relative employment and wages, and the microeconomics of individual behavior lend support to this notion. Once we introduce particular communities such as Flint, we begin to understand how locales bind, structure, and support residents according to where they live and work.[1] These empirical and theoretical arguments were used to establish a rather different conceptualization of the interregional migration national policy question, different that is from the conservative notions which dominate current debates. This discussion was based as well upon our earlier analysis of the ends of current conservative policy proposals, such as national economic efficiency.

If, as I have argued, the community means so much in understanding the migration processes and individuals' options, policies that promote the resilience of communities have a vital role to play in ensuring the welfare of society. Accordingly, community integrity could be interpreted as a necessary instrument of policy, and not only as a substantive policy goal in and of itself. Of course, we should be wary of immediately reducing such an argument to yet another "trickle-down" policy wherein, for example, jobs are created locally and the effects are thought to be multiplied throughout the community. The crucial argument is not a multiplier notion, rather a theoretical, even philosophical, idea: that there is an inevitable interdependence between place and individual behavior. For example, it was argued in Chapter 5 that individual relocation decisions are taken with respect to the conditioning structure of local labor market characteristics. Thus individuals may choose not to relocate for quite rational reasons related principally to the character of local labor markets. The possibility of choice, of being able to relocate and make a better life may be closed by the force of circumstances. The mobility option as an instrument or means of attaining the more general goal of individual choice and welfare can be integrated within the proposed policy agenda without necessarily agreeing with Coase (1960) that transactional efficiency should be the transcendent public policy objective. Again, to re-emphasize, it is a question of means and ends.

The integrated package of policy options presented in Chapter 6 was premised upon substantive values of social justice and individual welfare.[2] I take it as given that a "well-ordered" society (as in Rawls's 1979 terms) is one in which the government functions to ensure the material well-being of society's members. Summarily expressed, this Rawlsian imperative implies that social justice is not possible without government intervention. A more general argument could be that justice is a social good, that there is a moral imperative of collective security which is an intimate part of social life.[3] More significantly, but at the same time more generally, the notion of maximum individual welfare denotes a specific substantive conception of social justice. And, it also denotes a crucial role for government policy. In consequence, the nihilism of current conservative urban policy options is eschewed in favor of a specific agenda regarding the proper "ends" of society. Unfortunately, much of the debate over regional growth and decline takes place over the means or instruments of policy, like Coasian notions of market efficiency, rarely about the ends of public policy. This is the fundamental failing of the conservative urban agenda.

In this final chapter, I sketch possible substantive principles of a revitalized national urban policy, paying particular attention to interregional migration. It is necessarily a sketch because of the generality of debates over ends and the implied political values it deems important. Instead of approaching this task from the standard policy analytical paradigm of trade-offs, options, and the like, I argue the case for a particular urban policy recipe. Briefly, my argument is that because governments must ensure social justice, they then must be concerned with the welfare of individuals and their relative equality. I follow Dworkin's (1981) conception of a non-utilitarian vision of social equality that allows for individual choice with respect to location, a conception born out of the social order of everyday life. Basic to this notion of social justice are two propositions: (a) that when discussing the ends, not means, of public policy we inevitably deal with political values, not preferences; and, (b), that when discussing ends there can only be recipes of justice, not harmonious mixes of alternative preferences molded through consensual trade-offs. Both propositions imply a specific method of analysis wherein no attempt is made to sustain a consensual view of competing ends. The focus of this chapter is essentially idealistic and is concerned with the elements to a *good* public policy.[4]

AGAINST TRADE-OFFS

The first proposition, that the ends of public policy deal with values not preferences, need not detain us for long. Few academics would disagree with the notion that values are political variables which pervade not only how we analyze problems, and how we interpret conclusions, but also how we frame questions. As Mishan (1982) has recently noted, normative analysis, as opposed to positive analysis, is a false dichotomy. A more realistic stance is to view policy analysis as politics itself, and not as a substitute for politics. Despite its apparent simplicity, this issue is subtle and more complex than many would first imagine. It raises quite complex questions that have no immediate answers. For example, does a policy whose goal is equality of housing choice for all citizens regardless of race also mean heterogeneity in the mix and location of various races? If this is not the case, if it is argued that racial heterogeneity is not the same as equality of housing choice, then we have an argument of interpretation. Not only would such an interpretation have to consider the meaning(s) of equality, but also important would be an analysis of *means* and *ends*. That is, could it be that equality of housing choice is really an instrument for achieving spatial racial heterogeneity? Generally, Berlin (1969) and, more recently, Rae et al. (1982), have argued that concepts such as equality are vacuous unless invested with specific meaning, and, of course, specific contexts.[5]

The problem of deciding on the meaning of policy objectives is pervasive and cuts across many substantive and regulatory fields. A variety of strategies are used to give determinant meanings to policy ends. For example, a favorite mode of interpretation is to appeal to an outside (that is, programmatically neutral) arbiter such as the courts. From that perspective, the court is asked to rule on the true intent or meaning of a given piece of legislation, constitutional doctrine and the like. But here, as in all issues of policy adjudication, the problems of values and ideology intrude. Ely (1980), for instance, has suggested that adjudication is not value neutral, that the legal system is often very conservative in procedure and conservative in terms of values. He suggested that a way around this problem is to design neutral procedures for the adjudication of conflict so that outcomes are not biased. As many have protested, however, the design of procedures requires a prior definition of desired outcomes. If there is no idea of the best result there can be no useful procedures (Tribe 1980). Once we return the problem of interpretation to the political arena, then the politics of interpretation takes on the character of the underlying structure of political power. There can be no neutral adjudicator (Tushnet 1980).

A mode of interpretation that has had some currency in the past involves a return to the original intent of legislation or policy as the datum point for establishing the veracity of policy ends. For example, Houseman (1979), in a study on the "right of mobility," takes the reader through an exhaustive and elaborate investigation of original American and British constitutional documents to arrive at the true meaning of the "freedom of locomotion." As embodied in the Fourteenth Amendment to the U.S. Constitution, Houseman (1979) argued, this is an absolute right of all citizens to move where they wish; a principle found in sources such as Blackstone's *Commentaries on the Laws of England.*[6] The problems with original intent arguments are well known (*see* Brest 1980). Despite their apparent simplicity, it is impossible to understand the context in which previous policy ends were formulated without introducing the context of the present. Experience and history change our understanding of the meanings and possibilities of policies—their goals and means. Historical detective work begins with our values, which are borne out of the exigencies of current times. Inevitably, meaning has a historical, even spatial, setting that cannot be circumvented.

Consequently, interpretation of the ends of public policy is a political act. Similarly, choices between contending interpretations, even contending ends, are also political acts that depend more upon the nature of fundamental values than supposedly neutral rules of adjudication. Appeals to the neutrality of rules to discriminate between arguments also suffer from basic drawbacks. First, by establishing a rule, an order is imposed on what is appropriately included, and what is inappropriately excluded. No rule can be completely inclusive because it depends on finding commonalities in the various catagories and concepts arranged under its rubric. Second, a common metric of comparison is necessary. Yet values may be incommensurable and subject to disagreements concerning the very nature of the problem at hand, and to even the existence of a problem and its proposed solution. The common metric must be a consistent value or standard of justice. How else can we compare and adjudicate between competing interpretations of equality of mobility unless we have a substantive bench mark? From this view, it is clear that a common metric presupposes a solution, it is a procedure premised upon an outcome. Thus the definition of the metric is essentially the means of resolving conflict, but also inevitably the location of the chosen substantive value or interpretation of equality. To this extent, rules order and determine the resolution of competing interpretations.

Extending this logic further also means that trade-offs between substantive value positions presuppose a solution—an underlying metric. Thus it makes no sense to talk of policy trade-offs except at a naive and superficial level. To the extent that public policies are based upon different substantive values then they are independent of one another. This conclusion has a number of implications for conducting policy analysis. First, the notion of trade-offs presupposes a desirable end, and also a set of options for attaining that end. Now, it may well be true that there are preferred options but, of course, this implies that preferences are conceived in terms of a common metric. Consequently, *preferences* relate to means, not ends, and they entail shared, not contending, values. Second, the existence of independent policy ends implies that there can be no harmonious macro-solutions to overlapping, even contradictory, policies. As Berlin (1969) has noted, the conception of harmony is a fiction based upon a natural-system–oriented model of the world.[7] Although consensus may be a desirable attribute for many, denoting stability and order (for example, *see* Huntington 1981), there cannot be neutral technical solutions to conflicts over substantive ends. Third, and obviously related, is the fact that because ends entail independent substantive values, *how* they are combined is the crucial political question.

Returning for the moment to questions of regional justice and national economic efficiency, the only possibility of a trade-off between these two visions is if there is a common, albeit unstated, integral substantive value. Perhaps the underlying integrating value is maximum individual welfare. If so, then both regional justice and national efficiency are instruments, or means, not ends in themselves. In the first instance, the maximization of individual welfare in a locality might be achieved through policies of direct job creation targeted to areas of high unemployment. To the extent that these policies are successful in increasing local prosperity then, as the argument goes, individuals would directly or indirectly benefit. In the second instance, national economic efficiency, perhaps measured by total income generated, may require a highly spatially concentrated economic system. For example, it is quite possible that spatial concentration reduces market transaction costs by improving the coordination of buyers and sellers, as well as their knowledge of market opportunities (Clark 1980a).[8] Individual welfare would be advanced to the extent that increments in aggregate income are redistributed. Choice between these two policy options might be made through technical tests of which is better, perhaps even considerations of disruption costs versus net benefits, and so on—conventional cost-benefit analysis. Even here there are questions of relative distribution, but none of substantive ends.

It is also entirely plausible that regional equity and national economic efficiency are separate substantive values in and of themselves. I argued in Chapter 2 that national efficiency is a rather weak normative goal, subject to charges of fetishism and naivete, yet held, no doubt, by some (perhaps the federal government which has most to gain in terms of power and legitimacy; Clark and Dear 1984). A trade-off is totally implausible in this context. Why should the Midwest give up its claim to regional equity if this means the advancement of its nemesis? Yet if it is argued that regional equity is the substantive goal, and national efficiency an instrument, why would an end and a means for it be traded off? After all, the means is supposed to serve the end. If not, the means should be discarded. Here, then, is the fundamental problem with notions of trade-offs and substantive ends. *If regional equity and national efficiency are indeed competing values, there is no common metric to enable any trade-off.* If these two concepts are means, then which is more desirable will be decided according to how it advances a third, unstated end, given political preferences for the distribution of costs and benefits. If, on the other hand, one is an end, the other a means (the most likely combination wherein regional equity is the end, national efficiency a means), trade-offs are inconceivable.

How plausible is community integrity as a substantive value? I argued previously that it is a means to an end, enabling people to live where they desire. More broadly, this goal could be stated as advancing individual choice or freedom. On the other hand, it is clear that some philosophers and citizens would argue that community integrity is a *good* thing; that the continuity and existence of social association is a necessary feature of human life, and without the protection of community integrity, individuals would be made worse off. Their loss would be qualitative in this instance, but nevertheless very real. Urban sociologists have often contended that community integrity is a crucial attribute of individual life, and manifests itself in social associations as diverse as church groups and street-corner gangs. In other instances, community integrity has been used as a surrogate for more general goals. For example, some writers have noted that community association expresses an underlying *good* value of political participation, the taking control of one's life. The community is thought alternatively to be an *incubator* and the *medium* of social life. Although these notions have been attacked in recent times as mere historical artifacts of an era where social life has been highly geographically constrained, the community "good" still retains its promoters.

Strong community identity and association has been promoted as means of maintaining the physical and cultural character of urban life. Through the diversity engendered by different ethnic, racial, and social backgrounds, communities have been valued for their continuity in preserving valuable social infrastructure. Again, community integrity can be interpreted as a means to an end, although there is some debate in the philosophical literature about the inherent *good* of inter-community heterogeneity. For example, Nozick (1974) has argued for a society composed of individuals of like preferences, wherein the diversity of communities provides a choice of life and social association. In Nozick's theory, communities are a means of ensuring liberty, consent, and, ultimately, democracy. But also important for Nozick is the conception of association that goes beyond an instrumental quality. For many political philosophers, radical and conservative alike, the community is the cornerstone of society.[9] Mansbridge (1980), a radical socialist, has lauded the cooperative democracy of small towns, and Nozick (1974) a conservative libertarian, argues for the freedom embodied in community choice. Clearly, community integrity is as often a means as an end. while national maximum wealth can hardly be seriously considered an end, but instead more likely a means.

COMMUNITY AND EQUALITY

Community integrity, whatever the philosophical and empirical rationales, cannot be the overriding goal of public policy. Social justice cannot be held hostage of exclusive utopian visions of community resilience. Even given the extraordinary costs of urban economic decline that threaten the Midwest over the next decade, community integrity cannot be bought by restricting the choices of their residents, however indirectly conceived. The lack of mobility assistance and the absence of retraining and job-search facilities would be essentially policies of neglect or worse of restricted choice. Based on the conceptions of social justice presented in Chapter 6, it is clear that such policies would promote inequality, rather than equality as such. For example, some sectors of commerce in the Midwest have strongly opposed relocation policies, arguing that the vitality of their communities is at risk. And it is true that the shrinking economic and population base of places like Flint has forced many commercial enterprises into bankruptcy. Balkanizing poverty, however, is no solution to the needs of social justice and equality. To understand what options might be plausible in this instance requires a more detailed discussion of what equality means. But in doing so, I immediately enter the realm of idealist and normative values of my own choosing. I do so in order to demonstrate wider theoretical and political facets of public policy. I do not mean to impose my own values in the guise of "science" or "good" policy analysis.

My definition of equality is based upon Dworkin's (1981) conception of equality of resources (EOR). Simply defined, EOR requires that *distribution and redistribution proceed to the point where no further transfer would leave individual shares of total resources more equal.* When contrasted to the utilitarian notion of equality of welfare (EOW), the following characteristics of EOR emerge. First, EOR is a rule-oriented social standard of equality that depends upon a common metric between individuals for its application. Thus shares of income, employment opportunities, even the existence of certain choices could be used to indicate comparative equality. On the other hand, EOW is a subjective, individualist conception of equality. It supposes that people should be equally happy, based upon their own tastes and preferences. As such, the EOW model is utilitarian, while EOR is not. Second, EOR is premised upon a given set of social resources but, at the same time, it does not take into account the prior distribution of resources. In contrast, EOW may require that those with expensive tastes be given more resources than those with more frugal tastes. Given that consumption preferences are highly income-contingent, the *prior* definition of income will determine the nature of redistribution.

Third, this equality measure is *social,* as opposed to individualistic, in presupposing political solutions to the rank and order of substantive values, and how (the means) EOR is to be achieved. Moreover, it presupposes political equality so that outcomes, whether in terms of ends or means, reflect the true interests of the majority. The minority may disagree, but be equally free to express and hold to their views as others. The contrasts with the EOW standard are stark in this instance. Utilitarian individualist models of equality assume a consensual agreement on the underlying substantive end. There can be no political process because non-consensual political behavior would imply gaming and, perhaps, even the denial of the equality of others. A gaming response might be to change preferences once they are fulfilled according to prior tastes and preferences. In doing so, one person would accumulate more and more over time. In addition, some altruism is required for individuals to recognize the claims of others to their tastes. Once different political goals (the ends) are introduced, then politics does not matter. Either way, the EOW standard eschews the political process for what can only be a *metaphysical* conception. It allows for no human agency.

Fourth, EOR policies are inevitably based upon the existing social wealth. In contrast, EOW is unconditional; that is, it presupposes that enough wealth exists so that all preferences can be met. Again, it is obvious that equality under an EOW regime is largely external to the existing economic structure, whereas an EOR regime is based upon an historical conception of society. Dworkin (1981) also argued that his vision of EOR should not be mistaken for more well known *starting-gate* models of equality. A popular example of a starting-gate model is equality of opportunity (EOO), wherein every citizen is given an equal chance at the beginning of a period and then left to their own devices. In the extreme, EOO is an inequality model justified by claims of equality.[10] By starting people with equal chances, subsequent inequality, due to an unequal distribution of ambition, luck, and even circumstances (like living in Flint, Michigan) is thought to be either inevitable (as in "people are unequal by nature") or irrelevant, or both. In subsequent time periods moves to change the resulting distribution are often judged to be unjust (as in "changing the rules midstream") and invalid. Thus starting-gate models of equality imply inequality and ultimately powerlessness.

The EOR model proposed by Dworkin (1981) has the following *formal* properties. He proposed an initial redistribution so that all people are equal according to some EOR standard. Then, given a range of preferences and tastes, he allows for trading and exchange to a point where no one would want another's bundle of goods. Through this exchange system EOR would evolve according to people's preferences. But by invoking an envy test, equality would be maintained by virtue of the conscious choices of those concerned. Preferences in this context are the choices of individuals, given an EOR premised upon the initial level of social wealth. For this model to work, three specific conditions need to be met. First, the force of circumstance should not hinder any person's ability to play the market. Simply put, all people must be able to participate equally, even if this means compensating people for various handicaps. For example, being initially located in Flint should not hinder one's ability to trade or exchange. More obviously, physical or mental handicaps must be obviated. Second, the market itself must be efficient in the sense that transaction costs are at a minimum. This requires little explanation except to note again the relevance of Coase ((1960).

Third, the envy test must be continuous rather than discrete.[11] This condition is necessary to avoid the pitfalls of starting-gate models of equality. By maintaining an ongoing envy test, the veracity of choice is maintained, and no individual is put at a disadvantage by reason of external circumstances. That inequality will result from this structure cannot be in doubt. But the distinguishing feature of this model is that resulting inequality will be a function of individual decisions regarding their best lives. Thus, for example, some people may wish to remain in Flint by reason of social identity, etc., thereby reducing their lifetime chances for greater income or economic advancement. Their choice to do so under these conditions must be *free,* not conditional upon the force of local circumstances, and it must be legitimized by the envy test. Notice that if the structure of the market solution begins to diverge from the preferences of those involved the system can be altered, whether by starting again at the EOR point or even by revision of both the means and ends of public policy. Individuals in the system are neither trapped by the initial distribution or by the character of events over time.

What then are the conditions for freedom of choice? It is this attribute that justifies the veracity of the envy test as well as the resulting distribution of resources. Isaiah Berlin (1969, p. 130) noted that the extent of individual freedom in this context depends on:

(a) the number of possibilities open to any person; (b) the ease to which possibilities may be achieved; (c) the importance and relevance of those possiblities given specific circumstances; (d) how amenable possibilities are to human agency; and, (e) the significance of these possibilities in terms of the overarching social values of society itself.[12]

These conditions imply that freedom is contextual and set within the structure of social experience. There are no ahistorical or fundamental human rights separate from the social experience of individuals (Clark 1982a). It is also the case that there can be no absolute measure of freedom of choice, rather it is a relative concept, like equality of resources. We have then come full circle from an initial discussion of the primacy of choice in Chapter 6, to a more general and then particular discussion of equality in Chapter 7, and again the conditions for choice in this section. But here we have emphasized that freedom of choice is a necessary condition (a means) of social justice.

One way of understanding the importance of these conditions is to reconsider the choices of people located in Flint. Given the collapse of the local economy the number of possibilities (for employment, monetary rewards, even life styles) open to an individual are more limited in number and perhaps quality than, for example, people who live in Dallas. Just because this is true, it does not mean that a Flint resident relocating in Dallas would necessarily do better than remaining in Flint. The ease of achieving these possibilities may be so restricted for Flint workers in Dallas that choice is otherwise highly constricted. Similarly, just improving the number of jobs available in Flint by opening an Auto-World will not likely alter the range of options open to unemployed auto workers. Rather, these options are more likely to be irrelevant and will not alter the specific circumstances faced by local unemployed residents. The only possibility here is to alter either the jobs themselves or the skills of the unemployed. The latter course is less problematic than the former. Finally, but as crucial, it is obvious that the development of large numbers of unskilled jobs in Flint may be insignificant given the pervasive *social* belief in skilled unionized employment as the best option that has developed in Flint over the last fifty years.

There is then an immediacy in the relevance of this freedom of choice criteria that goes beyond theoretical analysis. And, for the model of equality proposed above, these conditions are crucial for the efficacy of the public policies that aim to create an EOR standard for social justice. It would be misleading, however, to imagine that these conditions can be easily achieved. EDA, CETA, and Trade Readjustment programs have all attempted to increase the number of options open to local residents in depressed communities. At this level they have been quite successful. Yet once we introduce specific circumstances, relevance, and human agency it becomes clear that EDA in particular has failed to adequately target those who are most in need. Strategies of "trickle down" hardly deal with the barriers to individual choice and the relevance questions. The Trade Readjustment Act programs have been more successful in these terms although the Act has not been funded to near the level required. Much more problematic has been the efficacy of policies of local economic development with regard to local social values. In other instances, they have been ignored as the whole concept of community has been devalued as a legitimate substantive end.

Urban policy can hardly but fail without a full appreciation of the complexity of choices and options. Furthermore, some of the criteria imply significant social conceptions of *good* options that maintain the fundamental importance of social context. By that, I mean that options are not only considered in terms of individual choices, that their relevance is judged by normative standards that are relative to the locality and social situation. To suppose these criteria are irrelevant, or perhaps unimportant, is to mistake my entire argument. Essentially, individuals are conceived in terms of their social character, and to place an order on these criteria is to impose a normative value of what *should* be important and unimportant. I do not deny the inevitability of this process. It must also be recognized, however, that there can be no neutral arbiter concerning the relevance of competing normative conceptions of the *good* society. That is, if the Midwest Congressional Coalition argues for community standards of relevance against other interest groups (such as the Southwest Economic Conference) who argue national efficiency, the argument is purely political—related to different substantive ends or, less critically, different means.

In this context, it must be emphasized that the market-choice form noted above should not be taken as implying a specific neoclassical or classical commodity market.[13] It is used as a device for administratively organizing the exchange process so necessary for an interdependent society. Although it embodies, functionally and formally, individual liberty and consent (so important to Posner 1981), there need be no market in a conventional sense. The government could organize exchange through arbitrary redistribution until, through trial and error, all preferences were satisfied. Similarly, the market conception does not immediately indicate the type of market that would best facilitate exchange. For example, we could envisage an auction, perhaps a *bourse*. The choice is, in Berlin's (1969) terms, merely a technical matter; in Dworkin's (1981) terms, the choice is a matter of policy (the "best" means of achieving a good allocation of community resources).

ENDS AND MEANS

The notions of justice, individual choice, and community integrity presented above depend upon a particular theory of social rights. To distinguish between my notion and that of utilitarianism, a more general discussion is required of the structure of community and social relationships. The conception of legitimate individual choice and a conflict between individual rights and the community good, arises out of a certain theory of society. Individuals in utilitarian theory are actually fully constituted as human beings outside the immediate structure of society. Nozick's (1974) theory of the role of individuals and institutions is particularly instructive on this point. He asserted that society only has a character after an agreement has been reached amongst free individuals over what they desire. In essence, individuals form alliances (communities) based upon overlapping preferences, and then logically form what we would identify as society. These communities are loose associations of individuals protected by a representative and minimalist state. Preferences can, of course, change, and so can the nature and identity of the individuals that make up alliances. In addition, the state's role is severely circumscribed, basically existing to enforce rights of mutual existence and non-imperialism.

With free mobility and choice, a long-run equilibrium should result such that an individual's preferences exactly map his/her chosen conception of the relationship between individuals and the community. Put bluntly, according to his logic the community is only the sum of its individual members. Since rights in Nozick's theory reside with the individual, the community good is inevitably compromised.

Although Rawls (1971) is not enamored with utilitarianism, his model has some similarities with Nozick's in that the former author's conception of a social contract requires autonomous, choice–oriented individuals who base their decision for association upon mutual advantages. Calculating whether or not to associate with others is, for Rawls, akin to cost/benefit analysis. And, again, individuals make their decisions of social contract outside society. As in Nozick's theory, individuals for Rawls are fully constituted prior (in logical time) to the community. Of course, Rawls assumed there are moral obligations involved in association (unlike Nozick) that relate to this notion of an original position. This original position is hardly a description of reality, nor is it intended as such, rather it is a reference point for evaluating principles of justice; particularly, with respect to those who are least well off. Again, however, rights begin with the individual. As society is introduced the prospect of a clash between individual rights and the community good is developed. Note, however, the values inherent in association, for Rawls, like Nozick, are defined in terms of individual rights prior to the community's social structure.

The key problem with both Nozick and Rawls is their separation of the individual from society in their respective original positions. It is not simply that such a notion is unrealistic; the issue is deeper and essentially philosophical. How is it possible to have individuals as human beings separate and constituted prior to the social relations that constitute them as calculating and emotional actors? The alternative position is that such a separation is inconceivable. Accordingly, individuals only have meaning as human beings to the extent to which they are part of a community. Individuals do not choose to belong to community; in point of fact, there is no choice because it is the social relations that define the individual not a collection of individuals defining the community. Interdependence rather than independence is the key building block of what can be termed the community. My argument can then be distinguished from utilitarian and social contract theories because it conceives of the relationship of individuals to the community in terms of their mutual and contextural obligations born out of their social relations.

Thus, the notion of choice with respect to individuals and their possible social association is not the issue. Social relations are assumed to be inherent in the human experience. Similarly, individuals are not considered as independent autonomous agents, rather individuals are analyzed as being inextricably bound by the mutual bonds of interdependence. This should not be taken as implying that interdependence in any way limits the extent and existence of conflict over the moral principles that guide community policy. There are, and must be, continual conflict over what constitutes the community good, individual claims regarding needs and deserts, and role of individuals. When Duncan Kennedy (1979) noted the problem of the "fundamental contradiction," he framed it in terms of what the individual has to give up for social association. Complete individual freedom, according to Kennedy, is impossible because we need others—their preferences, wishes, and intimate contact—for human development. While it may be romantic to consider ourselves as outsiders, even that position is taken with reference to society.

My alternative is obviously to analyze individuals in terms of their social character. Inherent in this approach is the analysis of the social obligations of individuals derived out of social interdependence, whereby individuals act in the interests of others and themselves with reference to their social relationships. At the first level of appearance [defined in Clark (1981b) as being the realm of moral rights], we have expectations of ourselves and our fellow citizens summarily in the notion of a community. Moral expectations are also expressed as social obligations—rights, if you like, which must be observed and maintained for the reproduction of social relations. Thus, the rights accorded an individual can only be defined contextually: defined in terms of social relations and expectations of moral concern, derived out of the particular social context. This implies two further conditions.

First, collective coercion by the community of particular individuals can be legitimized in the name of the interdependence implicit in human relations. Obviously, such a notion requires consent. Social obligations can fall more heavily on one group more than another.

As long as the means by which social (as opposed to individual) decisions are agreed upon (perhaps according to the universality rule as in Rawls's original position), then sacrifices can be made. Second, rather than assume individual rights and the community good to be antithetical, the conclusion here is that individual rights themselves can only be identified in terms of a particular community. This does not necessarily mean that the community will be protected from adverse effects of individual action. In point of fact the existence of adverse effects must be related to the social structure of power that allows certain outcomes.

At this point it might be protested that this definition of rights as contextual obligations is simply an extension of positivistic empiricalism. That is, because rights are contextual they can only be defined in particular instances. There are no ultimate moral arbiters of right or wrong according to this logic as there are no original positions independent of social life. This is partly true. It should be noted, however, that social obligations can have a large moral component. Further, rights as obligations can also mean that not only are we concerned with how people act, but, as well, obligations embody normative values—expectations of how individuals ought to act, and of how the community good ought to be achieved. This aspect is missing from positivistic theories of rights and interpretation.

The implications of the foregoing discussion of equality and social justice for national and regional policies are twofold. First, a deliberate political choice is inherent in any set of policies that presume to achieve a specific substantive end. Second, there are clusters of congruent values that, in total, represent specific mixes of substantive goals. These clusters might be termed recipes in that it is their particular relationships to one another that structure their political potency. For example, an important cluster is best indicated by the notion community integrity. This is composed of an assorted set of ends and means that together form a specific mix of values and options. For some, community integrity is a means to an end: the welfare of local residents mediated through their social context. Some believe community integrity embodies cultural aspects of human existence that can never be individual, but inherently social. This conception is of community integrity as a *good,* in and of itself. The congruence of different sets of means and ends provides the basis for political action and, to a lesser extent, internal conflict over the dominance of various preferences.

Congruence is possible only if the underlying social values do not destroy the possibilities of achieving one another. And there must be an integrating conception that provides form to the recipe. The specificity of different recipes of social justice also indicates an inevitability of conflict between different sets of congruencies. The most obvious conflict is between what I have termed community integrity and maximum national wealth. To a certain extent, both might be objects of similar policy instruments, like minimizing transaction costs of exchange, improving individual choice, and so forth. But, in total, these two ensembles represent drastically different conceptions of the best policy, the best goal, and the best society. In general they are images of society as much as they are objects of specific policy instruments. When debates ensue over policy there is an inevitable confusion over ends and means; much of this confusion is a product of ignoring the congruences between ends and means, even if they may appear similar between recipes. The issue here is simply that once we deal with clusters of substantive ends there can be no common metric of decision. It is not a technical question.

We noted earlier, in a related context, that trade-offs are implausible. Such a notion depends not only upon a common metric, but also an assumption that ends can be harmonized. Not only are values and ends contingent upon experience, but they are held as more or less integrated world views: as organizing principles of social justice and equity. Thus, harmony is hardly likely: more likely is political conflict over the desirability of different recipes of policies. Ultimately, disagreement expressed in this study regarding the veracity of conservative urban policies stems more from its specific recipe of policies than with specific instruments of policy. For example, one can hardly disagree with the desirability of improving market efficiency. The Coasian model draws, quite clearly, the implications of speeding the spatial-temporal efficiency of market transactions. Similarly, one can hardly disagree with mobility programs that enable greater freedom of choice. Both conceptions are relative, not absolute measures of desirable attributes. But, as well, both are means to different ends. Another example is the idea that national growth is surrogate for individual welfare. Of course this is true, but how it is actually implemented depends on its specific relationship with other congruent ends and means: as recipes of public policy.

SUMMARY

This chapter dealt with the problems of defining social justice and equality. It was necessary to develop these notions, applicable to the questions of interregional migration and national urban policy, because proposed solutions to public policy dilemmas imply *normative,* and not positive, conceptions of good policy. The underlying problem with both the *Urban America in the Eighties* Panel report and the 1982 *President's National Urban Policy Report* is their impossible arrogance. They suppose to set out a clear and unequivocal agenda for public policy while at the same time denying the validity of alternative visions of community and society. These reports suppose that an empirical case can be made for their assertions, without of course providing the evidence. In consequence, both reports are difficult to justify on the very terms they assume to be without controversy. The reports take as an article of faith that the "free" market will work out "efficient" solutions. Yet Berlin's (1969) axiom remains entirely appropriate: "freedom for the pike is death for the minnows." In these terms, there can be no justice and no equality: the rich get richer and the poor, poorer as some communities grow and others are destroyed by callous indifference to the disastrous economic conditions of less privileged regions.

From empirical assumptions to substantive conceptions of social justice, both reports were subjected to rigorous scrutiny. They suppose that governments cannot intervene in the economy without mistake, that government intervention brings worse unintended consequences than *good* planned outcomes. But they mistake poor implementation for unnecessary intervention. By this I mean that a good society in any general sense must ensure the basic needs of society. The reports presume that such needs will be met through maximum national wealth, and with a minimal role for government. Similarly, they assume (albeit implicitly) that compensation is the best policy given a certain national wealth. By invoking Pareto optimality the reports deem the problem solved. Yet the problems have hardly begun, because there can be no neutrality in such a solution. Mishan (1982) has rightly noted that the Pareto criterion is not the ethically neutral notion sought by consensual-oriented policy analysts and policy makers.

Ultimately, the problems with the conservative urban agenda are to be found in their confusion of ends and means. They suppose that national wealth maximization is alternatively a means and an end—a way of ensuring the prosperity of society and a good thing in and of itself. From that position, both reports then suppose trade-offs are possible, if undesirable. But here again there are difficulties because at times they trade-off means and ends, which is patently absurd, and, at other times, they seem to trade off competing ends despite the problems of adjudication and interpretation that require standards and rules of substantive justice. Here, the reports are compromised by their dependence upon a false metric or standard of comparison.

My argument for a substantive notion of social justice and equality is hardly uncontroversial. But, at the same time, it is premised upon a framework of policy evaluation that may be more general than the policy it supports. The policy I argued for in this chapter is simply the sustenance of individual choice, whether it be for continued residence or relocation. As a means, I promoted *community integrity,* primarily for empirical reasons, and more general theoretical notions of social context and individuality. But arguments can be made for community integrity as an end in and of itself.

What is readily apparent is that congruent policy ends and means can be conceived as highly specific recipes for social justice that embody fundamental political values. Thus, trade-offs were eschewed in favor of distinct recipes for justice, and contrasts drawn between particular definitions of equality. In this context, I argued for equality of resources (EOR) wherein standards of equality are based upon social, as opposed to subjective, visions of material well-being. From that point, I argued for a *market* for preferences and resources; thus, the efficiency of market transactions is a prerequisite for achieving ends. To the extent to which public policy follows this recipe, a far more intricate set of policies needs to be formulated targeting means and ends without compromising individual freedom of choice and community integrity.

NOTES

1. Foucault (1980) has suggested that the notion of space as a community, as an arena of action, is best understood as a political metaphor wherein power is given a concrete dimension in order to illustrate its instrumentality. He argued that spatial categories enable "one to grasp precisely the points at which discourses are transformed in, through and on the basis of relations of power" (p. 70).

2. Even so, I made no attempt to specify the particular definition of social justice I assume to be important and transcendent above all else. Although Rawls was introduced in support of the "good society" concept, I do not assume that his theory of justice is the only legitimate theory. In fact, as will become clear, I disagree with the Rawlsian vision of justice. Those seeking a general overview of the question of social justice are referred to Pettit (1980).

3. More particularly, the state is assumed to provide at least the needs of people— those conditions necessary for the preservation and development of human beings— and perhaps even deserts—relative claims of advantage and disadvantage (Galston 1980).

4. Nozick (1981, p. 555) defined idealism in the following terms: "Values exist, but their existence and their character are both somehow dependent upon us, upon our choices, attitudes, commitments, structurings, or whatever." In some instances, idealism has been equated with irrelevance; that being idealistic is like tilting at windmills. Yet, such criticism is unwarranted on at least two counts. First, it is only by defining or *constructing* a political option can reasoned logic be brought to bear on both reality and its competing images. Second, emphasis on idealism forces us to confront the inherent politics of values and *how* images themselves are constructed. Of course, some idealistic visions may have little bearing upon reality, and may have little in common with existing conceptions of society. What I intend here is an exploration of social justice that has some of its roots in widely held, albeit not consensual, beliefs.

5. For example, Rae et al. (1982) argue that "the universal use of 'equality' as a category of thought depends upon its very abstractness, its formal emptiness" (p. 3).

6. For a formal definition of the Privileges and Immunities clause of Section 1 of the Fourteenth Amendment, see the prologue of the Civil Rights Act of 1866, Chapter 21, 14 Stat. 27; cf. Blackstone's *Commentaries*, (1765-1769) pp. 129-38.

7. Williams (1982, Ch. 5) has argued that the plurality of values and their incommensurability should not be thought of as being cause for despair. Rather, "value-conflict is not necessarily pathological at all, but something necessarily involved in human values, and to be taken as central by an adequate understanding of them." Harmony is then rather unlikely except in the hierarchical order imposed by the political process. Similarly, movements that seek technical solutions to conflict must be viewed with the utmost suspicion. At this point, it might be claimed by the reader that surely *harmony* is itself an ideal world; that, in my terms, it is just as valid as

my *disharmony* view. That argument would be rather romantic, however, in that (defined by Nozick 1981, p. 555) it is assumed that "values exist independently of us, but inchoately. We choose or determine their precise character; we sculpt and delineate them."

8.   Here is a contrast between orthodox conceptions of the science of economics and a more radical notion that is beginning to emerge in the literature. The former conceives the task of economics to be efficient allocation of scarce resources, the latter conceives the task of economics to be the *just* coordination of economic activity.

9.   There is, nevertheless, some ambiguity in the philosophical literature concerning the relative importance of community and individualism. Both Rawls and Nozick have been accused of hyperindividualism in that for those authors, individuals come before (in time and space) community (*see* Clark 1982a, and Sandel 1982). Thus, there is an unrealistic conception of individuals separate from their society—if you like, separate from the social values that give individuals their identity (Putnam 1981 explores a similar issue in somewhat different terms, "brains-in-a-vat"). The radical literature, on the other hand, supposes fully determined social life, derived from the exigencies of the mode of production. Neither position seems entirely plausible.

10.   Berlin (1969, p. 124) makes the point that simple rules of freedom are not benign whatever their immediate rationale; he put the issue succinctly as "freedom for the pike is death for the minnows."

11.   This analysis has some similarities to a recent theory of fairness proposed by Baumol (1982) and developed from Foley (1967). The basis of their model is to be found in the old adage: "I cut [the cake], you choose [your slice or share]!" Although their theory remains utilitarian, the implied envy test is not dissimilar to that proposed by Dworkin (1981).

12.   Berlin (1969, p. 124) puts this issue as "freedom for an Oxford don . . . is a very different thing from freedom for an Egyptian peasant."

13.   See Hahn (1982) for a sceptical (social-oriented) review of the utilitarian claims of market equity and justice. He rightly notes the indeterminancy of utilitarianism on the grounds that "there seems [to be] no higher principle which can decide between the *ex post* and *ex ante* approach . . . partly because the rankings of actions will not be independent of the person doing the ranking" (p. 198). Put another way, utilitarianism supposes individual and subjective valuation of the merits of alternative public policy options without providing a way out of impasses created by opposing valuations. Since legitimacy resides solely with the individual, no social institution can undertake an ordering of priorities. No wonder utitlitarians *value* consensus higher than any other social norm, without it, there can be no *social,* as opposed to individual, public policy.

APPENDIX I:

Time-Series Models of Migration

There are many reviews of Box and Jenkins's (1976) time-series techniques and some applications to regional economic phenomena. Rather than repeat these extensive reviews, the modeling methodology and conceptual basis of the techniques used in Chapter 4 will only be briefly discussed. Bennett (1979) provided a more detailed discussion for the more technically conversant reader.

Assume that in-migration over time can be represented as a set of discrete deviations such that Z_t is the current observation and Z_{t-1}, Z_{t-2}, Z_{t-3}, etc., are previous observations. Because most economic processes are non-stationary, having no natural mean or constant variance, it may be necessary to difference the series so that

$$\nabla Z_t = Z_t - Z_{t-1} = (1 - B)Z_t$$

where ∇ is defined as the backward difference operator and B is the backward shift operator. Differencing of the series in this manner can be summarized as $d = 1$. This procedure has an analogue in economic theory where economic adjustment is the object of enquiry. That is, instead of dealing with the determinants of levels, the more interesting issue is often the determinants of changes or the pattern of adjustment to changes of independent variables (Sims 1982).

An autoregressive process is defined as one in which the current value of Z_t (in- or out-migration in this instance) is a function of previous values of the process plus a random shock. For example, let any $\tilde{Z}_t = Z_t - \mu$ is the mean about which the process varies, then

$$\tilde{Z}_t = \phi_1 \tilde{Z}_{t-1} + \phi_2 \tilde{Z}_{t-2} + \phi_3 \tilde{Z}_{t-3} + \ldots + \phi_p \tilde{Z}_{t-p} + a_t$$

where $\Phi_1 \ldots \Phi_p$ are the parameters of an autoregressive process of order p and a_t is a random shock at time t. Typically, demographic forecasting models are autoregressive

(AR) models of order p = 1 (using census data implies 5–10-year intervals). That is,

$$\tilde{Z}_t = \phi_1 \tilde{Z}_{t-1} + a_t$$

In more general terms, an AR process of order p can be represented by

$$\phi(B) = 1 - \phi_1 B - \phi_2 B^2 - \ldots - \phi_p B^p$$

or

$$\phi(B)\tilde{Z}_t = a_t$$

Moving average (MA) processes, on the other hand, express $\tilde{Z}_t$ as being dependent upon a finite number (q) of previous and current random shocks. That is,

$$\tilde{Z}_t = a_t - \theta_1 a_{t-1} - \theta_2 a_{t-2} - \ldots - \theta_q a_{t-q}$$

In time-series forecasting this does not mean that the weights $(1, -\Theta -\Theta_2,$ etc.) need total to unity or be positive. More generally,

$$\theta(B) = 1 - \theta_1 B - \theta_2 B^2 - \ldots \theta_q B^q$$

and

$$\tilde{Z}_t = \theta(B)a_t$$

A moving average process of order q = 1 would then be written as

$$\tilde{Z}_t = a_t - \theta_1 a_{t-1} = (1 - \theta_1 B)a_t$$

Imagine what such a process would imply about gross migration. Essentially, the volume or change in the volume of in-migration, would depend on the current random shock and on some weighted portion of the previous shock. Instead of depending on the past volume of in-migration, as in autoregressive models, random disturbances would generate each successive year's in-migration to a given state. Such a model would go against virtually all conventional assumptions regarding the smoothness of the time-path of labor force migration, not being dependent on long-run or previous patterns of migration.

It may be the case however that in-migration is actually a mixture of autoregressive and moving average processes. In that case, it would be represented such that

$$\tilde{Z}_t = \phi_1 \tilde{Z}_{t-1} + \ldots + \phi_p \tilde{Z}_{t-p} + a_t - \theta a_{t-1} \ldots - \theta_q a_{t-q}$$

or

$$\phi(B)\tilde{Z}_t = \theta(B)a_t$$

A relatively simply ARMA process of order p = 1, q = 1 would then be defined as

$$\tilde{Z}_t - \phi_1 \tilde{Z}_{t-1} = a_t - \theta_1 a_{t-1}$$

Finally, to account for non-stationarity, it may be necessary to difference the series such that

$$\phi(B) \, (1 \, - \, B)^d \tilde{Z}_t \, = \, \theta(B) a_t$$

or

$$\phi(B) \nabla^d \tilde{Z}_t \, = \, \theta(B) a_t$$

Tests of causality were also employed to help identify the directions and patterns of the relationships between capital growth and migration for each state. These types of tests have become more popular in recent years as a way of indicating and verifying theoretically derived relationships, particularly in economics (see Sims 1977; Caines et al. 1981; and Granger and Newbold 1977). They have also been suggested as useful diagnostic tools for constructing econometric forecasting models (Pierce 1977), although their applications in regional econometric modeling have been more limited (for one example see Green and Albrecht 1979; and the comments by L'Esperance 1979). The rising popularity of these methods should be understood as part of a more general trend of applying stochastic time-series techniques in geography and regional science. Indeed, the notion of causality that forms the core of these tests requires the adoption of a time-series perspective.

Granger and Newbold (1977) suggested two basic conditions for the assignation of causality. First, the future cannot cause the past. Strictly speaking, only the past can cause the present and future. Second, it is impossible to identify causality between two deterministic processes; causality is only sensibly applied to two or more stochastic processes. Given these two rules, causality between two series X_t (for example capital) and Y_t (for example in-migration) can be more specifically defined as follows. Let I_t represent a set of observed series that includes X_t, Y_t and any other series, subject to data availability, that might affect the interaction between X_t and Y_t as suggested by underlying theory. In econometric analysis, these "other series" are analogous to variables introduced into a multiple regression equation so that their influence on the variables of interest might be held constant. Let $(X|I)$ represent the optimal prediction of X_{t+1}, using the information of I_t, with variance $\sigma^2(X|I)$. Also let $(X|I-Y)$ represent the optimal prediction of X_{t+1}, based on all the information in I_t except for the series Y_t. Then if may be concluded that Y_t causes X_t with respect to I_t if $\sigma^2(X|I-Y) > \sigma^2(X|I)$.

From this definition, it is clear that causality has a quite restricted meaning. Its application may not necessarily uncover "true" causality, and if limits or simplifications are imposed on the content of I_t, any resulting "causality" may in fact be spurious. Nevertheless, this method has the advantage of providing a testable definition and, in common with the overall philosophy of recent time-series approaches, it systematically induces the researcher to test alternative hypotheses that might potentially challenge the legitimacy of suspected or observed causal relationships. For example, it is not inconceivable (and given our previous discussion of the competitive market school, entirely predictable) that Y is found to cause X and X is found to cause Y, either instantaneously (coincidentally) or lagged over time. In these simultaneous cases causality is said to be two-way or characterized by feedback (Granger and Newbold 1975). The point is that causality need not be unequivocal even in the limited sense noted above unless and until the converse of the originally derived relationship is also tested and disproved. For the issue posed in Chapter 4, determining the direction of causality between capital and migration, these tests of causality are more powerful than a simple regression model; no a priori assumption is needed regarding the direction of causality.

APPENDIX II:

Mathematics of Job Search Theory

Based upon the discussion of search theory in Chapter 5, the prime motivation for searching is assumed to be possible gain in lifetime income. Individuals compare the utility of their present situation with the utility that could be expected after searching. The utility of the present situation is described by the utility function (Pissarides 1976, pp. 22–34),

$$U_t = U(M', w_o, \sum_0^t C_t)$$

where

U_t = utility at any time t;

M' = initial wealth;

w_o = effective wage rate at $t = o$, adjusted for welfare payments (perhaps unemployment insurance) and risk;

C_t = accumulated costs of search to time t, including out-of-pocket expenses, and foregone earnings ($C_o = O$, $t = O$); and

t = elementary search period in a sequential job search model, where $t = (1 \ldots T)$ and T is the search horizon.

This matching process could be conceived in terms of the average utility expected from successful and unsuccessful job searching, weighted by the probabilities of success and failure, respectively. The utility of a successful search (W_t) is equal to

$$W_t = 1/a_t \sum_{w_t > \tilde{w}_t} f(w_t) \ U^*(M', w_t, \sum_0^t C_t)$$

where

w_t = a wage offer by an individual firm;

$f(w_t)$ = distribution of wage offers across all firms, at time t;

$U^*(M', w_t)$ = chosen utility level at a given wage rate, constrained by contract (a function of the number of hours worked);

w_t = an individual's reservation wage (see below); and

a_t = the probability that an individual will accept a jobs offer in elementary search period t and is defined as

$$a_t = \sum_{w_t > \tilde{w}_t} f(w_t)$$

The utility of unsuccessful search is given as

$$U_t = U(M', w_o, \sum_0^t C_t)$$

Thus the expected value of search, V, is

$$V_t = a_t W_t + (1 - a_t) U_t$$

where a_t and $(1-a_t)$ are the probabilities of success and failure, respectively. Consequently a worker will search for a job only if

$$V_t > U(M', w_o, \sum_0^t C_t)$$

This states that workers will search for jobs only if by searching they can expect to improve their present lot.

The dependence of the reservation wage on the offered wage can be shown in the following terms (see Pissarides 1976):

Based upon the above

$$V = \sum_{w > \tilde{w}} f(w)U^*(M', w)$$

where

V = expected value of continued search,

w = a wage offered by a firm,

$f(w)$ = the distribution of wage offers across all firms, and

U^* = chosen utility level at each wage offer w, given initial wealth M'.

An individual will only accept a wage offer w_k if

$$U^*(M', w_k) \geq V = \sum_{w > \tilde{w}} f(w)U^*(M', w)$$

The reservation wage is that which satisfied Equation (II.7) as an equality. That is

$$U^*(M', w_k) = V = \sum_{w > \tilde{w}} f(w)U^*(M', w)$$

Consequently the supply of labor to any firm is a decreasing function of the wage rates of all other firms.

Bibliography

Almon, S. 1965. "The distributed lag between capital appropriations and expenditures." *Econometrica* 33: 178–96.

Alonso, W. 1971. "Equity and its relation to efficiency in urbanization." In J. Kain and J. Meyer, eds., *Essays in Regional Economics.* Cambridge: Harvard University Press.

_____. 1972. "Problems, purposes, and implicit policies for a national strategy of urbanization." In S.M. Mazie, ed., *Population Distribution and Society.* Washington, D.C.: USGPO.

_____. 1977. "Surprises and rethinkings of metropolitan growth: A comment." *International Regional Science Review* 2: 171–74.

_____. 1980. "Population as a system in regional development." *Papers and Proceedings, American Economic Review* 70: 405–09.

Alperovich, G., J. Bergsman, and C. Ehemann. 1975. "An econometric model of employment growth in metropolitan areas." *Environment and Planning A* 7: 833–62.

America's New Beginning: A Program for Economic Recovery. 1981. Washington, D.C.: USGPO.

Arrow, K. 1951. *Social Choice and Individual Values.* New York: John Wiley.

Ayres, R., and S. Miller. 1981. "The impacts of industrial robotics," CMU–RI–TR–81–7. The Robotics Institute. Pittsburgh: Carnegie-Mellon University.

Azariades, C. 1975. "Implicit contracts and underemployment equilibrium." *Journal of Political Economy* 83: 1183–1202.

Baily, M.N. 1974. "Wages and employment under uncertain demand." *Review of Economics and Statistics* 41: 37–50.

Bailyn, B. 1967. *The Ideological Origins of the American Revolution.* Cambridge: Harvard University Press.

Ballard, K., and G.L. Clark. 1981. "The short-run dynamics of inter-state migration: A space-time economic adjustment model of in-migration to fast growing states." *Regional Studies* 15: 213–28.

Ballard, K., R. Gustely, and R. Wendling. 1980. *NRIES: National-Regional Impact Evaluation System.* Washington, D.C.: USGPO.

Barnes, W. 1982. "Cautions from Britain: The EZ answer proves elusive." *Urban Innovation Abroad* (special supplement. May): 1–4.

Barro, R., and H. Grossman. 1976. *Money, Employment and Inflation.* Cambridge: Cambridge University Press.

Bartel, A. 1979. "The migration decision: What role does job mobility play?" *American Economic Review* 69: 775–86.

Barth, P.S. 1971. "A time series analysis of layoff rates." *Journal of Human Resources* 6: 448–65.

Bartlett, B.R. 1982. *Reaganomics: Supply-side Economics in Action.* New York: Quill.

Baumol, W. 1982. "Applied fairness theory and rationing policy." *American Economic Review* 72: 639–51.

Bebchuk, L.A. 1980. The pursuit of a bigger pie: Can everyone expect a bigger slice?" *Hofstra Law Review* 8: 671–709.

————. 1982. "The case for facilitating competing tender offers." *Harvard Law Review* 95: 1028–56.

Beitz, C.R. 1979. *Political Theory and International Relations.* New Haven: Yale University Press.

Bennett, R.J. 1979. *Spatial Time Series.* London: Pion.

Berger, R. 1977. *Government by Judiciary: The Transformation of the Fourteenth Amendment.* Cambridge: Harvard University Press.

Berlin, I. 1969. *Four Essays on Liberty.* Oxford: Oxford University Press.

————. 1981. *Concepts and Categories: Philosophical Essays.* Introduced by B. Williams, edited by H. Hardy. New York: Penguin.

Berns, L. 1981. "Thomas Hobbes." In L. Strauss and J. Cropsey, eds., *History of Political Philosophy.* 2nd ed. Chicago: University of Chicago Press.

Berry, B.J.L. 1964. "Cities as systems within systems of cities." In J. Friedmann and W. Alonso, eds., *Regional Development and Planning: A Reader.* Cambridge: MIT Press.

Birch, D. 1981. "Who creates jobs?" *The Public Interest* 65: 3–14.

Blanchard, O.J. 1980. "The monetary mechanism in the light of rational expectations." In S. Fischer, ed., *Rational Expectations and Public Policy.* Chicago: University of Chicago Press.

Blanco, C. 1963. "The determinants of interstate population movements." *Journal of Regional Science* 5: 77–84.

Bluestone, B., and B. Harrison. 1982. *The Deindustrialization of America.* New York: Basic Books.

Borts, G., and J. Stein. 1964. *Economic Growth in a Free Market.* New York: Columbia University Press.

Box, G., and G. Jenkins. 1976. *Time Series Analysis, Forecasting and Control.* San Francisco: Holden-Day.

Brechling, F.J.B. 1973. "Wage inflation and the structure of regional unemployment." *Journal of Money, Credit, and Banking* 5: 355–79.

Brenner, H. 1973. *Mental Illness and the Economy.* Cambridge: Harvard University Press.

Brest, P. 1980. "The misconceived quest for the original understanding." *Boston University Law Review* 60: 204–58.

————. 1982. "Interpretation and interest." *Stanford Law Review* 34: 765–73.

Browne, L.E., P. Mieszkowski, and R.F. Syron. 1980. "Regional investment patterns." *New England Economic Review* (July/August): 5–13.

Burdett, K. and B. Hool. 1982. "Effects of the inflation-unemployment trade-off." In R.H. Haveman and J.L. Palmer, eds., *Jobs for Disadvantaged Workers: The Economics of Employment Subsidies.* Washington, D.C.: Brookings Institution.

Burdett, K., and D. Mortensen. 1980. "Search, layoffs, and labor market equilibrium." *Journal of Political Economy* 88: 652–72.

Bureau of Economic Analysis. 1976. *Regional Work Force Characteristics and Migration Data.* Washington, D.C.: U.S. Department of Commerce.

————. 1980. "Regional and state projections of income, employment, and population to the year 2000." *Survey of Current Business* (Nov.): 44–70.

_____ . 1981. *BEA Regional Projections: 1980 OBERS.* Washington, D.C.: U.S. Department of Commerce.

Bureau of Industrial Economics. 1982. "Assumptions underlying the industrial outlook to 1986." *Industrial Outlook for 200 Industries with projections for 1986.* Washington, D.C.: U.S. Department of Commerce.

Bureau of Labor Statistics. 1977. *Employment and Earnings, States and Areas 1939-1975.* Washington, D.C.: U.S. Department of Labor.

Business Week. 1981. "One country, five separate economies." (June 1, special issue): 56-100.

Cagan, P. 1979. *Persistent Inflation.* New York: Columbia University Press.

Caines, P.E., C.W. Keng, and S.P. Sethi. 1981. "Causality analysis and multivariate autoregressive modeling with an application to supermarket sales analysis." *Journal of Economic Dynamics and Control* 3: 267-98.

Calabresi, G. 1968. "Transaction costs, resource allocation, and liability rules—a comment." *Journal of Law and Economics* 11: 67-73.

_____ . 1980. "About law and economics: A letter to Ronald Dworkin." *Hofstra Law Review* 8: 553-62.

Carleson, R.B. 1981. "Changes affecting state and local grants." *National Tax Journal* 34: 289-92.

Cartwright, D. 1978. "Major limitations of CWHS files and prospects for improvement." Washington, D.C.: U.S. Bureau of Economic Analysis.

Casetti, E. 1981. "A catastrophe model of regional dynamics." *Annals, Association of American Geographers* 70: 212-24.

Cebula, R.J., and R.K. Velder. 1973. "A note on migration, economic opportunity, and the quality of life." *Journal of Regional Science* 13: 205-11.

Choper, J.M. 1980. *Judicial Review and the National Political Process: A Functional Reconsideration of the Role of the Supreme Court.* Chicago: University of Chicago Press.

Clark, G.L. 1980a. "Capitalism and regional disparities." *Annals, Association of American Geographers* 70: 226-37.

_____ . 1980b. "Urban impact analysis." *The Professional Geographer* 32: 82-85.

_____ . 1981a. "Law, the state and the spatial integration of the United States." *Environment and Planning A* 13: 1197-1232.

_____ . 1981b. "A Hicksian model of labor turnover and local wage determination." *Environment and Planning A* 13: 563-74.

_____ . 1981c. "The employment relation and spatial division of labor: A hypothesis." *Annals, Association of American Geographers* 71: 412-24.

_____ . 1982a. "Rights, property, and community." *Economic Geography* 55: 120-38.

_____ . 1982b. "Volatility in the geographical structure of short-run U.S. interstate migration." *Environment and Planning A* 14: 145-67.

_____ . 1982c. "Dynamics of Interstate Labor Migration." *Annals, Association of American Geographers* 72: 297-313.

_____ . 1983. "Fluctuations and rigidities in local labor markets, part I: Theories and evidence." *Environment and Planning A* 15: 165-85.

Clark, G.L., and K. Ballard. 1980. "Modeling out-migration from depressed regions: The significance of origin and destination characteristics." *Environment and Planning A* 12: 799-812.

_____ . 1981. "The demand and supply of labor and interstate relative wages: An empirical analysis." *Economic Geography* 57: 95-112.

Clark, G.L., and M.J. Dear. 1984. *State Apparatus: Structures and Language of Legitimacy.* London: George Allen and Unwin (forthcoming).

Clark, G.L., and M. Gertler. 1983a. "Migration and capital." *Annals, Association of American Geographers* 73: 18-34.

_____ . 1983b. "Local labor markets: Theories and policies in the U.S. during the 1970s." *The Professional Geographer* (in press).

Clark, G.L., and J. Whiteman. 1983. "Why poor people do not move: Job search behavior and disequilibrium amongst local labor markets." *Environment and Planning A* 15: 85–104.

Clark, K., and L. Summers, 1979. "Labor market dynamics and unemployment: A reconsideration." *Brookings Papers on Economic Activity* no. 1, pp. 13–72.

Coase, R. 1960. "The problem of social cost." *Journal of Law and Economics* 3: 1–44.

————. 1974. "The lighthouse in economics." *Journal of Law and Economics* 17: 357–76.

————. 1981. "A comment." *Journal of Law and Economics* 24: 183–87.

Cochrane, D., and G.M. Orcutt. 1949. "Application of least squares regression to relationships containing autocorrelated error terms." *Journal, American Statistical Association* 44: 32–61.

Coleman, J.L. 1979. "Efficiency, exchange, and auction: Philosophic aspects of the economic approach to law." *California Law Review* 68: 221–49.

————. 1980. "Efficiency, utility, and wealth maximization." *Hofstra Law Review* 8: 509–52.

Committee on Population Redistribution. 1970 reissue. R.J. Goodrich et al., eds., *Report,* New York: Johnson reprint.

Congressional Budget Office. 1977. *Troubled Local Economies and the Distribution of Federal Dollars.* Washington, D.C.: USGPO.

————. 1982. *An Analysis of the President's Budgetary Proposals for Fiscal Year 1983.* Washington, D.C.: USGPO.

Congressional Quarterly. 1978. *Taxes, Jobs and Inflation.* Washington, D.C.: Congressional Quarterly, Inc.

Cooter, R. 1982. "The cost of Coase." *Journal of Legal Studies* 11: 1–33.

Dahlman, C.J. 1979. "The problem of externality." *Journal of Law and Economics* 22: 141–62.

Daniels, B. 1981. "An investigation of the impact of acquisition on the acquired firm." Counsel for Community Development Inc., Cambridge, MA (mimeo).

DaVanzo, J. 1981. "Microeconomic approaches to studying migration decisions." Rand Note N-1201-NICMD, Rand Corporation: Santa Monica, CA.

DaVanzo, J., and Hosek, J.R. 1981. "Does migration increase wage rates?—an analysis of alternative techniques for measuring wage gains to migration." Rand Note N-1582-NICHD, Rand Corp.: Santa Monica.

David, P.A. 1973. "Fortune, risk and the microeconomics of migration." Discussion paper 274. Department of Economics, Harvard University, Cambridge.

Department of Labor. 1982. *Report on the Job Search Relocation Experiment: Results and Prospects.* Washington, D.C.: USGPO.

Department of Manpower and Immigration. 1975. *International Migration and Immigrant Settlement.* Ottawa: Information Canada.

Dixon, R., and A.P. Thirlwall. 1975. "A model of regional growth rate differences on Kaldorian lines." *Oxford Economics Papers* 27: 201–14.

Doeringer, P., and M. Piore. 1971. *Internal Labor Markets and Manpower Analysis.* Lexington, MA: D.C. Heath.

Downs, A. 1979. "Urban policy." In J. Peckman, ed., *Setting National Priorities.* Washington, D.C.: Brookings Institution.

Dunlop, J. 1950. *Wage Determination Under Trade Unions.* Fairfield, NJ: Augustus M. Kelley.

Dworkin, G. 1979. "Paternalism." In P. Laslett and J. Fishkin, eds., *Philosophy, Politics and Society: Fifth Series.* New Haven: Yale University Press.

Dworkin, R. 1978. *Taking Rights Seriously.* Cambridge: Harvard University Press.

————. 1980a. "Is wealth a value?" *Journal of Legal Studies* 9: 191–225.

————. 1980b. "Why efficiency?" *Hofstra Law Review* 8: 563–90.

————. 1981. "What is equality: Part I, equality of welfare; Part II, equality of resources." *Philosophy and Public Affairs* 10: 185–246, 283–345.

Economic Council of Canada. 1977. *Living Together: A Study of Regional Disparities.* Ottawa: Supply and Services Canada.

——. 1982. "In short supply: Jobs and skills in the 1980's." *Au Courant* 3: 4–11.

Eisenberg, M.A. 1982. "The bargain principle and its limits." *Harvard Law Review* 95: 741–820.

Ely, J. 1980. *Democracy and Distrust.* Cambridge: Harvard University Press.

Feldstein, M.S. 1975. "The importance of temporary layoffs: An empirical analysis." *Brookings Papers on Economic Activity* no. 3, pp. 725–44.

Fielding, A.J. 1982. "Counterurbanization in Western Europe." *Progress in Planning* 17: 1–52.

Fields, G.S. 1976. "Labor force migration, unemployment, and job turnover." *Review of Economics and Statistics* 58: 407–15.

Fish, S. 1980. *Is There a Text in This Class?* Cambridge: Harvard University Press.

Fiss, O. 1982. "Objectivity and interpretation." *Stanford Law Review* 34: 739–63.

Foley, D. 1967. "Resource allocation and the public sector." *Yale Economic Essays* 7: 45–98.

Foucault, M. 1980. *Power/Knowledge: Selected Interviews and Other Writings 1972–1977.* New York: Pantheon Books.

Galston, W.A. 1980. *Justice and the Human Good.* Chicago: University of Chicago Press.

Garnick, D. 1981. "U.S. population distribution into the 21st century." Paper presented at the Conference on North American Housing Markets into the 21st Century, University of British Columbia, Vancouver.

General Accounting Office. 1981. *Small Businesses Are More Active as Inventors than as Innovators in the Innovation Process.* Gaithersburg, MD.: GAO.

——. 1982a. *Advances in Automation Prompt Concern over Increased U.S. Unemployment.* Gaithersburg, MD: GAO.

——. 1982b. *Revitalizing Distressed Areas Through Enterprise Zones: Many Uncertainties Exist.* Gaithersburg, MD: GAO.

Gertler, M. 1983. "Capital dynamics and regional development." Ph.D. dissertation, Harvard University, Cambridge, MA.

Gertler, M., and J. Whiteman. 1982. "Urban division of labor." Graduate School of Design, Harvard University, Cambridge, MA (mimeo).

Gilder, G. 1981. *Wealth and Poverty.* New York: Bantam Books.

Glasgow, D.G. 1981. *The Black Underclass: Poverty, Unemployment and Entrapment of Ghetto Youth.* New York: Vintage Books.

Gleave, D., and M. Cordey-Hayes. 1977. "Migration dynamics and labor market turnover." *Progress in Planning* 8: 1–95.

Goldberg, M. 1977. "Planees and planners: Towards a synthetic planning process." Working paper no. 4. Faculty of Commerce and Business Administration, University of British Columbia, Vancouver.

Gordon, I.R., and D. Lamont. 1982. "A model of labor-market interdependencies in the London region." *Environment and Planning A* 14: 237–64.

Granger, C.W.J. 1977. "Comment." *Journal, American Statistical Association* 72: 22–23.

Granger, C.W.J., and P. Newbold. 1975. "Economic forecasting: The atheist's viewpoint." In H. Renton, ed., *Modeling the Economy.* London: Heinemann.

——. 1977. *Forecasting Economic Time Series.* New York: Academic Press.

Green, R.J., and G.R. Albrecht. 1979. "Testing for causality in regional econometric models." *International Regional Science Review* 4: 155–63.

Greenwood, M.J. 1975. "Research on internal migration in the United States: A survey." *Journal of Economic Literature* 8: 397–433.

——. 1981. *Migration and Economic Growth in the United States.* New York: Academic Press.

Gustavus, S., and L.A. Brown. 1977. "Place attributes in a migration decision context." *Environment and Planning A* 9: 529–48.

Habermas, J. 1982. "A reply to my critics." In J.B. Thompson and D. Held, eds., *Habermas: Critical Debates.* Cambridge: MIT Press.

Hahn, F. 1982. "On some difficulties of the utilitarian economist." In A. Sen and B. Williams, eds., *Utilitarianism and Beyond.* Cambridge: Cambridge University Press.

Hall, R.E. 1980. "Employment fluctuations and wage rigidity." *Brookings Papers on Economic Activity* no. 1, pp. 91–123.

Hammermesh, D. 1976. *Jobless Pay and the Economy.* Baltimore: Johns Hopkins University Press.

Hanson, R. 1982. *The Evolution of National Urban Policy 1970–1980: Lessons from the Past.* Washington, D.C.: National Academy of Sciences Press.

Harz, L. 1955. *The Liberal Tradition in America.* New York: Harcourt, Brace and World.

Herzog, J. 1979. "Job search and relocation assistance pilot project." Rockville, MD: Westat (mimeo).

Hicks, D. 1982. "Reindustrialization and American urban policy in the 1980s." University of Texas, Dallas (mimeo).

Hicks, J.R. 1932. *The Theory of Wages.* London: Macmillan.

————. 1939. "The foundations of welfare economics." *Economic Journal* 49: 696–712.

Hobbes, T. 1962 ed. *Leviathan.* Edited by M. Oakeshott with an introduction by R.S. Peters. New York: Collier Books.

Holland, S. 1976. *Capital Versus the Regions.* London: Macmillan & Co.

Hookway, C. 1978. "Indeterminacy and interpretation." In C. Hookway and P. Pettit, eds., *Action and Interpretation: Studies in the Philosophy of the Social Sciences.* Cambridge: Cambridge University Press.

Horiba, Y., and R.C. Kirkpatrick. 1981. "Factor endowments, factor proportions, and the allocative efficiency of U.S. interregional trade." *Review of Economics and Statistics* 63: 178–87.

Houseman, G.L. 1979. *The Right of Mobility.* Port Washington, NY: Kennikat Press.

Huntington, S. 1981. *American Politics: The Promise of Disharmony.* Cambridge: Harvard University Press.

Iwai, K. 1981. *Disequilibrium Dynamics.* New Haven: Yale University Press.

Jackson, W.I. 1978. *Policy Analysis: A Political and Organizational Perspective.* New York: St. Martin's Press.

Joint Committee on Taxation. 1981. "Description of S.2298, Enterprise Zone Tax Act of 1981." U.S. Congress, Washington, D.C.

Just, R.E., D.C. Hueth, and A. Schmitz. 1982. *Applied Welfare Economics and Public Policy.* Englewood Cliffs, NJ: Prentice-Hall.

Kain, J.F. 1978. "Failure in diagnosis: A critique of Carter's national urban policy." Policy Note P78-2, John F. Kennedy School of Government, Harvard University, Cambridge, MA.

Kain, J.F., et al. 1976. "Simulation of the market effects of housing allowances." Research Report R77-1. City and Regional Planning Program, John F. Kennedy School of Government, Harvard University, Cambridge, MA.

Kalecki, M. 1971. *Essays on the Dynamics of Capitalist Economies.* Cambridge: Cambridge University Press.

Kaldor, N. 1939. "Welfare propositions and inter-personal comparisons of utility." *Economic Journal* 49: 549–52.

————. 1970. "The case for regional policies." *Scottish Journal of Political Economy* 17: 337–47.

Keeley, M.C. 1977. "The impact of income maintenance on geographical mobility: Preliminary analysis and empirical results from the Seattle and Denver income maintenance experiments." Research memorandum 47, Stanford Research Institute, Menlo Park, CA.

Kelman, M. 1979. "Consumption theory, production theory, and ideology in the Coase theorem." *Southern California Law Review* 52: 669–98.

Kennedy, D. 1976. "Form and substance in private law adjudication." *Harvard Law Review* 89: 1685–1778.

————. 1979. "The structure of Blackstone's Commentaries." *Buffalo Law Review* 23: 205–381.

————. 1981. "Cost-benefit analysis of entitlement problems: A critique." *Stanford Law Review* 33: 387–445.

King, L.J., and G.L. Clark. 1978. "Regional unemployment patterns and the spatial dimensions of macroeconomic policy." *Regional Studies* 12: 283–96.

Koyck, L.M. 1956. *Distributed Lags and Investment Analysis.* Amsterdam: North Holland Publ. Co.

Kraft, G.A., A. Williams, J. Kaler, and J. Meyer. 1971. "On the definition of a depressed area." In J. Kain and J. Meyer, eds., *Essays in Regional Economics.* Cambridge: Harvard University Press.

Kuhn, S. 1982. *Computer Manufacturing in New England.* Cambridge: Joint Center for Urban Studies of MIT and Harvard University.

Leontief, W. 1956. "Factor proportions and the structure of American trade: Further theoretical and empirical analysis." *Review of Economics and Statistics* 38: 386–407.

L'Esperance, W.L. 1979. "Comment." *International Regional Science Review* 4: 164–66.

Lilien, D.M. 1980. The cyclical pattern of temporary layoffs in U.S. manufacturing." *Review of Economics and Statistics* 62: 24–31.

Lowry, I. 1966. *Migration and Metropolitan Growth.* San Francisco: Chandler.

McCall, J.J. 1970. "Economics of information and job search." *Quarterly Journal of Economics* 84: 113–26.

McKay, J., and J. Whitelaw. 1977. "The role of large private and government organizations in generating flows of interregional migration: The case of Australia." *Economic Geography* 53: 28–44.

McKenzie, R.B. 1981. "The case for plant closures." *Policy Review* 15: 119–34.

MacKinnon, R.D., and P. Rogerson. 1980. "Vacancy chains, information filters, and interregional migration." *Environment and Planning A* 12: 649–58.

Mansbridge, J.J. 1980. *Beyond Adversial Democracy.* New York: Basic Books.

Markusen, A. 1978. "Class, rent, and sectoral conflict: Uneven development in western boomtowns." *Review of Radical Political Economics* 10: 117–29.

Martin, R.L., and J.E. Oeppen. 1975. "The identification of regional forecasting models using space-time correlation functions." *Transactions, Institute of British Geographers* 66: 95–118.

Massey, D. 1978. "Capital and locational change: The UK electrical engineering and electronics industry." *Review of Radical Political Economics* 10: 39–54.

Massey, D., and R. Meegan. 1982. *The Anatomy of Job Loss: The How, Why and Where of Employment Decline.* London: Methuen.

Meyer, J., R. Schmenner, and J. Meyer. 1980. "Business location decisions, capital market imperfections and development of central city employment." Joint Center for Urban Studies of MIT and Harvard University, Cambridge, MA (mimeo).

Miernyk, W. 1979. "A note on recent regional growth theories." *Journal of Regional Science* 19: 303–08.

————. 1982. *Regional Analysis and Regional Policy.* Cambridge: Oelgeschlager, Gunn & Hain.

Milne, W.J., N.J. Glickman, and F.G. Adams. 1980. "A framework for analyzing regional growth and decline: A multiregional econometric model of the United States." *Journal of Regional Science* 20: 173–89.

Ministry of Treasury and Economics. 1982. *Ontario Budget.* Toronto: Ontario Government Printer.

Mishan, E.J. 1982. "The new controversy about the rationale of economic evaluation." *Journal of Economic Issues* 16: 29–77.

Moynihan, D.P. 1977. *Congressional Record,* June 27, pp. S10829–34.

Moriarty, B. 1976. "The distributed lag between metropolitan-area employment and population growth." *Journal of Regional Science* 16: 195–212.

Morrison, P. 1972. "Migration from depressed areas: Its meaning for regional policy." Santa Monica, CA: Rand Corporation.

Mueller, C. 1982. *The Economics of Labor Migration: A Behavioral Analysis.* New York: Academic Press.

Muller, T.L. 1981a. "Regional impacts." In J.L. Palmer and I.V. Sawhill, eds., *The Reagan Experiment.* Washington, D.C.: The Urban Institute.

————. 1981b. "Regional-urban policy: Should the government intervene?" *The Urban Institute: Policy and Research Report* 11: 11–14.

Musgrave. R.A., and P. Musgrave. 1978. *Public Finance: Theory and Practice.* New York: McGraw-Hill.

Muth, R. 1971. "Migration: Chicken or egg?" *Southern Economic Journal* 37: 295–306.

Myrdal, G. 1957. *Economic Theory and Underdeveloped Regions.* London: Duckworth.

Nathan, R. 1981. "Reforming the federal grant-in-aid system for states and localities." *National Tax Journal* 34: 321–27.

National Journal. 1976. "Federal spending: The north's loss is the sunbelt's gain." (June 26).

National Research Council. 1982. *Critical Issues for National Urban Policy: A Reconnaissance and Agenda for Further Study.* Washington, D.C.: National Academy of Sciences Press.

National Tax-Limitation Committee. 1981. *Meeting America's Economic Crisis: A "Road Map" to Emergency Federal Spending Reductions* with a foreword by D. Stockman. Washington, D.C.

Nordlinger, E. 1981. *On the Autonomy of the Democratic State.* Cambridge: Harvard University Press.

Norris, C. 1982. *Deconstruction: Theory and Practice.* London: Methuen.

Note. 1980. "The right to travel—residence requirements and former residents." *Harvard Law Review* 93: 1585–94.

Nozick, R. 1974. *Anarchy, State, and Utopia.* New York: Harper & Row.

————. 1981. *Philosophical Explanations.* Cambridge: Harvard University Press.

Office of Management and Budget. 1981. *Fiscal Year 1982 Budget Revisions.* Washington, D.C.: Executive Office of the President.

Oi, W. 1962. "Labor as a quasi-fixed factor." *Journal of Political Economy* 70: 538–55.

————. 1976. "Residential location and labor supply." *Journal of Political Economy* 84: S221–38.

Olsen, E. 1971. *International Trade Theory and Regional Income Differences.* Amsterdam: North Holland Publ. Co.

Olson, M. 1965. *The Logic of Collective Action.* Cambridge: Harvard University Press.

O'Neill, D.M. 1973. *The Federal Government and Manpower: A Critical Look at the MDTA—Institutional and Job Corps Programs.* Washington, D.C.: American Enterprise Institute.

Ostergren, R.C. 1981. "Land and family in rural immigrant communities." *Annals, Association of American Geographers* 71: 400–11.

Parr, J. 1966. "Out-migration and the depressed area problem." *Land Economics* 3: 149–59.

Parsons, D.O. 1977. "Models of labor market turnover: A theoretical and empirical survey." *Research in Labor Economics* 1: 185–224.

Pechman, J., and others. 1981. "The nondefense budget." In J. Pechman, ed., *Setting National Priorities: The 1982 Budget.* Washington, D.C.: Brookings Institution.

Persky, J., and W. Klein. 1975. "Regional capital growth and some of those other things we never talk about." *Papers, Regional Science Association* 35: 181–90.

Pettit, P. 1980. *Judging Justice: An Introduction to Contemporary Political Philosophy.* London: Routledge and Kegan Paul.

Phillips, A.W. 1958. "The relationship between unemployment and the rate of change of money wage rates in the United Kingdom 1861–1957." *Economica* 25: 283–99.

Pierce, D.A. 1977. "Relationships—and the lack thereof—between economic time series, with special reference to money and interest rates." *Journal, American Statistical Association* 72: 11–22.

Pierce, N. 1976. "Northeast governors map battle plan for fight over federal funds." *National Journal* (Nov. 27): 1695–1703.

Piore, M.J. 1979a. "Conceptualization of labor market reality." In G. Swanson and J. Michaelson, eds., *Manpower Research and Labor Economics.* Beverly Hills: Sage Publishers.

————. 1979b. *Birds of Passage.* Cambridge: Cambridge University Press.

————. 1981. "The theory of macro-economic regulation and the current economic crisis in the United States." Working Paper no. 285, Department of Economics, MIT, Cambridge, MA.

Pissarides, C. 1976. *Labor Market Adjustment: Microeconomic Foundations of Short-run Neoclassical and Keynesian Dynamics.* Cambridge: Cambridge University Press.

Plaut, T.R. 1981. "An econometric model for forecasting regional population growth." *International Regional Science Review* 6: 53–70.

Pole, J.R. 1980. *American Individualism and the Promise of Progress.* Oxford: Clarendon Press.

Poole, R.W. 1981. "Community and regional development." In E.J. McAllister, ed., *Agenda for Progress: Examining Federal Spending.* Washington, D.C.: The Heritage Foundation.

Posner, R. 1981. *The Economics of Justice.* Cambridge: Harvard University Press.

President's Commission for a National Agenda for the Eighties. 1980. *Urban America in the Eighties: Perspectives and Prospects.* Washington, D.C.: USGPO.

President's National Urban Policy Report. 1978. Washington, D.C.: USGPO.

President's National Urban Policy Report. 1980. Washington, D.C.: USGPO.

President's National Urban Policy Report. 1982. Washington, D.C.: USGPO.

Putnam, H. 1981. *Reason, Truth and History.* Cambridge: Cambridge University Press.

Rae, D., with D. Yates, J. Hochschild, J. Morone, and C. Fessler. 1982. *Equalities.* Cambridge: Harvard University Press.

Rawls, J. 1971. *A Theory of Justice.* Cambridge: Harvard University Press.

————. 1979. "A well-ordered society." In P. Laslett and J. Fishkin, eds., *Philosophy, Politics and Society: Fifth Series.* New Haven: Yale University Press.

Rees, A., and G.P. Schultz. 1970. *Workers and Wages in an Urban Labor Market.* Chicago: Chicago University Press.

Rees, J. 1979. "Regional industrial shifts in the U.S. and the internal generation of manufacturing in growth centers of the southwest." In W. Wheaton, ed., *Interregional Movements and Regional Growth.* Washington, D.C.: Urban Institute.

Renshaw, V. 1970. "The role of migration in labor market adjustment." Ph.D. dissertation. MIT, Cambridge, MA.

————. 1978. "Possible biases associated with errors in migration data compiled from CWHS." Bureau of Economic Analysis, Washington, D.C.

Richardson, H. 1973. *Regional Growth Theory.* London: Macmillan & Co.

Rogers, A. 1979. *Essays on the Formal Demography of Migration and Population Redistribution.* Laxenburg, Austria: International Institute of Applied Systems Analysis.

Rogerson, P., and R.D. MacKinnon. 1982. "Interregional migration models with source and interaction information." *Environment and Planning A* 14: 445–54.

Romans, J.T. 1965. *Capital Exports and Growth Among U.S. Regions.* Middletown, CT: Wesleyan University Press.

Rosen, S. 1969. *Nihilism: A Philosophical Essay.* New Haven: Yale University Press.

Rosenheim, M.K. 1969. "Mobility after *Shapiro v. Thompson.*" In P.B. Kurland, ed., *The Supreme Court Review.* Chicago: University of Chicago Press.

Rossiter, C. 1982. *Conservatism in America.* Rev. 2nd ed. with a foreword by George Will. Cambridge: Harvard University Press.

Rothschild, M., and J.E. Stiglitz. 1970. "Increasing risk: A definition." *Journal of Economic Theory* 2: 225–43.

Ryan, M. 1982. *Marxism and Deconstruction: A Critical Articulation.* Baltimore: Johns Hopkins University Press.

Safarian, A.E. 1980. "Ten markets or one? Regional barriers to economic activity in Canada." Discussion paper, Ontario Economic Council, Toronto.

Sandel, M.J. 1982. *Liberalism and the Limits of Justice.* Cambridge: Cambridge University Press.

Saunders, R.S. 1981. "Permanent layoffs: Some issues in the policy debate." Discussion paper, Ontario Economic Council, Toronto.

Scanlon, T.M. 1982. "Contractualism and utilitarianism." In A. Sen and B. Williams, eds., *Utilitarianism and Beyond.* Cambridge: Cambridge University Press.

Schelling, T.C. 1961. *The Strategy of Conflict.* Cambridge: Harvard University Press.

———. 1978. *Micromotives and Microbehavior.* New York: W.W. Norton.

Schwartz, G.G. 1982. "Revitalizing cities through national sectoral strategies." In D. Hicks and N.J. Glickman, eds., *Prospects for Economic and Urban-Regional Transformation: Transition to the 21st Century* (forthcoming).

Scitovsky, E. 1941. "A note on welfare propositions in economics." *Review of Economic Studies* 9: 77–88.

Schultz, T.W. 1980. "Nobel lecture: The economics of being poor." *Journal of Political Economy* 88: 639–51.

Select Committee on Population. 1978. *Domestic Consequences of United States Population Change.* U.S. House of Representatives, Washington, D.C.: USGPO.

Simon, H. 1951. "A formal theory of the employment relationship." *Econometrica* 19: 293–305.

Sims, C. 1974. "Distributed lags." In M. Intriligator and D. Kendrick, eds., *Frontiers in Quantitative Economics.* Amsterdam: North Holland Publ. Co.

———. 1977. "Comment." *Journal, American Statistical Association* 72: 23–24.

———. 1982. "Policy analysis with econometric models." *Brookings Papers in Economic Activity* no. 1, pp. 107–64.

Slater, P. 1975. "A hierarchical regionalization of Russian administrative units using 1966–69 migration data." *Soviet Geography* 16: 453–65.

———. 1976. "A hierarchical regionalization of Japanese prefectures using 1972 interprefectural migration flows." *Regional Studies* 10: 123–32.

———. 1981. "Combinatorial procedures for structuring internal migration and other transaction flows." *Quality and Quantity* 15: 179–202.

Stanback, T.M., and T.J. Noyelle. 1982. *Cities in Transition: Changing Job Structures in Atlanta, Denver, Buffalo, Phoenix, Columbus (Ohio), Nashville and Charlotte.* Totowa, NJ: Allanheld, Osmun.

Soja, E. 1980. "The socio-spatial dialectic." *Annals, Association of American Geographers* 70: 205–25.

Stigler, G. 1972. "The law and economics of public policy: A plea to the scholars." *Journal of Legal Studies* 1: 1–12.

Stokey, E., and R. Zeckhauser. 1978. *A Primer for Policy Analysis.* New York: W.W. Norton.

Thurow, L. 1980. *Zero-Sum Society.* New York: Viking-Penguin.

Tiao, G., C. Box, M. Grupe, G. Hudak, W. Bell, and I. Chang. (n.d.) *The Wisconsin Multiple Time Series WMTS-1. Program.* Madison: University of Wisconsin.

Tribe, L.H. 1972. "Policy science: Analysis or ideology?" *Philosophy and Public Affairs* 2: 66–110.

———. 1973. "Technological assessment and the fourth discontinuity: The limits of instrumental rationality." *Southern California Law Review* 46: 617–60.

———. 1980. "The puzzling persistence of process-based constitutional theories." *Yale Law Journal* 89: 1063–80.

Tullock, G. 1980. "Two kinds of legal efficiency." *Hofstra Law Review* 8: 659–70.

Tushnet, M. 1980. "Darkness on the edge of town: The contributions of John Hart Ely to constitutional theory." *Yale Law Journal* 89: 1037–62.

Urban and Regional Policy Group. 1978. *A New Partnership to Conserve America's Communities.* Washington, D.C.: U.S. Department of Housing and Urban Development.

Vehorn, C. 1977. *The Regional Distribution of Federal Grants-in-Aid.* Columbus, OH: Academy for Contemporary Problems.

Verba, S., and N. Nie 1972. *Participation in America.* New York: Harper & Row.

Vernez, G., R. Vaughan, B. Burright, and S. Coleman. 1977. "Regional cycles and employment effects of public works investments." R-2052-EDA, Rand Corp.: Santa Monica, CA.

Vernon, R. 1979. "Unintended consequences." *Political Theory* 7: 57–73.

Vining, D. 1974. "Spatial distribution of population and its characteristic evolution over time: Some evidence from Japan." *Papers, Regional Science Association* 35: 157–78.

————. 1981. "Review of *Interregional Movements and Regional Growth* edited by W. Wheaton." *Environment and Planning A* 13: 1177–80.

Vining, D., and A. Strauss. 1977. "A demonstration that the current deconcentration of population in the United States is a clean break with the past." *Environment and Planning A* 9: 751–58.

Viscusi, W.K. 1976. "Adaptive models of job search." Discussion paper 80, Public Policy Program, John F. Kennedy School of Government, Harvard University, Cambridge, MA.

Walker, R.A. 1978. "Two sources of uneven development under advanced capitalism: Spatial differentiation and capital mobility." *Review of Radical Political Economics* 10: 28–38.

Walker, R.A., and M. Storper. 1981. "Capital and industrial location." *Progress in Human Geography* 5: 473–509.

Weinberger, J. 1975. "Hobbes's doctrine of method." *American Political Science Review* 69: 1337–53.

Weiss, C.H. 1978. "Improving the linkage between social research and public policy." In L.E. Lynn Jr., ed., *Knowlege and Policy: The Uncertain Connections.* Washington, D.C.: National Academy of Sciences Press.

Westat, Inc. 1979. *Second Annual Report on the Job Search Relocation Assistance Project.* Rockville, MD.: Westat.

Wheaton, W. 1979. "Metropolitan growth, unemployment, and interregional factor mobility." In W. Wheaton, ed., *Interregional Movements and Regional Growth.* Washington, D.C.: The Urban Institute.

Williams, B. 1981. *Moral Luck: Philosophical Papers 1973–80.* Cambridge: Cambridge University Press.

Williamson, J. 1965. "Regional inequality and the process of national growth." *Economic Development and Cultural Change* 13: 1–45.

Williamson, J., and P.H. Lindert. 1980. *American Inequality: A Macroeconomic History.* New York: Academic Press.

Williamson, O. 1975. *Markets and Hierarchies.* New York: Free Press.

————. 1979. "Transaction cost economics: The governance of contractual relations." *Journal of Law and Economics* 22: 233–61.

Wilson, J.Q., ed. 1980. *The Politics of Regulation.* New York: Basic Books.

Wolman, H.L., and A.E. Merget. 1980. "The presidency and policy formulation: President Carter and the urban policy." *Presidential Studies Quarterly* 10: 403–13.

Wrigley, N., and R.J. Bennett, eds. 1981. *Quantitative Geography.* London: Routledge and Kegan Paul.

Zelinsky, W. 1977. "Coping with the migration turnaround: The theoretical challenge." *International Regional Science Review* 2: 175–78.

Index

/